Leadership, Discourse, and Ethnicity

OXFORD STUDIES IN SOCIOLINGUISTICS

General Editors:
Nikolas Coupland
Adam Jaworski
Cardiff University

Recently Published in the Series:
Sociolinguistic Variation: Critical Reflections
Edited by Carmen Fought

Prescribing under Pressure: Parent-Physician Conversations and Antibiotics
Tanya Stivers

Discourse and Practice: New Tools for Critical Discourse Analysis
Theo van Leeuwen

Beyond Yellow English: Toward a Linguistic Anthropology of Asian Pacific America
Edited by Angela Reyes and Adrienne Lo

Stance: Sociolinguistic Perspectives
Edited by Alexandra Jaffe

Investigating Variation: The Effects of Social Organization and Social Setting
Nancy C. Dorian

Television Dramatic Dialogue: A Sociolinguistic Study
Kay Richardson

Language Without Rights
Lionel Wee

Paths to Post-Nationalism
Monica Heller

Language Myths and the History of English
Richard J. Watts

The "War on Terror" Narrative
Adam Hodges

Digital Discourse: Language in the New Media
Edited by Crispin Thurlow and Kristine Mroczek

Leadership, Discourse, and Ethnicity
Janet Holmes, Meredith Marra, and Bernadette Vine

LEADERSHIP, DISCOURSE, AND ETHNICITY

Janet Holmes, Meredith Marra, and Bernadette Vine

OXFORD
UNIVERSITY PRESS

OXFORD
UNIVERSITY PRESS

Oxford University Press, Inc., publishes works that further
Oxford University's objective of excellence
in research, scholarship, and education.

Oxford   New York
Auckland   Cape Town   Dar es Salaam   Hong Kong   Karachi
Kuala Lumpur   Madrid   Melbourne   Mexico City   Nairobi
New Delhi   Shanghai   Taipei   Toronto

With offices in
Argentina   Austria   Brazil   Chile   Czech Republic   France   Greece
Guatemala   Hungary   Italy   Japan   Poland   Portugal   Singapore
South Korea   Switzerland   Thailand   Turkey   Ukraine   Vietnam

Published by Oxford University Press, Inc.
198 Madison Avenue, New York, New York 10016

www.oup.com

Oxford is a registered trademark of Oxford University Press

Library of Congress Cataloging-in-Publication Data
Holmes, Janet, 1947-
Leadership, discourse and ethnicity / Janet Holmes, Meredith Marra, and Bernadette Vine.
    p. cm.—(Oxford studies in sociolinguistics)
Includes bibliographical references and index.
ISBN 978-0-19-973075-9 (alk. paper)—ISBN 978-0-19-973074-2 (pbk. : alk. paper)
1. Communication in management.   2. Diversity in the workplace.
3. Leadership.   4. Sociolinguistics.   I. Marra, Meredith, 1974-
II. Vine, Bernadette.   III. Title.
HD30.3.H65 2011
306.44—dc22   2010054133

1 3 5 7 9 8 6 4 2

Printed in the United States of America
on acid-free paper

CONTENTS

TABLES AND FIGURES

TABLES

FIGURES

ACKNOWLEDGMENTS

This book is based primarily on research undertaken by the three co-authors who constitute the core team of the Wellington Language in the Workplace (LWP) Project. However, it also draws in places on collaborative work with other members of the wider research project team. This work is specifically acknowledged in the footnotes and the references, but the LWP Project's collaborative approach means our debt to others in the research team remains a large one. Any errors or infelicities are, on the other hand, entirely our responsibility.

We would particularly like to thank the following members of the wider research team for their valuable contributions to the research from which this book derives: Professor Brad Jackson and Dale Pfeifer, for stimulating and helpful discussions on leadership issues; and Dr Stephanie Schnurr and Dr Julia de Bres, both of whom worked with us in the area of cross-cultural miscommunication. We also acknowledge, with great appreciation, the work of Sharon Marsden who has provided consistent and high-quality support in a variety of capacities, including editorial assistance and assembly of the reference list for this book.

We express appreciation to the research associates of the LWP Project (some of whom cannot be named because of issues of confidentiality), including Maria Stubbe for her contribution to the foundational research on which this project builds. We are also extremely grateful to our Māori research advisors: Harima Fraser has been involved as a research associate since the first stages of the LWP research; Mike Hollings and Brian Morris have provided ongoing support and encouragement; and Mary Boyce, whose life as a Pākehā immersed in Māori workplaces, has enabled her to share invaluable insights with us from her perspective as scholar, researcher, and workplace practitioner. In addition, many colleagues have provided valuable input during this project, including Ray Harlow, Elaine Vine, Derek Wallace, and Jane Bryson. Thanks also to Hamish Clayton, Sarah Dunstan, Bernie Hambleton, Rachel Scholes and Vivien Trott, colleagues who provided excellent administrative support. We are pleased to acknowledge Robert Cross from Image Services at Victoria University of Wellington for creating the cover photo.

Over the years of data collection, the LWP project has employed a number of very enthusiastic and competent research assistants, who have helped us collect, catalogue, transcribe, and analyse the data. They include Anna Costley, Tina Chiles, Bart Cox, Maurice Hutton, Gabriel Julian Brougham, Leilarna Kingsley, George Major, Marianne, Anthea Morrison, and Bobby Semau. We are also fortunate to have had a number of very able and enthusiastic Māori research assistants who have been generous with their knowledge and skills over the past six years: Kelly Keane, Te Atawhai Kumar, Arihia McClutchie, Crystal Parata, Maika Te Amo, Reuben Tipoki, Paranihia (Frances) Walker, Te Rangimārie Williams. They have worked alongside us in a range of contexts, especially collecting the data, transcribing, and in some cases translating and discussing our interpretations.

Finally and most importantly we obviously owe a huge debt to our workplace participants who did the actual recording or allowed their workplace interactions to be recorded, and who gave so generously of their time to provide ethnographic information and feedback on our analyses. They cannot be named explicitly, because we have agreed to keep them anonymous, but we are extremely grateful to them for the pleasure of the research collaboration and for what we have learned from working with them.

The research for this book was made possible by a Marsden grant administered by the Royal Society of New Zealand. We express our gratitude for this as well as to the Victoria University Research Fund that has provided consistent support for our research over many years.

Janet Holmes
Meredith Marra
Bernadette Vine

Leadership, Discourse, and Ethnicity

CHAPTER 1

Approaching the Analysis of Leadership and Ethnicity

He aha te kai a te rangatira? He kōrero, he kōrero, he kōrero
What is the food of the leader? It is eloquent talk, it is discussion,
it is communication.[1]

Leadership has been the focus of innumerable studies over many centuries, but surprisingly few have considered how talk contributes to effective leadership. Even fewer have examined how leaders talk in organisations with distinctive ethnic values and objectives. This book looks in detail at leadership discourse in the workplace and focuses, in particular, on how leaders communicate in "ethnicised" organisations. In ethnicised workplaces, ethnicity acts as a taken-for-granted backdrop, crucial for interpreting everyday workplace communication; ethnic values underpin the guidelines or norms that influence the way people interact and the ways in which they construct different aspects of their identity, including their ethnicity (Schnurr, Marra and Holmes, 2007). As one Māori leader said during a meeting when discussing priorities, "Basically I'm here to do stuff for Māori". This book explores how such a commitment is apparent in different leadership styles, and the ways in which ethnicity is instantiated in workplace talk.

A good starting point for our exploration is the following pair of excerpts from the opening of a team meeting in a New Zealand commercial organisation with a commitment to furthering the aspirations of the indigenous Māori population.[2]

---

1. One version of a well-known Māori proverb checked and translated by one of our Māori research advisors.
2. Māori are the indigenous people of New Zealand, constituting 14.7 percent of the population (*www.stats.govt.nz*, 2006).

EXAMPLE 1.1A³

Context: Kiwi Productions: Team meeting. Rangi is the meeting chair. Quentin is the team manager. At the start of the meeting, Natalie, a member of our research team, is collecting background information sheets from the meeting members

1		[5 minutes of small talk among meeting members]
2	Quentin:	you've got mine Natalie eh…
3		who's your family?
4	Natalie:	Carter his //name's Carter\
5	Quentin:	/oh\\ it is too oh okay
6		so which one's your father?
7	Natalie:	Danny
8	Quentin:	oh Danny's your dad
9		[indicates through intonation he knows him]
10	Natalie:	yeah
11	Quentin:	oh okay…
12		[Natalie leaves]
13	Quentin:	it's not a common name…
14	Irihapeti:	um is it Māori no?
15	Quentin:	no
16	Paula:	Irish
17	Quentin:	yeah ( )
18	Paula:	no see my brother had a a mate Johnny Carter
19		at school and I knew they'd be related
20		//because\ it's quite an unusual name
21	Quentin:	/yeah\\
22	Paula:	some cousin or something…

This excerpt illustrates a number of typical features of the opening stages of a meeting in any New Zealand commercial company. As people gather for the meeting they engage in small talk, discussing such topics as the weather, holiday plans, and what they have been doing over the weekend (Holmes and Stubbe, 2003a; Marra, 2008a). The meeting participants also express interest in the family of the researcher, and they establish a connection through the fact that Quentin knows her father. After she leaves, they continue to discuss links with the family. When Jemima, the last person expected, arrives, Rangi opens the meeting with a formal *karakia* ("prayer, recitation") in Māori.⁴

---

3. Transcription conventions are provided in the appendix at the end of the book.
4. The karakia is a significant component of the opening of the meeting, which is discussed in detail in chapter 4. Māori words in this book are italicized on first occurrence only. They are listed with translations in the glossary at the end of the book.

EXAMPLE 1.1B

Context: Kiwi Productions: Team meeting (continues on from 1.1a)

23		[Jemima arrives shaking an umbrella]
24	Jemima:	just had to rescue the office staff
25		from the weather
26		[several comments about the weather]
27	Rangi:	[opening karakia in Māori language]
28		yeah I just heard from Terina
29		*kua mate ia* ["he passed away"]
30	Quentin:	mm *ka aroha* ["how sad"]
31		[background talk]
32		[Paula points to the pile of papers
33		in front of Jemima]
34	Paula:	so you obviously had a good weekend Jemima
35	Jemima:	yeah I got I got the um + other twelve pages
36		[laughs] sitting here too
37	Rangi:	right *ki a koe* Quentin
38		["right over to you Quentin"]
39	Quentin:	*kia ora kia ora tātou kia ora hoki tātou*
40		*mō te āhua o (ā) tātou mahi i tērā Paraire*
41		["greetings greetings everyone and a big thank you to everyone for the effort that was put into last Friday"]

After this opening karakia, Rangi allocates the first turn to Quentin, and Quentin begins speaking to the first agenda item. Like the small talk preceding the meetings, these are components that this workplace meeting shares with many other meetings in our database.

However, as the excerpts illustrate, there are also a number of features that distinguish this meeting from others and that indicate that this is a workplace where Māori values and Māori ways of doing things prevail. The most obvious is the use of the Māori language. Māori is not spoken by many New Zealanders, and, apart from brief routine greetings, it is rarely heard in the workplace.[5] Unusually, then, team members in this organisation are bilingual, and they switch comfortably between English and Māori throughout their meetings. A second distinctive feature is the use of the formal karakia to signal the start of the meeting. The structure and content

---

5. Although the 2006 New Zealand Census figures report a small increase in the number of Māori people who claim to be able to speak Māori, surveys of the health of the language by Te Puni Kōkiri, the Ministry of Maori Development, indicate that fewer than 10 percent of Māori adults can speak Māori fluently, and there are very few domains in which it is possible to use the language.

of these components of Māori meetings are discussed in chapter 4. Here it is simply worth noting that Rangi's karakia is quite typical in that it makes reference to those present, to their families, to the sick, and to someone who has recently died. The karakia ends by asking for a blessing on this specific meeting. This serves as a formal declaration of the start of the meeting. The equivalent of this opening in most New Zealand meetings is a very brief and informal statement by the chair such as *okay let's go, right let's get started*, or *okay let's make a start* (Holmes and Stubbe, 2003a; Marra, 2008a; Bilbow, 1998; Barnes, 2007). Clearly, Māori ways of opening meetings are rather different.

Two other features also deserve brief comment. As noted, the team devoted some time to establish a link with the researcher. Although this could happen in many New Zealand contexts, it is totally predictable that it should occur in a Māori context. Relationships, especially through kinship, are a fundamental means of establishing connection in Māori culture. The brief exchange in Example 1.1a is thus significant in establishing a basis for Natalie's acceptance by the group. Second, it is relevant that Quentin begins his turn with a very positive expression of gratitude to the team for their performance the previous week. As we shall see, this too is typical of this workplace, which is characterised by a very supportive and positive culture. These excerpts, then, highlight a range of features whose significance will become increasingly apparent in the discussions that follow in this book.

LEADERSHIP AND LEADERSHIP DISCOURSE

Workplace interaction is fundamentally about spoken and written communication, and for those involved in leadership positions, spoken communication clearly predominates. According to one study, leaders spend on average "between 62 percent and 89 percent of their time in face-to-face communication", and "between one-third and two-thirds of their time communicating with their subordinates" in the workplace (Gardner and Terry, 1996: 153). Despite this, research that focuses on how leaders talk at work is relatively new (e.g., see Ford, 2006; Baxter, 2010). As discussed in chapter 3, research on leadership has been predominantly concerned with the characteristics of "good" leaders, and with how they are perceived by others. Surveys and interviews have been the favoured research tools for investigating these issues, with little attention to the ways in which leaders actually behave, and even less to how they interact and communicate with others at work. This book, thus, offers a new perspective on leadership in the workplace.

It is useful to begin with a brief consideration of the term *leadership*. Although the terms *leadership* and *management* are treated as interchangeable in many contexts, most leadership scholars make a clear distinction between them. Zaleznik (1977), for example, suggests that leaders develop vision and drive change, whereas managers monitor progress and solve problems. Others have suggested that leadership involves providing inspiration and setting new directions and objectives for an organisation, whereas management involves planning and organising to implement the processes that will help achieve the objectives (e.g., Drucker, 1955). More recently, Jackson and Parry (2008: 19) emphasise a need for both leadership and management. As discussed in chapter 3, current research adopts a more dynamic perspective, analysing leadership as a process, a way of providing direction and enacting authority in ongoing interaction with others. Consequently, regardless of their job titles, many individuals may display leadership behaviour in particular contexts. One way in which this is apparent is through their talk.

Our detailed analyses of the way language is used by people identified as effective leaders demonstrate a range of diverse competencies. Not only does their talk orient to the transactional goal of achieving workplace objectives, but also it exemplifies relational skills, taking account of interpersonal aspects of communication, such as establishing and maintaining rapport with colleagues.[6] In other words, leadership can be viewed as a discursive performance that integrates the achievement of transactional objectives with more relational aspects of workplace interaction. In Example 1.1b, for instance, Rangi uses the formal karakia to bring the small talk to a close and direct people's attention to the business at hand, thus achieving his transactional objectives. However, the transition is gradual, with time allowed for people to comment on the recent death that is referred to, for example, *how sad* (line 30), followed by a humourous comment from Paula pointing to the evidence that Jemima had been working hard: *you obviously had a good weekend Jemima* (line 34), before Rangi shifts to business by assigning Quentin the first turn to talk. In other words, Rangi's discourse pays careful attention to relational aspects of interaction with his colleagues as well as the achievement of his workplace objectives.

Leadership is, thus, conceptualised as a dynamic, transformational process or activity that draws on a range of discursive strategies in order to integrate different aspects of effective communication in everyday interaction.[7] Using an interactional sociolinguistics framework together with a social constructionist approach (discussed further later), this book elaborates these points drawing on recorded material collected from a range of leaders in New Zealand workplaces.

6. See, for example, Holmes and Stubbe (2003a), Holmes, Schnurr, Chan and Chiles, (2003), Schnurr (2005), Marra, Schnurr and Holmes (2006). See also Dwyer (1993), Robbins, Millett, Cacioppe and Waters-Marsh (1998), Fairhurst and Sarr (1996), Sayers (1997), Fairhurst (2007).

7. We are conscious that the term *effective* communication is problematic. What is considered effective varies from one context to another and depends on whose perspective is adopted. From a task-oriented perspective, *effective* might be considered as equivalent to *successful*, whereas, from a relational perspective, it might be a synonym of *harmonious*; if time is a central consideration, *effective* might be equivalent to *efficient*, although *effective* might mean "clear and direct" when message is the focus. Our definition of *effective talk* aligns with our focus on context, i.e., it is the colleagues, subordinates, or even the competitors of our leaders who define them as effective, using criteria relevant for the specific community of practice of which they are members. The data analysis is thus the basis for what counts as effective in any particular context.

CULTURE AND ETHNICITY

This book is concerned with illuminating different ways of performing leadership, and especially ways of constructing leadership in workplaces in which distinctive cultural values prevail. Inevitably, then, we must grasp the nettle of defining what we mean by *culture* and *ethnicity*, and consider their relevance at different levels of analysis. Ting-Toomey (1999: 10) defines culture as "a learned meaning system that consists of patterns of traditions, beliefs, values, norms, and symbols that are passed on from one generation to the next and are shared to varying degrees by interacting members of a community". Using a social constructionist approach, Kramsch (1998) emphasises the negotiated and fluid nature of culture, noting that a shared culture entails membership of a community that is linguistically mediated and dynamic (see also Erez and Gati, 2004). As Sarangi (2009: 96) says, "language is not just a carrier of cultural values and norms ... it plays a constitutive role in sustaining and changing cultural practices". This fluid and dynamic approach permits us to consider how cultural traditions, beliefs, values, norms, and symbols are instantiated and negotiated in the discourse of the different groupings relevant to our research.

In the New Zealand context, at least the following need to be distinguished: New Zealand culture, Māori culture, and Pākehā culture.[8] Additionally, in the context of our research, we must consider organisational culture and the culture of a work team or community of practice (CofP).[9] Although some characteristics distinguish these different groupings, there are also many overlaps in the features of behaviour that instantiate their cultural norms and values. In the analyses in this book, we pay attention to these overlaps, as well as identifying points at which participants appear to be enacting the distinctive cultural norms of a specific group.

In discussions of leadership to date, culture has been analysed predominantly at the macro-level—Western culture, American culture, New Zealand culture (e.g., Hofstede, 1997; Hofstede and Hofstede, 2005; House, Hanges, Javidan, Dorfman and Gupta, 2004; Chhokar, Brodbek and House, 2007). Chan (2005) describes aspects of the intersection between national and workplace culture in different sociocultural contexts. By contrast, in this book we adopt a predominantly micro-level, more dynamic approach to culture, and one that reflects the interplay of various understandings of culture.

---

8. Pākehā is the Māori term for the majority group of European, mainly British, people who colonised New Zealand in the nineteenth century.
9. The term *community of practice* is associated with the work of Lave and Wenger (1991) and Wenger (1998). Eckert and McConnell-Ginet (1992) provide a useful definition: "an aggregate of people who come together around mutual engagement in an endeavour. Ways of doing things, ways of talking, beliefs, values, power relations—in short, practices—emerge in the course of this mutual endeavour. As a social construct, a CofP is different from the traditional community, primarily because it is defined simultaneously by its membership and by the practice in which that membership engages" (1992: 464).

One issue that needs to be explicitly addressed at this point, is the use of the term *Māori culture*. As Sir Tipene O'Reagan points out, the concept of "Māori" as applied to people "is essentially a Pākehā invention. The only need to distinguish a group of people as Māori came with the arrival of another group. Prior to that, we were Kahungunu, Ngāti Porou, Ngāti Whātua, Ngāi Tahu" (Diamond, 2003: 25). In other words, Māori people identified with their *iwi* or tribes, not as a homogeneous ethnic group, Māori. This is still true in many contexts, as noted in the discussion of Example 7.3 in chapter 7. For many Māori, their tribal affiliations are extremely significant. However, it is also true that the gradual domination of New Zealand by Pākehā immigrants throughout the nineteenth and twentieth centuries and the imposition of Pākehā ways of doing things in public spheres led to a recognition by Māori people of what iwi shared, their culturally distinctive ways of doing things. In current usage, there are many contexts in which both Māori and Pākehā make effective and appropriate use of the term *Māori culture*. We consider that this book constitutes such a context, and those who worked with us in our Māori workplaces concur with this usage.

Turning to more specific levels of analysis, to a greater or lesser extent, every organisation develops a distinctive culture, and within the organisation, particular workplace teams often develop as distinct CofPs (Wenger, 1998; Holmes and Stubbe, 2003a, b) with particular ways of doing things and "systems of shared understandings" (Metge and Kinloch, 1978: 8). Interactional norms are negotiated, and newcomers and outsiders are vulnerable to potential transgressions. The distinctive culture of a CofP is constantly being instantiated in ongoing talk and action, continually modified by large and small acts in regular social interaction within ongoing exchanges. In other words, discourse plays a central role in constructing culture.

At New Zealand (NZ) Productions, for example, a Pākehā organisation, team meetings typically begin with small talk on a range of topics, including work-related catch-up talk, as people gradually arrive. When everyone is present, there is typically a short sharp transition to business, as illustrated in Example 1.2.

EXAMPLE 1.2

Context: NZ Productions: Team meeting. Veronica comes in to inquire about an invoice

1	Roger:	getting warm again eh
2	Molly:	[laughs]: oh I know: it was cold this morning
3		outside ++ [coughs]
4		when I got home from the gym
5		and I had a shower I was so hot
6		I was still really sweating really bad
7		so I had to stand outside

8	Roger:	yeah cool down yeah
9	Molly:	I got dressed and I said to my partner
10		[sighs]: oh: I just gotta sit out here
11		and have my cup of tea [laughs]: he said
12		he said are you crazy woman I says look at me:
13	Imogen:	yeah but you'd //be standing outside with a\
14	Molly:	/I said I've just been to the\\ gym for an hour
15		and I //says\
16	Imogen:	/but with\\ you're you're drinking a cup of tea
17		that'll just make you hot
18	Molly:	[laughs]: yeah:
19	Veronica:	I just got this from the promoters
20		they're chasing a invoice for goods for [company]
21	Imogen:	for the ones we're still producing?
22	Veronica:	apparently came through in January
23		she thought it had already been done +++
24	Imogen:	we did [drawls]: do: some
25		we did some in December
26		and we're doing some more now
27	Veronica:	doing some now so they're not done
28	Imogen:	but they're not fin- they'll be delivered today…
29	Chrissie:	good company actually +
30	Paul:	shoot Rog
31	Roger:	er we got a hundred and sixty one quotes
32		some of the bigger ones…

Integrating into this CofP involves learning how to contribute appropriately to the small talk and premeeting business talk. Note, for instance, that Imogen contributes to the small talk between Molly and Roger but then quickly orients to Veronica's transactional query. Community membership also involves accurately identifying the brief marker of the transition to the business meeting as soon as it occurs. In this case, the signal is simply *shoot Rog* (line 30). All team members recognise this as the start of the meeting and begin to pay attention as Roger opens with the first official agenda item. Because Roger's report is always the first item on the agenda, the brief *shoot Rog* is quite sufficient as a meeting opening marker if you are a team member. Membership of the CofP means being familiar with the particular ways of doing things that help define the distinctive workplace culture. And the concept of CofP facilitates our focus on dynamic workplace practices as instantiated in discourse.

In this research, we make use of the notion of the "*ethnicised*" CofP (Schnurr, Marra, and Holmes, 2007; Holmes, Marra, and Schnurr, 2008), a workplace where people behave in ways that accord with the cultural norms and values of their ethnic group. This concept provides a means of taking account of the impact that the ethnicity and ethnic orientation, as well as the ethnic values and beliefs of the workforce, may have on the discursive performance of organisational members, and in particular workplace leaders.[10] We suggest that, although leaders from ethnically diverse organisations may draw on a similar range of discursive strategies when "doing leadership", they often differ in the precise ways in which they make use of these strategies, or in the ways in which they instantiate these strategies from context to context. So, for example, in our data, the way in which the leader in a Māori team of professional designers provides critical feedback to team members is typically considerably less explicit than that from the Pākehā leader of a professional IT team.[11] In other words, leaders typically construct their professional identities in ways that are consistent with their ethnic identities and orientations, by behaving in ways that reinforce (or sometimes contest) the norms developed in the leaders' CofPs, and which are embedded in the wider context of their organisations' cultures.

ETHNICITY AND LEADERSHIP

There has been relatively little research exploring the ways in which indigenous people conceptualise and enact leadership.[12] Avolio and Yammarino (2002: 402) point to the dearth of studies in this area:

> our understanding of leadership in different ethnic and racial groups is also in its infancy. As a field, we are presented with some great opportunities to explore whether leaders of colour lead differently from white leaders; how women leaders lead differently from men leaders; how leaders in one culture lead differently from leaders in another culture, etc. So much of our work in leadership had been conducted with primarily samples of white male and some white female leaders and followers.

In New Zealand, many people's experience of workplace leadership is typically Pākehā, and often male, leadership. Relatively few have worked with Māori in leadership roles. Because Māori people are a numerical minority in New Zealand, and workplaces that operate according to Māori principles of interaction are few and far between, it is Pākehā communicative norms that generally predominate (Metge, 1995). Thus, many Pākehā are unaware of the areas and dimensions of potential difference in the ways leadership is enacted in different ethnic contexts. In this book, we attempt to identify features of the communication styles of effective Māori

10. This concept is further elaborated in later chapters.
11. We treat Pākehā as an ethnicity, socially constructed through behaviour and discourse in the same way as other more salient ethnicities (see Fought, 2006: 112 ff).
12. But see Baragwanath, Lee, Dugdale, Brewer and Heath (2001), Ka'ai and Reilly (2004), Mahuika (1992), Nga Tuara (1992), Sinclair (2005), Walker (1993), Warner and Grint (2006). Note, too, as recognised by Warner and Grint (2006: 225), that many textbooks point to the importance of avoiding overgeneralisation in this area.

leaders that tend to be overlooked or misinterpreted when viewed through a main-stream management lens. We focus especially on discourse features that are valued in Māori work contexts by Māori employees.

We emphasise at the start that, although ethnicity is a focus of the analysis, the concept of ethnicity is not taken for granted: people's ethnicity is not treated as a pre-determined social category. The sociologists Omi and Winant (1994: 14) argue that "the definition of the terms 'ethnic group' and 'ethnicity' is muddy". One way of managing the muddiness is to approach ethnicity as a dynamic and active process that is evident in the way people behave in ongoing interaction (Blommaert, 2005, 2007; Fought, 2006; De Fina, 2007). Being Pākehā or Māori is a process that involves others and that requires constant appropriate performance in specific con-texts. As De Fina suggests, "there are no unified criteria that can universally define ethnic boundaries; rather these are creatively invoked and negotiated by individ-uals and groups in response to their evolving social roles and circumstances" (2007: 373). This is very clear from the observation of interactions in the Māori organisa-tions that have been the focus of our analysis. Ethnicity permeates workplace com-munication in these organisations; ethnic values influence the way people interact, and the ways in which they enact leadership. In interview, for example, Yvonne, the managing director of a Māori organisation, was asked to comment on the leader-ship strengths of her most senior manager, Quentin. The points she picked out were his extensive knowledge of *tikanga Māori* ("Māori ways of doing things"), and of *te reo Māori* ("Māori language"), as well as his ability to step up and provide direction, reassurance, and stability in a crisis.

EXAMPLE 1.3

Context: Kiwi Productions: Interview with Yvonne, managing director

1	Yvonne:	Quentin of course plays a really important part
2		in our company with regard to *tikanga Māori*
3		um in that and he takes quite a leadership role
4		in that and that has increased as well over time...
5		yeah in a way I think you know it's funny
6		sometimes a crisis shows you what people are made of...
7		using [Māori] ceremony to get through difficult times...
8		and I think the staff really valued it and it got them
9		got everyone through it

In his own interview, Quentin indicated high awareness of this responsibility to provide "cultural leadership", to "really help Kiwi Productions walk the talk" by providing guidance to staff in areas involving tikanga Māori. He gives an example of the death of a colleague's daughter as just such a crisis and describes how he led the staff as they "worked through a lot of things" in a distinctively Māori way. The precise issue is discussed further in chapter 7 (see Examples 7.5, 7.6, 7.7).

It is clear that, in this CofP, walking the talk means behaving in ways that are consistent with Māori values, such as the high priority given to *manaakitanga* ("hospitality"), caring for people and nurturing relationships, and *whanaungatanga* ("relationships"), looking after family "and being very careful about how others are treated" (Mead, 2003: 29). Being a good leader involves more than providing direction for the organisation's business; it entails actively supporting people in ways that go well beyond what is usual in Pākehā organisations, especially those who are needy due to sickness or bereavement. These themes recurred frequently in our analyses of leadership responsibilities in Māori organisations.

Finally, it is worth noting that these values permeate Māori workplaces, as will become very apparent in later chapters. Whether they identify as Māori or Pākehā for census purposes, employees in ethnicised Māori organisations enact their professional identities in more or less Māori ways in workplace interaction. This approach to researching ethnicity in workplace interaction underpins the model we have developed for the purposes of our analysis. In the next section, we discuss the components of this model.

THEORETICAL FRAMEWORK AND ANALYTICAL MODEL

The theoretical model we have developed for analysing workplace discourse reflects a "realist" position on the relationship between structure and agency (Coupland, 2001; Reed, 2005; Ehrlich, 2008; Cameron, 2009). In very general terms, "real world material conditions and social relations . . . constrain and shape the discursive construction of organisational reality in any particular socio-historical situation" (Reed, 2005: 1629). We construct our social reality within the constraints of particular social and historical conditions; in other words, our behaviour, which includes our talk, is constrained by the parameters of broad societal norms and "inherited structures" of belief, power, opportunity, and so on (Cameron, 2009: 15). We construct our social identities within the constraints of culturally available, sense-making frameworks or "discourses" (Ehrlich, 2008: 160). Our model identifies these social constraints on interactional behaviour at different levels of generality, from the broadest and most encompassing societal or institutional level through to the more specific level of CofPs or workplace teams (cf. Vaara, 2003; Hecht, Warren, Jung and Krieger, 2005; Wodak, 2008: 208). We illustrate the relevance of the various components with brief specific examples.

At the societal or institutional level there are at least two relevant interactional norms that influence the way people communicate. First, there is a general expectation in New Zealand society, reflected in everyday common-sense discourses, that English is the normal or usual language of communication in most societal domains. There are very few exceptions to this: for example, Māori is the preferred language on the *marae* ("traditional meeting ground"), and church services may be held in a community language. Second, New Zealand society subscribes to an egalitarian ideology, and one consequence of this is a general expectation that formality is kept to a minimum.[13] Hence, only very ceremonial events, such as the opening of Parliament and university graduations, and proceedings or ceremonies in legal and religious domains are governed by institutionalised formal rules of interaction.

At the organisational level, there are further discourse norms, including those that relate to the degree of formality of meetings at different levels of the organisational hierarchy. In some organisations, for instance, board meetings at the most senior level are conducted with relative formality: for example, a written agenda circulated to participants in advance, together with the formal minutes of the previous meeting, the expectation that all members will attend or will send apologies in advance. In such organisations, the chair of the meeting generally conducts the meeting by beginning on time and moving systematically through the items on the agenda; decisions are typically formally voted on and recorded. In other organisations, board meetings are not so formal. The agenda may be written on a white board, jotted on a piece of paper by the meeting chair, or simply based on discourse conventions; there is no formal requirement to send apologies in advance, progress through the agenda may not be strictly systematic, and decisions may be reached relatively informally rather than by formal vote. Obviously, variations of these patterns are possible in different organisations.

At the CofP level, the interactional discourse norms of particular workplace teams are relevant. This may be most evident in discourse features such as the amount and kind of small talk that precedes meetings, different degrees of tolerance of variation in their starting time, the use of terms of address that indicate in-group membership, use of technical jargon specific to the sector, and particular preferred styles and types of humour (Holmes and Marra, 2002a). In one organisation in which we worked, for example, the manager was teasingly referred to as Queen Clara, and much humour, such as references to "royal" edicts, derived from this shared knowledge (Holmes and Marra, 2006). In another organisation, the phrase "the Len factor" operated as shorthand for bureaucratic delay on the progress of documents through the system. Our recordings captured the first use of this phrase when its meaning was made explicit, as well as subsequent uses when it had become an established element of in-group jargon. In some organisations, what we perceived as technical jargon was endemic. The following excerpt from a meeting at Kiwi Consultations illustrates this well. The content of the discussion was largely opaque to us as outsiders.

---

13. See Trevor-Roberts, Ashkanasy and Kennedy (2003).

EXAMPLE 1.4

Context: Kiwi Consultations: Team meeting

1	Rowan:	we've been going through draft of brief
2		and attaching relevant documents that were
3		referred to in the brief
4		which for the most part are all the key documents
5		but they're not all the strictly relevant documents
6		might be just correspondence or whatever
7		which doesn't necessarily advance the issues
8		but it's a broad //test\ of relevance
9	F1:	/mm\\
10	F2:	mm
11	F3:	mm
12	Candice:	so is part of the problem a distinction
13		where people are approaching discovery
14		from an OIA perspective
15		rather than a litigation perspective
16	Rowan:	um that I mean that's an issue
17		at the [organisation] end
18	Candice:	not only [organisation]
19	Rowan:	I mean this is this is just
20		well I don't I don't know if that's (an issue here)
21		it's just this was just a process //process\ issue
22		I think
23	Candice:	/mm\\

It is easy for outsiders to identify the insiders' jargon and the evidence of shared understandings in an on-task excerpt such as this: *draft of brief, test of relevance, problem of distinction, discovery,* and so on. Although we can guess at the meaning of an *OIA perspective* (Official Information Act), *litigation perspective* (line 15), and a *process issue* (line 21), outsiders can have no appreciation of their significance in the specific context of this discussion. The minimal feedback (lines 9, 10, 11), as well as Candice's substantial and collaborative response (lines 12–15, 18) to Rowan's outline of the issue clearly indicates that the participants are engaged and paying attention. This short excerpt nicely illustrates, then, how familiarity with specific technical terminology can distinguish one CofP from another.

Finally, at the level of a specific interaction, a number of detailed contextual features are relevant. These include:

- The relationship between the participants (relative statuses, degree of solidarity, relative roles/social identities)

- The formality of the setting
- The topic of discussion (e.g., technical, personal)
- The discourse context

These are most satisfactorily analysed using the dynamic approach advocated by Eckert (2008) and Blommaert (2007), which analyses roles and social identities in particular social contexts by examining the available stances that participants adopt throughout an interaction. Ways of talking are associated with particular roles, stances (e.g., authoritative, consultative, deferential, polite), activities, or behaviours (cf. Ochs, 1992). Ways of speaking develop associations that mean they are interpreted as indices of ethnicity or leadership, and different facets of identity are instantiated and negotiated in any specific interaction. We bring this sociocultural knowledge to our interactions, and we use it to assess and interpret the linguistic behaviour of participants. Ethnicity and leadership are components of social meaning, aspects of social identity conveyed indirectly, through a range of stances indexed by the choice of particular linguistic and discursive features, which may, of course, be multifunctional (Holmes, 1997, 2006; Holmes and Marra, forthcoming).[14]

Eckert's approach provides, then, a dynamic way of characterising the different components or facets of social identity (professional, ethnic, gender, age, etc.) that people are constantly indexing in workplace interaction. By activating different stances, participants dynamically construct complex workplace identities, which take account of the norms of the specific discourse context in which they are interacting as well as the specific interactional goals they wish to achieve from moment to moment. In some cases, this entails the complex integration of components from diverse identities, the construction of multiple and hybridised social identities across a range of social categories such as gender, ethnicity, culture, class, religion, and so on. Relevantly, in the context of this analysis, Lemke (2008: 33) suggests, "hybridity represents a compromise by the individual among the pressures and forces of multiple cultures and institutions which are seeking to control our identities".

So, for example, the norms of interaction between the managing director and the finance manager of a company are influenced by their relative status; by how long they have been working together; by whether they are interacting at a formal meeting with others present or in a one-to-one interaction in the finance manager's office; by whether, at any moment, they are discussing financial, organisational, strategic, social, or personal issues; and by what has immediately preceded the

14. In elaborating how the concept of indexical field may contribute to an understanding of how people use linguistic features in interaction, Eckert (2008: 469–470) proposes that speakers convey through their linguistic choices both "permanent qualities" (e.g., educated, articulate, elegant), and momentary and situated stances (e.g., polite, angry, emphatic, careful). She emphasises the fluidity of these categories: people who are habitually angry, she suggests, "may become angry…people through *stance accretion*", anger becomes a permanent component of their identity or habitual persona. Or, as Lemke says, "[w]hat links the long term to the short is precisely recurrence" (2008: 25).

discussion and what is expected to follow it (e.g., a board meeting or morning coffee). All these contextual factors potentially influence the stances adopted and thus the features of their discourse: for example, the managing director may be more likely to index status and power, adopting an authoritative stance expressed through direct imperatives if a board meeting is to follow and time is short, and especially if they have already spent some time preparing and have thus developed a common understanding of what needs to be done (see Vine, 2004, 2009). Social identity theory, then, provides a useful bridge between social structure and individual action (Bargiela-Chiappini, 2004: 39; see also Jenkins, 1996; Bucholtz and Hall, 2005; Locher, 2008).

Cross-cutting all these potential components is the influence of Māori discourse norms, which a good deal of material from our database suggests constitute a relevant taken-for-granted background for many New Zealand interactions. Most New Zealanders are aware that Māori norms for appropriate interaction differ from those of the majority Pākehā group. Most obviously, for instance, any Māori ceremony begins with a formal greeting of some kind, however brief, and New Zealanders are well aware of this. During a planning meeting, for instance, members of one of our Pākehā organisations explicitly refer to the ritual elements required if they decide to adopt a formal Māori welcome. The *haka* ("war dance") that precedes national rugby games, in which the All Black team participates, is another manifestation of this influence that is familiar to all New Zealanders, as well as rugby fans worldwide. However, there are also other more subtle ways in which Māori interactional norms affect the ways in which New Zealanders conduct their discourse. These can be analysed by drawing on some of the cultural dimensions of interaction identified in House's (2005: 21) model. See Figure 1.1.

The model provides five potentially universal dimensions for analysing cross-cultural differences: degrees of directness, degrees of explicitness, the degree to which a communication is oriented toward self rather than other-oriented, the degree to which it is oriented toward content rather than toward the addressees, and the extent to which the discourse is characterised by verbal routines as opposed to ad hoc formulations. House (2005) used these dimensions to compare interactions between German-speaking subjects with interactions between English-speaking subjects. She concluded that (British) English speakers tend to interact in ways that are less direct, less explicit, less self-referenced and content oriented, and more prone to resort to verbal routines than German speakers (House, 2005: 21).

Indirect	———————	Direct
Orientation to other	———————	Orientation to self
Orientation to addressee	———————	Orientation to content
Implicitness	———————	Explicitness
Verbal routines	———————	Adhoc formulations

Figure 1.1
Toward a Model of Dimensions of Ethnic Contrast—Continua for Analysis (after House, 2005)

Our research suggests that some of these dimensions can usefully be applied to the analysis of interaction in New Zealand workplaces. The dimensions of degrees of directness and degrees of explicitness are particularly useful. We have found, for example, that in many workplace contexts, Pākehā New Zealand English speakers (and especially people with predominantly British heritage) tend to be more direct and more explicit than Māori New Zealanders in stating what needs to be done, for example, in criticising the work of colleagues, or in disagreeing with a proposal. This supports the argument that such norms are culturally relative and must be carefully examined in the dynamic interactional contexts in which talk occurs. On the other hand, our analyses suggest that the dimensions of orientation to self versus orientation to other, and orientation to content versus orientation to addressees are confounded to some extent. We will illustrate in subsequent chapters some of the ways in which Pākehā workplace interactions are often characterised by a relatively high degree of self-orientation compared to similar interactions in Māori workplaces in which Māori cultural values tend to inhibit self-promotion. However, the dimension of orientation to content versus orientation to addressees does not seem to offer much additional leverage. We have, therefore, omitted this dimension from our model. The final dimension of ad hoc formulation versus verbal routines proved particularly useful because it characterises relevant features of discourse in a range of different workplace contexts, including meetings in Māori and Pākehā organisations. In Example 1.1b, for instance, the karakia with which Rangi opens the meeting makes specific reference to a well-known Māori person who had recently died. As he notes on finishing the karakia, "I just heard from Terina...*kua mate ia* ['he passed away']" (lines 29–30). This is just one indication of the way that Rangi tailored the karakia to fit the particular participants and the particular context.

At two points, this model provides for considerations relating to the indexical functions of language (e.g., as a marker of group membership), as well as consideration of the extent to which it is possible to demonstrate individual agency within the structures of the higher order constraints. First, in providing for the analysis of the relationship between participants, the model provides scope for examining how particular dimensions of similarity and difference, including, ethnicity, age, gender, status, and power are actively negotiated in interaction (cf. Eckert, 2008). Second, the dimension of "orientation to self versus other" permits detailed consideration of the kind of social identity that participants are constructing in specific interactions within the wider contextual, situational and institutional constraints.

It will be apparent that social identity is a core concept within this model, which provides a framework for exploring the dynamic and complex relationship between, for example, ethnic, gender and professional identities (Corder and Meyerhoff, 2007; Spreckels and Kotthoff, 2007; Ehrlich, 2008). The model also permits consideration of dimensions, such as directness and explicitness, which have been consistently identified as important in models of politeness or rapport management, especially in recent research in this area which adopts a social

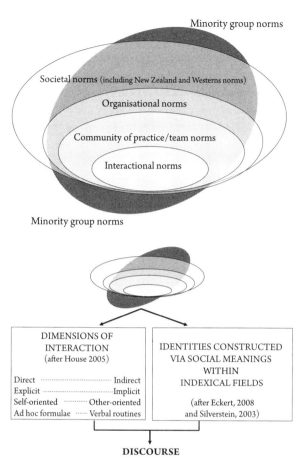

Minority group norms

Societal **norms** (including New Zealand and Westerns norms)

Organisational norms

Community of practice/team norms

Interactional norms

Minority group norms

DIMENSIONS OF INTERACTION (after House 2005)	IDENTITIES CONSTRUCTED VIA SOCIAL MEANINGS WITHIN INDEXICAL FIELDS
Direct .... Indirect Explicit ....Implicit Self-oriented ·········· Other-oriented Ad hoc formulae ····· Verbal routines	(after Eckert, 2008 and Silverstein, 2003)

DISCOURSE

Figure 1.2
A Multilayered Model of Intercultural Interaction

constructionist approach to the analysis of cross-cultural and intercultural interaction (e.g., Spencer-Oatey, 2008; Watts, 2005). See Figure 1.2.

The model suggests that preexisting institutional structures and their associated discourse norms inevitably constrain the discourse options available to participants in any interaction. The choices available are influenced by a wide range of historical, institutional, social, and cultural discursive constraints.[15]

This complex and multidimensional framework facilitates analysis of the ways in which leaders in different workplaces enact and negotiate their leadership roles through discourse in specific interactions, in particular social contexts, within specific CofPs. By closely examining discourse at the micro-level of individual workplace interactions, it is possible to see how what Goffman (1974) terms the "interaction order" intersects with institutionally ordered social relationships

---

15. See also Fairhurst (2007).

(Cook-Gumperz, 2001: 119–120), as the model indicates. Analysis within this model can illuminate, for instance, to what extent leaders share power and control at different points with other senior managers who act as co-leaders in enacting particular aspects of leadership performance, as well as ways in which leaders exploit specific formal or informal discourse features in constructing particular stances to index, for instance, authority or "mateship" (Phillips, 1996).

The model includes reference to minority group norms. As the preceding discussion has made clear, the relevant norms for our research are those of Māori culture. Cultural values are very important in interpreting leadership performance in different organisations. It is important to note that social dimensions, such as gender and power, are also relevant to the interpretation of what is going on in particular interactions in different CofPs in our dataset. This is often apparent, not only in the discourse of workplace meetings, but also in the different workplace narratives that leaders produce in different contexts and in different CofPs, as we have demonstrated (Marra and Holmes, 2005; Holmes, 2009). In sum, leaders skilfully draw on a range of discursive strategies and styles to achieve their leadership objectives, and they take account of the different ways in which societal constraints, ethnicity, and CofP norms interact in particular sociocultural contexts. We conceptualise workplace communication, then, as the result of balancing creativity and constraint, where the constraints can be characterised at many different levels of generality (cf. Eisenberg and Goodall, 2004). In the next section we provide an outline of our approach to the analysis of workplace discourse, a social constructionist approach within the framework of interactional sociolinguistics.

DISCOURSE ANALYSIS

Our approach to discourse analysis has its roots in interactional sociolinguistics, an approach that was pioneered by the sociolinguist John Gumperz (1982a; 1982b; 1996), building on the work of the sociologist Erving Goffman (1963, 1974). This approach analyses discourse in its wider sociocultural context, and it draws on the analysts' knowledge of the community and its norms in interpreting what is going on in an interaction.[16] As succinctly summarised by Schiffrin (1994: 105):

> Goffman's focus on social interaction complements Gumperz's focus on situated inference: Goffman describes the form and meaning of the social and interpersonal contexts that provide presuppositions for the decoding of meaning. The understanding of those contexts can allow us to more fully identify the contextual presuppositions that figure in hearers' inferences of speaker's meaning.

16. See Schiffrin (1994); Swann and Leap (2000); and Holmes (2008) for overviews of Interactional Sociolinguistics.

What this means in practice is that both contextual information and the use of fine-grained analytic tools contribute to understanding and interpreting how meaning is negotiated between participants in interaction.

Because interactional sociolinguistics focuses on the ways in which relationships are seen to be negotiated and maintained through talk, it is well placed to analyse the discourse of leadership in different cultural contexts. Interactional sociolinguistics is ethnographically oriented, taking account of the analyst's understanding of the sociocultural context of the interaction under investigation, and making use of micro-level analytic techniques to explore how participants negotiate meaning through talk. In undertaking the analysis of any interaction, we draw on a range of background and self-reported information gathered through participant observation, interview, and discussion to support our detailed discourse analyses and interpretations of talk in action.

Using this approach, we analyse authentic everyday workplace talk for evidence of the social relationships between speakers, and the discursive construction of different facets of their social identities, examining both what they say and how they say it. The analysis involves paying particular attention to the clues people use to interpret conversational interaction within its ethnographic context. This ranges from considerations of content, narrative structure, humour, and turn-taking patterns to detailed analysis of pronoun use, discourse markers (e.g., *oh, okay, well*), pauses, hesitations, and paralinguistic behaviour, as well as other relevant discourse features.

The ways in which relationships and social identities are negotiated and maintained through talk are clearly key components of interactional sociolinguistics. Interaction and identity construction are conceptualised as dynamic interactional processes where meanings and intentions are jointly and progressively negotiated between the individuals involved in a given interaction. As Linell (2001: 160) says:

> ...what is apparent when we take a close analytic look at the practice of actual interaction among real persons is that both the persons and the situations in which they interact are never fully determined. They are continually in production, under construction, through the boot-strapping processes of contextualisation, shifts in footing, and adaptation by interlocutors to each other's actions.

This social constructionist approach frames communication as a process that is instrumental in the creation of our social worlds, rather than simply an activity that we do within them. It emphasises the dynamic aspects of interaction, and the constantly changing and developing nature of social identities, social categories and group boundaries, a process in which talk clearly plays an essential part (e.g., Butler, 1990; Blommaert, 2007; Ehrlich, 2008; Cameron, 2009). Social constructionism is also basic to the concept of the CofP introduced earlier. Leadership is a relational process predicated on asymmetrical power relations between leaders and those they work with. A social constructionist approach within an interactional sociolinguistic framework provides a productive means of analysing how people enact, reflect, and reinforce their positions as leaders through their talk at work in differently ethnicised workplaces.

Finally, in discussing our analytical approach, it is important to note that we have consistently endeavoured to bring a critical dimension to the analysis of workplace interaction (Pennycook, 2001; Sarangi, 2006). Our detailed interactional sociolinguistic analysis of workplace discourse is undertaken with attention to the pressures of institutional discourse and power structures, and especially the pressures experienced by Māori, a socially nondominant, indigenous ethnic group, to conform to majority group discursive norms and expectations. This was relevant in all phases of the research, not least in developing an appropriate research methodology, as described in chapter 2. In the same vein, we are aware of the need to be constantly reflexive in our approach, in order to avoid imposing inappropriate or normative judgments and evaluations in the process of interpreting what is going on. Analysts must be supremely sensitive and open to alternative interpretations. Triangulation of the data is one safeguard in this respect: a range of sources provides alternative interpretations and perspectives on what was said, heard, intended, inferred, and so on. This has been a crucial component of our research, which will become apparent. In the next section, we briefly describe the Language in the Workplace Project and its goals, as well as our database.

THE WELLINGTON LANGUAGE IN THE WORKPLACE PROJECT

The data used as the basis of the analyses in this book was collected as part of the Language in the Workplace Project, based at Victoria University of Wellington in New Zealand.[17] The broad objectives of the project are to describe characteristics of effective communication in New Zealand workplaces, to identify causes of miscommunication, and to disseminate the results of the analysis for the benefit of workplace practitioners.[18] Despite the recent growth of interest in workplace interaction,[19] there has been relatively little research that focuses on how people actually communicate verbally with their colleagues at work on a daily basis, and even less on how leaders use talk to accomplish their objectives. This book makes a contribution to this area.

At the time of writing, our database comprises approximately 2,000 interactions recorded in more than 20 New Zealand workplaces, including government departments, factories, small businesses, semipublic or nongovernment organisations (NGOs), and private, commercial organisations. The interactions include both

17. See *http://www.victoria.ac.nz/lals/lwp* for further information.
18. What is considered "effective" is defined by colleagues, organisations and industry results. See Holmes and Stubbe (2003a) for a discussion of this appreciative inquiry approach.
19. See Holmes (2011) for a recent comprehensive overview of workplace discourse research.

business talk and social talk, informal talk and meetings of many different sizes and kinds, with participants from a wide range of different levels in the workplace hierarchy. The total corpus includes interactions from some workplaces with a relatively high proportion of women, some with a relatively high proportion of Māori workers, and a number with an ethnic and gender balance more closely reflecting the New Zealand norm. This rich corpus thus includes material from Māori workplaces, from workplaces with a strong sympathy for Māori concerns, and from bicultural workplaces, all of which have assisted in providing valuable verification or "warrants" (Toulmin, 2003; Cameron, 2009; Swann, 2009) for the analyses in this book, which compare interaction in two specific Māori workplaces with two parallel Pākehā workplaces, as described in chapter 2. In the next section, we provide an indication of the content of the rest of the book.

OUTLINE OF THE CONTENTS OF THE BOOK

Chapter 2 describes our database and methodology, and especially the different ways in which the data was collected in differently ethnicised workplaces. The discussion explores the issues that arise when majority group researchers work with participants who consciously foster attention to minority cultural norms and ethnically distinctive ways of doing things in the workplace. Working with an ethnically different group inevitably complicates every component of the research process, from formulation of the research questions through data collection to analysis and interpretation of the findings. The specific methodological challenges that we encountered in researching leadership in Māori workplaces are discussed, as well as the insights that we gained working together with our Māori participants.

Chapter 3 examines the way leadership is constructed through workplace talk. Following a review of the literature on leadership, the chapter illustrates how discourse analysis can provide insights into the ways in which leaders construct their identity in different CofPs. There is discussion of the relevance of talk in enacting transactional and relational dimensions of leadership identity—dimensions widely regarded as key in evaluating effective leadership performance. This chapter also introduces consideration of cultural factors in leadership performance, providing some initial evidence of the critical influence of Māori culture on ways in which Māori leadership is enacted in Māori CofPs.

Transactionally oriented talk is the focus of chapter 4, which illustrates how leaders achieve their organisational goals through task-focused workplace meetings. This chapter illustrates the pervasive influence of contextual factors on the ways in which leaders construct their leadership identity in order to meet organisational goals in ethnically different workplaces. The chapter first examines the unmarked norm, namely the ways in which leadership is enacted in Pākehā business meetings, focusing for exemplification on the opening and closing phases. These norms are then contrasted with those apparent in the Māori workplaces in our dataset, where the opening and closing sections provide an opportunity for the discursive enactment of ethnic values and norms. Culturally different turn-taking patterns are also examined, illustrated, in particular, by a discussion of dissimilar perceptions of what counts as appropriate feedback as opposed to intrusive interrupting.

Chapter 5 focuses on relational talk at work and illustrates the different ways in which leaders attend to workplace relationships in Māori and Pākehā workplaces. The analysis examines, in particular, how leaders use social talk and humour as strategies for maintaining and strengthening collegial relationships in their everyday workplace interactions. Similarities and differences in the ways in which relational practice is enacted at work are discussed, focusing on the influence of the distinctive values of the ethnicised workplaces.

Chapter 6 examines the concept of co-leadership, demonstrating that, in some organisations, different facets of leadership are shared among two or more senior members of a workplace team. The range of ways in which co-leadership is discursively enacted, including the ways in which co-leadership interacts with ethnicity, is examined and illustrated. We outline how co-leadership actually works in practice within particular organisations, identifying just which aspects of control and power are shared and which are not delegated. In all four of the workplaces we examine, there are co-leadership partnerships, although each is different. These partnerships reflect societal, organisational, and CofP norms as well as the particular strengths of the individual leaders involved.

Chapter 7 focuses in detail on the influence of an ethnicised workplace culture on the ways in which leadership is constructed in Māori CofPs. The analysis in this chapter illustrates the important point that, although there are a number of identifiable discursive patterns that characterise Māori ways of enacting leadership, as explored in earlier chapters, there is also considerable variation and diversity in the way different Māori leaders construct their leadership role. The chapter illustrates a number of ways in which Māori values pervade aspects of interaction in the Māori organisations with which we worked, while also suggesting that no New Zealand workplace can be impervious to these values.

The implications of the research for leadership, workplace communication, and intercultural pragmatics are explored in the final chapter. Our analyses throughout the book indicate a number of areas of potential miscommunication and unintentional offense in intercultural interaction.[20] This chapter examines some of the sociopragmatic implications of these insights for those working in intercultural contexts, whether as researchers, as employers and employees, or as colleagues. We describe what we, as Pākehā researchers, learned about intercultural and cross-cultural communication from three perspectives: first, in terms of developing

---

20. In our usage "intercultural interaction" refers to interactions involving participants from more than one culture, while research on "cross-cultural interaction" compares the interactional norms of different cultural groups.

flexible methodologies; second, in relation to the specific ways in which leaders attended to different dimensions of leadership performance in different workplace contexts; and, third, in terms of what we learned from Pākehā employees working as minority group members in Māori CofPs.

The research described in this book is intended to make a contribution to the areas of leadership and cross-cultural pragmatics, and specifically to our understanding of what constitutes effective leadership in different sociocultural contexts, and how this is accomplished through everyday workplace discourse. By analysing the complexities of the ways in which people actively construct their relationships at work, we aim "to map both distinctive and universal values" (Harris and Bargiela-Chiappini, 1997: 5) as evident in workplace interaction in differently ethnicised CofPs.

CHAPTER 2

Collecting the Data

Ka ketekete te kākā, ka koekoe te tūī, ka kūkū te kererū.
The kākā chatters, the tūī sings, the kererū (native pigeon) coos.

This proverb highlights difference and diversity: each bird has its own voice and way of expressing itself. In this chapter we discuss the importance of acknowledging and respecting diversity in the context of undertaking research.

The model outlined in chapter 1 integrates the social constructionist stance that we have adopted throughout our research. Using this dynamic approach, the concept of ethnicity is problematised, and a variety of contextual factors (including the specific community of practice (CofP)) come into focus as we approach the analysis of the interaction of leadership, discourse, and ethnicity. A social constructionist stance also supports the investigation of how leadership is enacted in talk, moving beyond the more traditional data sources of interviews, surveys, and questionnaires, and concentrating instead on the analysis of discourse in its social context. Our attention is on what leaders *do* in different CofPs, rather than what they *say* they do. In undertaking this analysis, then, our well-established methodology, with its focus on naturally occurring data collected from authentic settings, proved entirely appropriate. As this chapter describes, getting access to this kind of data relies crucially on positive and productive working relationships with leaders and their colleagues.

Over the many years that we have been researching workplace communication, we have typically handed over control of the data collection procedure to our participants, asking them to audio-record a range of their talk as it occurs in their everyday working life. The goals of the research are negotiated with workplace participants who become collaborators, research partners, and consultants. In the particular phase of the research described in this book, we made considerable efforts to ensure that the approach we have adapted and refined over many years was appropriately developed for working in non-Pākehā workplaces. Because our goal is a cross-cultural examination of leadership at work, investigating what it means to be an effective leader in comparable Māori and Pākehā workplaces, we were very aware of the significance of ethnicity as a social factor that required attention in the research design and data collection procedures.[1] As Pākehā researchers, our customary approach inevitably followed Pākehā social norms, including the often unacknowledged "rules" that influenced what we considered appropriate ways of behaving in relation to those with whom we were working. Undertaking research with Māori participants required us to critically reflect on the inherent assumptions built into the standard Language in the Workplace procedures.

In this chapter we describe the dataset used in our analysis, and the procedures used for collecting the data. We discuss some of the central methodological and analytical issues raised by the research, including the importance of identifying and contesting assumptions inherent in our usual methodology, and we outline our response to the ethical and cultural considerations that arose in working with Māori participants.

THE DATASET

We set out to investigate the leadership styles of Pākehā and Māori at work and to explore what effective Māori leaders do that might be overlooked when their leadership and communication styles are viewed through a mainstream lens. Our approach involved case studies of leaders in four organisations, one Māori and one Pākehā from each of two sectors. By Māori workplaces, we mean not just workplaces where a majority of the employees are Māori, but rather, as described in chapter 1, "ethnicised" CofPs: that is, workplaces with a conscious orientation to Māori cultural norms and goals, where Māori ways of doing things prevail and the communicative behaviours exhibited by participants are typically consistent with Māori cultural values and beliefs (Schnurr et al., 2007). As noted in chapter 1, Māori people are a numerical minority in New Zealand, and workplaces that operate according to Māori principles of interaction are few and far between; it is Pākehā communicative norms that generally predominate (Metge, 1995). In identifying suitable organisations for our dataset, we first set about securing cooperation with two Māori workplaces, and found comparable Pākehā organisations that met our criteria. Hence, the two Pākehā organisations were selected to be as close a match as possible to the Māori workplaces in terms of their core business, size, and organisational structure.

The four organisations finally included in the dataset, thus, included two workplaces (one Māori and one Pākehā) oriented to creative media-type outputs, whereas the other two orient to knowledge work and negotiation. They were all of

1. "Cross-cultural" refers to our comparison of Māori and Pākehā workplaces; in each workplace we also investigate intracultural communication.

Table 2.1 THE DATASET OF INTERACTIONS
USED IN THE FOUR CASE STUDIES

		Ethnicity (the organisation self-identifies as):	
		Māori	Pākehā
Sector:	Creates outputs	**Kiwi Productions**	**NZ Productions**
		Leaders' interactions	Leaders' interactions
		(2 leaders) 640 mins	(2 leaders) 617 mins
		Team meetings	Team meetings
		(4 teams) 1,479 mins	(3 teams) 1,078 mins
		Interviews	Interviews
		(4 leaders) 150 mins	(3 leaders) 226 mins
	Knowledge and negotiation	**Kiwi Consultations**	**NZ Consultations**
		Leaders' interactions	Leaders' interactions
		(2 leaders) 551 mins	(2 leaders) 374 mins
		Team meetings	Team meetings
		(2 teams) 561 mins	(1 team) 170 mins
		Interviews	Interviews
		(2 leaders) 185 mins	(1 leader) 33 mins

similar size (25–50 employees), and, by chance, all located in a compact section of the local city centre. Our subsequent analysis provided considerable support for this two-by-two research matrix, with similarities based both on ethnicity and on sector. So, for example, the two Māori organisations shared many features: for example, a manifest awareness of Māori values such as humility and emphasis on the group over the individual. Organisations in the same sector shared other features, including both workplaces where the core business involved negotiation and consultation had a strong team-based approach to their daily operations, with group members sharing specialised base-line expertise and achieving their goals collaboratively.

In each workplace our goal was to collect data from at least two leaders in one-to-one interactions and in team meetings. In all cases, we collected more data than anticipated. The resulting dataset, as outlined in Table 2.1, includes audio recordings of small, relatively informal work-related meetings and discussions involving two or three people, as well as larger and longer meetings of each leader's team that were both audiotaped and videotaped. In addition, for all four workplaces, a rich fund of ethnographic information was gathered by means of extensive ethnographic notes collected during the research collaborations, as well as follow-up interviews and, where possible, focus groups or debriefing sessions covering a range of topics and issues. The core dataset is, consequently, supplemented with a great deal of useful additional material that proved very valuable in interpreting the data.

For the kind of systematic and detailed analysis conducted in this kind of research, this constitutes a particularly extensive and rich dataset (Bargiela-Chiappini,

Nickerson and Planken, 2007). Engaging with organisations as research collaborators and assisting them to record their own interactions generally result in very good quality data, as well as encouraging a high level of trust and cooperation, which is enhanced through negotiation and triangulation with participants in the analysis and feedback phases.

Both Māori workplaces were white-collar professional organisations with primarily commercial objectives. They were similar in size with a hierarchy of responsibility, comprising a number of managers, each of whom reported to the Chief Executive Officer (CEO) or managing director. These workplaces, pseudonymed Kiwi Productions and Kiwi Consultations, were selected because of their explicit commitment to furthering Māori objectives. Most of those working in both organisations identified as Māori, and ethnicity was an important and omni-relevant aspect of workplace interaction. Their *kaupapa* ("objectives, priorities, core business") is Māori oriented, and the organisations are committed to promoting Māori values and furthering Māori goals (cf. Bryson and O'Neil, 2008). In both cases, these goals are to promote Māori issues within a mainstream and, consequently, Pākehā-dominated industry.

Tables 2.2 and 2.3 summarise the data collected from leaders at each of the Māori organisations. Within the dataset, we have extensive recordings from one team at Kiwi Productions who regularly use Māori in their workplace meetings,

Table 2.2 THE DATASET FROM KIWI PRODUCTIONS

Leaders (in Hierarchical Order)	Ethnicity of Leaders	Leaders' Data
Yvonne (Managing Director)	Māori	One-to-one interactions, meetings, Interview
Quentin (Senior Manager)	Māori	One-to-one interactions, meetings, interview
Gretel (Manager)	Pākehā	Meetings, interview
Rangi (Manager)	Māori	Meetings, interview

Table 2.3 THE DATASET FROM KIWI CONSULTATIONS

Leaders (in Hierarchical Order)	Ethnicity of Leaders	Leaders' Data
Daniel (Chief Executive Officer)	Māori	One-to-one interactions, meetings, interview
Frank "Ants" Anton (Senior Manager)	Pākehā	One-to-one interactions, meetings, interview

and, overall, the Māori language is used for more extended communication more often in this organisation. In the majority of contexts, however, the Māori workplace participants with whom we have worked typically use English as their principal working language. Māori greetings (*mōrena, kia ora*) are frequently heard in both workplaces, as well as widely known Māori words and phrases such as *kai* ("food") and *kei te pai* ("that's good"); and a *pōwhiri* ("formal welcome") or *whakatau* ("welcome") is standard for any new staff member. Moreover, and significantly, the role of Māori cultural norms is evident in all aspects of the interaction in both Māori workplaces, regardless of the relative amount of Māori and English used.

A key research finding is the extensive influence of ethnicity on workplace interaction in the form of a fundamental commitment to distinctive cultural beliefs, values, and ways of doing things. Thus, through their talk and their behaviour toward their colleagues within and outside the workplace, members of both organisations construct the workplace as Māori space (cf. Valentine, 2002; Bell, Binnie, Cream and Valentine, 1994). Both workplaces have Māori symbols etched in the glass on their windows, with more traditional symbols at Kiwi Productions and more modern artistic symbols at Kiwi Consultations. Additionally, at Kiwi Consultations, artifacts, visual Māori symbols, and paintings make a strong contribution to this construction, whereas Māori books, posters, and art play a similar role at Kiwi Productions.

However, there are also differences that reflect the somewhat different orientations of these two Māori organisations to the wider community, and these are also evident to some extent in the communicative norms that prevail in each CofP. In Kiwi Productions, for example, tikanga Māori plays a significant and explicit role in the day-to-day operations of the organisation, whereas this is not so obviously the case in Kiwi Consultations. Professional relationships in Kiwi Productions appear to be expressed more formally than in Kiwi Consultations, and a more contestive and aggressively challenging style of interaction prevails in Kiwi Consultations meetings than in Kiwi Productions meetings. It is important to bear in mind, then, that, although in this book we are exploring points of contrast between Māori and Pākehā leaders in their CofPs, any activity type in any specific workplace will be characterised by features that may place it in a unique position in a spectrum of Māori versus Pākehā dimensions of contrast.

Like their Māori counterparts, the two Pākehā organisations selected for our research (pseudonymed NZ Productions and NZ Consultations) were white-collar professional organisations, with explicitly articulated hierarchical relationships at the macro-level.

Most significantly, although the hierarchy is identifiable in static measures with formal, organisational charts, and easily articulated relationships, as demonstrated in Tables 2.4 and 2.5, these power asymmetries were less observable in the interactional practices of these organisations. There were named managers and management teams who were responsible and accountable for decisions and their

Table 2.4 THE DATASET FROM NZ PRODUCTIONS

Leaders (in Hierarchical Order)	Ethnicity of Leaders	Leaders' Data
Seamus (Managing Director)	Pākehā	Meetings, interview
Jaeson (General Manager)	Pākehā	One-to-one interactions, meetings, interview
Rob (Business Development Manager)	Pākehā	Meetings
Paul (Senior Manager)	Cook Island Māori	One-to-one interactions, meetings, interview

Table 2.5 THE DATASET FROM NZ CONSULTATIONS

Leaders (in Hierarchical Order)	Ethnicity of Leaders	Leaders' Data
Angelina (Division Manager)	Pākehā	One-to-one interactions, meetings
Suzanne (Senior Manager)	Pākehā	One-to-one interactions, meetings, interview

implementation, but there was also a heightened sense of egalitarianism that imbued their regular operations. In other words, at the micro-level, in their everyday practices, colleagues consulted, negotiated, and sought consensus, discursively treating one another as equals. At NZ Consultations, for example, Angelina, the division manager, was extremely consultative in style, and respectful of her colleagues' expertise, as illustrated in chapter 6. As a specific example, in team meetings she would carefully check how much information she needed to provide as background to an issue, so that she did not waste her colleagues' time. This perhaps indicates the salience of the tall poppy syndrome in Australasian (and some Scandinavian) societies in particular (Holmes, Vine, and Marra, 2009; Jackson and Parry, 2001). According to this oft-cited principle, Pākehā New Zealanders do not comfortably tolerate explicit demonstrations of power. Although power differences clearly exist, the enactment of power is typically indirect and hedged with the goal of reducing the power distance and emphasising an (artificial) level playing field (see Holmes, 2007a). Again, it seems, ethnicity may be an influence on the ways in which people orient to aspects of workplace interaction.

Given its explicit significance as a raison d'être of the work of the Māori organisations, as well as its more subtle, but no less important, influence on what were considered appropriate ways of interacting in different organisations, ethnicity was inevitably a central consideration in all aspects of our research design and data collection.

COLLECTING DATA IN MĀORI AND PĀKEHĀ WORKPLACES[2]

The Language in the Workplace Project team has been engaged in collecting and analysing workplace discourse since its inception in 1996. Throughout the project, the methodology has consistently adopted two important principles: (1) identifying issues of interest to both the organisations and the researchers, who cooperate in developing agreed research objectives; and (2) building strong relationships with volunteers in organisations (Stubbe, 1998a, 2001; Holmes and Stubbe, 2003a). The participatory research design takes up the call to negotiate research motivations and outcomes with participants. Our goal is to "break down the division between the researcher and the community" (Cameron, 1985: 2), to avoid researching *on*, and instead to research *with* our participants.

The principles, methods, and goals of the original design have been thoroughly described elsewhere (Stubbe, 1998a, 2001; Holmes and Stubbe, 2003a; Marra, 2008b), but for completeness we provide a brief summary here. The most distinctive feature of our approach is our solution to "the observer's paradox" (Labov, 1972): we ask the participants themselves to take control of the data collection in order to obtain material that is as little affected by the recording process as possible. To record meetings, we set up our video cameras in the meeting room before anyone arrives, and we then disappear until after the meetings are over. These procedures also help resolve another source of tension that faced us when we first began our research in Pākehā workplaces. Majority group communicative norms and values dictated that we needed to be as unobtrusive as possible, and consequently we promised our workplace participants that we would not interfere with their normal business, or add time to their working day. Having participants audio-record their normal workplace interactions, and setting up videorecorders in advance of meetings meant we did not intrude into people's workspace, and the recordings entailed no additional work time for them. Essentially we tried to be invisible around the workplace while our participants cooperatively collected our data.

On the other hand, we wanted to collect as much ethnographic detail as possible about each workplace. Our goal was "thick description" (Geertz, 1973) of the context of the talk that participants were recording for us. We also needed the assistance of our participants to check our interpretations of the data. To resolve this dilemma, we used a (usually female) research assistant, matched as far as possible in social characteristics to the participants themselves, to collect ethnographic data. While observing and making notes on the workplace routines, spaces, and comings and goings, she would also undertake everyday tasks such as copying material, making coffee, doing errands, and so on. Again, the goal was to fade into the background. Even our follow-up interviews were designed to be focused and brief in order to intrude as little as possible on the time of our participants. This method was very

2. The following sections draw on material presented in Marra (2008b).

successful in Pākehā workplaces where people appreciated efforts to minimise the impact of our research on their business.

Always learning from experience, our methodology became increasingly stream-lined, and we felt particularly confident of its effectiveness in white-collar work-places where the cultures of the organisations were similar to those of our personal workplace experiences. As the data collection expanded beyond government departments and corporate organisations into factory, medical, and IT settings, our concerns were typically practical, discovering methods for handling noisy environ-ments and mobile workforces, and capturing the benefits of new technologies. In each case, consulting throughout with the workplace participants, we made decisions on ways of adapting the data collection procedures to meet the challenges identified, while still adhering to the underlining research philosophy (e.g., Stubbe, 2001; Marra, 2008b). With all our participants, we consistently aspired for collabo-ration, mutually beneficial relationships, and, most significantly, the development of ongoing and lasting trust. In all these different workplace contexts, our practice was to minimise our intrusion as researchers into the work environment, a feature that, on reflection, indicated the Pākehā norms within which we were operating. For the workplaces with which we worked for the first decade of the project's life, then, the cultural orientation of the organisations was predominantly Pākehā dominated, arguably the unmarked norm for much of New Zealand society, and our approach worked well.[3]

When we began to consider extending our research to Māori workplaces, we knew that we needed to adapt our approach to take account of different expecta-tions of appropriate behaviour, and a different type of relationship between ourselves as academic researchers and our Māori co-participants. We were also very aware of the danger of unconsciously privileging our outsider Pākehā analytical perspectives over the insights and perceptions of the indigenous Māori co-participants when interpreting the meaning and significance of the research material. One way of addressing these challenges is through "a social-relations approach" to ethical research with minority groups (Garner, Raschka and Sercombe, 2006: 69). This model provides a means of evaluating the kinds of social relationships in which we inevitably engage when we work with Māori participants as co-researchers. It draws attention to areas of potential problems and misunderstanding due to the taken-for-granted nature of many aspects of the research process for majority-group aca-demics. It raises questions such as the following:

> What kind of social relationships are appropriate between the academic researchers, the workplace participants, and the Māori research assistants? Are they colleagues, friends, advisors, consultants, experts?

3. There were just two exceptions among over 20 workplaces: a government department, which was strongly influenced by the public sector environment, and a Māori team, which operated within the constraints of another government agency.

How do these relationships develop over time?

What are the costs and benefits of participating in the research for each party?

Who has power and authority in different situations?

Who decides, for instance, what will be recorded and for how long?

What are the academic researchers expected to contribute to the workplaces where they are working?

What social and professional obligations do they incur from their workplace participants' perspectives?

What skills are they expected to develop and share?

These questions can be raised for any participatory research, and they clearly indicate the complexity of the research process, but they are especially pertinent when majority group researchers work with people from a socially nondominant group.

Māori researchers have been at pains to point out the abuses suffered by indigenous peoples in the name of research in previous decades, and they have actively advocated ways of researching with Māori partners that are "respectful, ethical, sympathetic and useful" (Smith, 1999: 9). This was a challenge that we were keen to take up and that was well aligned with the core methodological principles we adhere to, even if somewhat different in application. The most important factor helping us to meet our goal of ethical responsibility in relation to working with Māori organisations has been the growing role of a Māori research team within the wider research group.[4] Even during earlier phases of our research, when our focus was effective communication in New Zealand workplaces more generally, we were fortunate to have the support of Māori advisors and colleagues. Harima Fraser from Te Puni Kōkiri (Ministry of Māori Development), for example, and Mike Hollings who has worked at three different government organisations during the period of our research, have both been involved in the planning of this project from the original initiative. An invaluable team of advisors, research associates, and research assistants continue to provide guidance in all aspects of the methodological design, ensuring that we approach, interact, and consult with Māori workplaces in culturally appropriate ways. Our Māori advisors confirmed that we would need to develop a very different kind of relationship with participants in Māori workplaces compared to our Pākehā workplaces.

As Smith (1999) indicates in her discussion of Kaupapa Māori research (a framework of culturally appropriate guiding principles), when working with Māori people, researchers who wish to be respectful are expected to engage with their participants; to build relationships; and to share information, knowledge, and skills (cf. Garner et al., 2006). In the Māori workplaces we were expected to be visible; to be seen around the workplace; *he kanohi kitea* ("seen faces"); to be

4. We have expressed our sincere appreciation to these team members for their contributions in the acknowledgments at the beginning of this book.

regularly available for discussion, explanation, and interpretation throughout the data-collection process and afterward. The nonintrusive methodology we had developed for use in Pākehā workplaces was, in many respects, inappropriate in the Māori workplaces. At every step, from initial contact through to writing up material for publication, behaving in a politic and appropriate way with our Māori co-researchers was a very different experience from the experience with our Pākehā participants.

Working with Māori co-researchers involves what Sarangi (2006: 204) has called "thick participation" or "continuity of involvement in a research setting". It means establishing an ongoing commitment and recognising the development of mutual obligations. The involvement does not end when the data is collected, nor even when the analysis is completed. The relationship between the academic researchers and workplace participants is not fixed, but is rather a developing one that is constantly negotiated as the research progresses. It also involves accepting that the perspectives of each about what is important at any particular point may differ (cf. Garner et al., 2006: 70). Thus, we learned that developing what is considered appropriate behaviour as researchers within ethnically different workplaces is a complex and demanding, but also a rewarding, process.

Given these challenges, it is understandable that there was a period in the 1980s and 1990s when New Zealand research on issues relating to the Māori population almost completely disappeared, despite the growing recognition of the importance of this cultural group as New Zealand's indigenous population. Critical reasons for what appeared to be an implicit ban on such research were a growing understanding of the effects of the power differential between the typically Pākehā researchers and those being researched, a recognition of the exploitative nature of much previous research, and a challenge by Māori researchers to the claims of objectivity by Pākehā researchers in Māori contexts (Smith, 1999; Pringle, 2005). One result of this backlash, which originated largely from the Māori population themselves, was the significant support given to Kaupapa Māori research, an approach that calls for a "decolonization" of methodologies (Smith, 1999).

At its most basic, this approach argues that ethically responsible Māori research should be carried out in a way that is culturally framed, and that acknowledges a Māori worldview; it gives "primacy to an Indigenous Māori paradigm" and forces the researcher to approach topics "from an alternate [Māori] philosophic orientation" (Ruwhiu and Wolfgramm, 2006: 51). In seminal work on Kaupapa Māori research, Smith (1999: 120) set out a framework prescribing the adoption of culturally specific ideas:

1. *Aroha ki te tangata* (a respect for people).
2. *Kanohi kitea* (the seen face, i.e., present yourself to people face to face).
3. *Titiro, whakarongo...kōrero* (look, listen...speak).
4. *Manaaki ki te tangata* (share and host people, be generous).
5. *Kia tūpato* (be cautious).

6. *Kaua e takahia te mana o te tangata* (do not trample over the *mana*[5] of people).
7. *Kaua e māhaki* (don't flaunt your knowledge).[6]

These guidelines draw on a range of Māori cultural values, and are, significantly, expressed in recognisable proverbs (an important form of expression with high currency in Māori culture).[7] As noted earlier, these guidelines, which largely advocate respect and engagement, appear to be reasonable and obvious goals for any ethical researcher. Their application in Māori settings, however, requires a deeper understanding of the subtle messages conveyed by proverbs profoundly embedded in Māori culture, and expressing fundamental Māori values.

In practice, enacting these principles meant that every step in our research process required some kind of adaptation. The principles speak to the very heart of the research motivation, and cannot simply be addressed by minor tweaking of research methods which emerge from a Western worldview (Ruwhiu and Wolfgramm, 2006). For example, as noted, to show respect in our Pākehā organisations, we aimed to be unobtrusive. Our goal, aimed at minimising observer effects, was always to avoid imposing on busy participants, and we, therefore, aimed to be practically invisible in the data-collection phase. In Smith's outline of Kaupapa Māori research, however, this behaviour could be considered disrespectful. To show respect, we needed to make efforts to build solidarity with our workplace colleagues. This meant "fronting up" in the organisations to show our commitment to the research goals of benefiting Māori, by being visible and available, being involved, as well as accepting hospitality and reciprocating in turn. The data collection practice in Māori workplaces involved regular visits and phone calls (in addition to e-mail contact), shared morning teas, corridor chats, and follow-up interactive workshops (in addition to written reports or formal presentations) to negotiate understandings and share information. Our most satisfying interactions emerged from discussions designed to elicit the perspectives of workplace participants about what was important. Workshop excerpts from the recorded material, and exploration of possible interpretations with our Māori participants were strategies that recognised the different knowledge and skills that we each brought to the table, resulting in a richer

5. *Mana* can be loosely translated as power, prestige, or authority that is earned (not assigned) and is closely related to respect. This term is used widely in New Zealand English, although its complexities are not typically carried over from Māori.
6. Linda Tuhiwai Smith's book has had significant influence within academia, and focuses particularly on methodology. The principles of Kaupapa Māori research have developed and been expanded within the work of a range of theorists, and they are especially recognised within the area of education, e.g., Graham Hingangaroa Smith (1990) and Russell Bishop (2005). We have added macrons to *kōrero, tūpato* and *māhaki* on the advice of our Maori experts. It is possible the book's publisher inadvertently omitted them.
7. One of our participants commented on the importance of proverbs and the difficulty of using them in English (as opposed to Māori). She noted that she uses proverbs frequently in Māori because they express so much, based on shared cultural understandings. When translated into English, however, she described them as sounding "daggy", that is, clumsy and weird.

and more culturally sensitive set of interpretations. For example, Yvonne, the managing director of Kiwi Productions, one of the Māori organisations in our dataset, wrote in an e-mail after one such discussion, "I was really interested in what you picked up about Gretel which even our HR adviser hadn't quite picked", suggesting that our analysis was providing insights that she found valuable, and that confirmed her own perceptions.

INTERPRETING THE DATA

As noted earlier, in line with Cameron, Frazer, Harvey, Rampton, and Richardson (1992)'s call to researchers, our goal has been to adopt a process that promotes collaborative research "with" our participants rather than to engage in paternalistic research "on" research subjects. Following Garner et al.'s (2006) model for sociolinguists, we critically examined the research relationship we wished to establish with our workplace participants and advisors. Despite consistently operating with a philosophy of building ongoing relationships with organisations, the relationships that we developed with Pākehā and Māori workplaces differed. In Pākehā workplaces, we typically highlighted the costs and benefits of our research for the organisation; the benefits for us as researchers were treated as so obvious that they were never mentioned. We argued, and Pākehā contributors generally accepted, that members of participating organisations typically benefited by sharing the insights our analyses could offer about their workplace communicative behaviour. Although discussion with participants always aided analysis, in these contexts, we were typically regarded as experts with knowledge to impart in exchange for cooperation, and with the potential to provide material for practical applications, such as workplace communication workshops.

In Māori workplaces, the research relationship evolved in a somewhat different direction. As Pākehā researchers in Māori territory we were aware of our potentially hegemonic assumptions and behaviours, and the many subtle ways in which our discourse and behaviours might unwittingly instantiate asymmetrical power relations (van Dijk, 1993; Wodak, 1995; Fairclough, 2003). To ignore the influence of ethnicity on the interaction of leaders would be to relegate its role to the status of Blommaert's (2005) forgotten contexts, and yet, for the participants in the Māori organisations, in particular, their ethnicity was relevant in all aspects of their workplace talk. Interpreting talk in Māori workplaces with integrity was thus a considerable challenge for us as researchers.

By applying a methodology that was as consistent with Kaupapa Māori research as possible, and that emphasised mutual respect and engagement, the ongoing relationship placed much greater emphasis on actively nurturing the growth of solidarity among all involved. Thus, although the underlying principles remain the same, the enactment of these principles was very diverse. To be accepted takes time, and respect is earned through repeated displays of appropriate behaviour. In every way, our goal was to become accepted group members. For us, as Pākehā researchers, the largest obstacle was undoubtedly our own cultural backgrounds. As the late James Ritchie, a much-admired and respected (by both Māori and Pākehā) New Zealand sociologist, noted in his discussion of becoming bicultural, "[in] the Māori world I am an outsider, a visitor, and always will be" (1992: 51). Being aware of this limitation is an important first step.

We remain committed to the benefits of close discourse analysis to our under-standing of workplace communication. This is especially important for challenging naïve Pākehā interpretations of what is going on, and exhibiting the potential bene-fits of understanding different cultural frames. In a perfect world, the kind of inves-tigations we undertook would be carried out by Māori researchers trained in discourse analytic techniques. As Pākehā researchers, we offered skills in exploring workplace interaction and in highlighting differences, and we, therefore, worked with Māori research assistants as much as possible to share those skills. In practice, however, at the interpretation stage in particular, we were heavily reliant on the gen-erosity of insiders in providing potential explanations and insights into the diverse ways in which cultural norms permeated Māori workplace discourse.

RESEARCHING WORKPLACE INTERACTION
IN SOCIOCULTURAL CONTEXT

The methodological design we have outlined reflects our conceptualisation of inter-actions as being influenced by multiple layers of context; we have deliberately attempted to take into account *at least* the levels of the model outlined in chapter 1 in our methodology. Starting from the micro-level, we have ensured that we have a range of interaction types within the recordings, following the reasoning that our interactional behaviour is affected by the discourse context in which it is produced and negotiated. This means we have collected one-to-one interactions including social and corridor talk, meetings, as well as informal debriefing sessions and formal interviews. Each type of event, or genre, has its own norms for interacting, and we needed to capture the range of discourse contexts in which our leaders were inter-acting at work.

The "rules" for these interaction types are, nevertheless, negotiated by members of different CofPs. As House (2005: 15) notes, adopting "a dynamic psycho-social view of a mutually reflexive relationship between talk and context" means acknowl-edging that "talk and the interpretive and inferential processes it generates [shape] context as much as context shapes talk". From this perspective, building a social identity appropriate for your community can be viewed as a construction or creation of workplace talk. We have, therefore, focused specifically in each of our four data sites on the community or communities in which the leaders operate, that is, selecting teams with a shared linguistic repertoire that has developed over time, with regular mutual and ongoing engagement, and with a common enterprise or purpose (Wenger, 1998; Eckert and McConnell-Ginet, 1992). In determining the relevance of these factors, we have considered shared understandings by communities: when or if it is appropriate to use the Māori language, the ways in which turn taking occurs in meetings, running jokes, the use of anecdotes for business purposes, and so on. Of greatest significance for our research design, however, was the orientation to culturally salient norms that imbued the interaction patterns at our two Māori organisations; for these organisations, adhering to tikanga, alongside their explicit goal of helping Māori people, formed a large part of the joint enterprise of the organisation, warranting ethnicity as a particular focus for our research.

To acknowledge this orientation, the notion of an ethnicised CofP has been a core consideration for the ways in which we have approached the research, and a significant component of the adaptations we have made in the implementation of the Language in the Workplace data collection philosophy. The most influential factor in our decisions has been the recognition of the Kaupapa Māori framework and its guiding principles, and the generous assistance provided by our Māori colleagues and collaborators. To sum up the differences between our approach with Māori and Pākehā organisations, we can draw a rough but useful analogy with the distinction between positive and negative politeness in the Brown and Levinson (1987) sense: in the Pākehā organisations we aimed to be unobtrusive and invisible, respecting the independence of the participants and their right not to be imposed on; in the Māori organisations our goal was to be integrated and present members of the group, with a strong emphasis on solidarity.

Although we have focused in the previous sections on the challenges of working with Māori participants, it is important to acknowledge assumptions in our design that reflect macro-level societal norms. As Pākehā researchers, such norms went unquestioned in our early research because they were the broad institutional and social norms to which all Pākehā organisations orient in their day-to-day operations. The assumptions underlying the tall poppy syndrome, and the consequent indirectness with which some leaders "do" power, influenced the way in which we approached the data collection in Pākehā settings. University researchers with titles such as Doctor and Professor, for example, cannot always easily make themselves invisible within organisations. Consequently, we introduced ourselves with first names, and we sought and emphasised existing social network connections wherever possible. The first-name egalitarian society, on which New Zealand prides itself, alongside the dense, multiplex social networks that characterise many sections of New Zealand society, meant that adopting this approach aided our quest to remain unobtrusive and maintain a low profile.

Our attention to the Kaupapa Māori framework, which challenges a western worldview (Ruwhiu and Wolgramm, 2006; Bishop, 2005), provided an important means of contesting such dominant, hegemonic assumptions. There is no one-size-fits-all approach to methodology or data collection, and behaving as ethical and sensitive researchers entails recognising the differences in each organisation and context in which we undertake research. The adaptable and participatory nature of our data-collection procedures, as originally conceived, inescapably entail developing appropriate procedures and methods for effective collection of naturally occurring workplace data.[8] The phase of our research reported in this book provided a particularly demanding test for them, but with commensurate rewards in terms of extending the boundaries of our knowledge and understanding of the research process, as we have outlined in this chapter.

HOW WE USE THE DATA IN THIS BOOK

Throughout this book, we use excerpts drawn from the recordings collected at the four workplaces to illustrate our claims. The extracts are taken from naturally occurring communicative events, typically the informal and formal meetings in which the focus leaders engage. They are supplemented, when useful, with excerpts from interviews with the focus leaders. After recordings are collected, they are catalogued, and broadly described, and then relevant material is transcribed, analysed, and discussed with participants (Holmes and Stubbe, 2003a; Marra, 2008b). Our warrant for the selection derives from our confidence that the excerpts are typical and representative, based on our extensive familiarity with the data, as well as the reassurance on this issue provided by our participants with whom we have discussed our interpretation of recorded material wherever possible, as described earlier.[9]

To facilitate understanding, we label each extract according to the workplace from which the data was taken using the organisational pseudonyms described earlier, whereby "Kiwi" indicates a Māori-focused organisation, and "NZ" signifies an organisation with an unmarked Pākehā orientation. The sector within which the organisation operates is noted as "Productions" or "Consultations". We have aimed to provide enough contextual information to help readers make sense of the extracts, while not distracting from the interactions themselves. Finally, the transcription conventions follow an established list described in Vine, Johnson, O'Brien, and Robertson (2002), with a simplified set provided as an appendix.

In her profile of the Language in the Workplace Project, Francesca Bargiela-Chiappini and her colleagues describe our analytic approach as data driven "in order to say something useful about the interactions under analysis rather than relying on one particular theory" (Bargiela-Chiappini et al., 2007: 123). Evidence of this will be apparent in our discussions of the data excerpts, although it will also be clear that the analyses have been consistently interpreted within an overarching social-constructionist framework. Moreover, it is important to bear in mind that

8. We acknowledge with appreciation Maria Stubbe's valuable contribution to the development of the design (see Stubbe, 1998a), as well as the strong influence of Michael Clyne's research in multilingual research sites in Australia.
9. The issue of "warranting" is well discussed in Cameron (2009), McRae (2009), and Swann (2009).

our analyses rely not only on our interpretations as independent researchers, but also on integrating Kaupapa Māori guidelines, taking account of the interpretations of our workplace collaborators and the advisory team, research assistants, and colleagues.

Our analysis has also benefited from insights provided by previous research on workplace discourse. There is a considerable amount of research describing majority group norms available to support our interpretations of the social meaning of workplace talk in Pākehā organisations.[10] Moreover, linguists have identified a number of linguistic features, pragmatic particles, and discourse patterns associated with Māori English, the name given to an ethnically marked variety of New Zealand English (see Benton, 1991; Kennedy and Yamazaki, 1999; Macalister, 2003). However, this is simply not the case for Māori discourse; research on Māori communication patterns, especially in nontraditional contexts, is sparse. This partly reflects the relative dearth of research in the 1980s and 1990s resulting from the reaction to research by majority group members on indigenous groups. However, the work of two researchers in the area of (social) anthropology has provided some particularly useful starting points. Anne Salmond's important study of Māori ceremony (Salmond, 1975) included influential work on rituals of encounter (Salmond, 1974), which has informed much of our analysis of meeting openings and closings. Joan Metge has produced a number of groundbreaking "handbooks" to make potential sources of cultural misunderstanding between Māori and Pākehā explicit, in particular *Talking Past Each Other* (with Patricia Kinloch in 1978) and more recently *Kōrero Tahi Talking Together* (Metge, 2001). However, with only a small number of published scholarly resources on which to draw for corroboration, our interpretations must be tentative.

Sensitively analysing data provided by people from culturally different backgrounds is a complex matter requiring considerable thought and care. We have defined our main task in relation to the Māori data as identifying which strategies contribute to effective interaction in Māori workplaces. There are many answers to this beguilingly simple-looking question. As sociolinguists, we argue that what is considered effective communication is a matter of perspective (see chapter 1, note 7), and the precise form that effective communication takes depends on a variety of considerations, including who is talking to whom and in what kind of context. It depends on what each participant is trying to achieve in the interaction, and it depends on their workplace culture or the taken-for-granted interactional norms that provide a framework for workplace talk. This will be apparent throughout this book, and it is illustrated well in the next chapter, which begins our exploration of ways in which leadership is constructed through workplace talk.

10. See Holmes (2011) for a recent review of this research.

CHAPTER 3

Constructing Leadership through Language

"I have never wanted to be an anchor for people, I have always wanted to be the person that can enable them".[1]

L eadership is a dynamic concept that has been studied from a myriad of perspectives across diverse disciplines. The language of leadership, however, is a relatively neglected area of research. In this chapter, we provide a brief survey of studies of leadership, identifying the potential role of language in leadership construction. The transactional and relational dimensions of effective leadership are briefly outlined as useful background for chapters 4 and 5, and the key role of language in enacting and indexing different facets of leadership identity is explored. Building on our own research, we highlight the crucial role of discourse in the enactment of leadership identity, and the contribution that discourse analysis can make to understanding leadership behaviour.

This chapter also includes discussion of the importance of cultural factors in leadership performance. There are many similarities in the ways that Māori and Pākehā leaders discursively index their leadership identities, but there are also some important differences that indicate the critical influence of Māori culture on ways in which Māori leadership is enacted in Māori communities of practice (CofPs). Two such issues are examined in the last section of the chapter.

1. Iritana Te Rangi Tawhiwhirangi in Diamond (2003: 91).

APPROACHES TO LEADERSHIP

Leadership Studies

Researchers in the fields of organisational behaviour and leadership studies (e.g., Alvesson and Billing, 1997; Parry, 2001; Sinclair, 1998) have typically defined leadership as the ability to influence others, and the notions of good or effective leadership have been measured in terms of organisational outcomes (Hede, 2001). Four major theories can be identified within this research: trait theories, behavioural theories, contingency theories, and implicit leadership theories. Trait theories focus on the "attributes of leaders such as personality, motives, values and skills" (Yukl, 2002: 11), although attempts to define relevant characteristics have "failed to find any traits that would guarantee leadership success" (Yukl, 2002: 12). Behavioural theories moved the emphasis to what leaders *do* rather than what they *are* (Northouse, 1997: 51). Contingency theories take account of the situation, a factor ignored in both trait and behavioural approaches, whereas implicit leadership theories have returned to trait theories but with an added dimension: they focus on "beliefs and assumptions about the characteristics of effective leaders" (Yukl, 2002: 129).

Though different labels are used, most leadership research identifies two fundamental dimensions underlying effective leadership behaviour. The first of these is the "task behaviours" dimension (Yukl, 2002), or what we refer to in sociolinguistic terms as "transactional skills" (Holmes and Stubbe, 2003a: 53). This transactional dimension refers to behaviours oriented to achieving workplace objectives, getting done what needs to be done. Leaders clearly need to be able to provide direction to others, and ensure decisions are made and implemented. This is vital to the successful running of organisations and businesses.

The second dimension has been described as "maintenance behaviours" (Yukl, 2002), or in sociolinguistic terms "relational behaviours" or "relational practice" (Fletcher, 1999). Relevant relational behaviours involve a range of interpersonal aspects of communication, that is, they are people-oriented behaviours, ways of indicating "concern for people" and relationships (Blake and Mouton, 1978). This dimension includes behaviours aimed at developing and maintaining rapport with colleagues and clients (Hede, 2001; Antonakis, Avolio, and Sivasubramaniam, 2003).

Both these dimensions have been identified as crucial to leadership success, and language is of paramount importance when considering the enactment of these behaviours. One of our leaders commented in interview on the importance of communicating effectively with his staff: "I believe if I'm a good communicator then, you know, I go a long way toward being successful at my job". Leadership scholars also acknowledge the importance of language in leadership (e.g., Berson and Avolio, 2004; Hackman and Johnson, 2004), but the language of leadership has been little studied within the fields of organisational behaviour and leadership studies. Indeed, traditionally there has been a tendency to neglect or overlook the language of leadership and the discourse strategies used to perform leadership. Most research in the area has involved interviews and surveys and has not examined naturally occurring workplace discourse. The "turn to discourse" in this area has been relatively recent (e.g., Ford, 2006; Fairhurst, 2007).

The work of Gail Fairhurst (2007) has been important in this respect. She identifies and refers to traditional leadership research as "leadership psychology", where the primary emphasis is upon the individual and the focus is almost exclusively within the cognitive realm of human endeavour. Her own interest, however, lies in the more recent, yet rapidly developing, approach of "discursive leadership", which, by contrast, is oriented toward discourse and communication. In exploring discursive leadership, Fairhurst (2007) suggests that, in very broad terms, discourse can take two forms (see also Gee, 1999). "Discourse" (or big "D" Discourse) relates to general and enduring systems for the formation and articulation of ideas in a historically situated time. This approach derives from and is well exemplified by the work of Michel Foucault (1982, 1988). The other form, "discourse" (or little "d" discourse) refers to talk and text in social practices within specific local contexts. Using this approach, the language that is being used by the actors and the interaction processes themselves become the central concern for the analyst (Potter and Wetherell, 1987). Fairhurst (2007) identifies a range of techniques for analysing little "d" discourse: sociolinguistics, ethnomethodology, conversation analysis, speech act schematics, interaction analysis, and semiotics. These areas are outside the traditional frameworks of leadership studies, but the valuable insights that they provide are beginning to be acknowledged (Jackson, Pfeifer, and Vine, 2006; Fairhurst, 2007).

Leadership and Narrative

Fairhurst (2007: chapter 6) explores the intersection of big "D" Discourse and little "d" discourse with a study of narrative, the one area of language use that has been investigated by leadership scholars. In particular, "hero stories" (Jackson and Parry, 2001) have been identified as a paradigmatic means of constructing inspirational leadership (see Example 3.2 below). Leaders use narratives as a way of sense making in an organisation; they provide a contextualising history, as well as a means of teaching about how things are done in an organisation, and how followers are expected to think (Boje, 1991; Dennehy, 1999; Fleming, 2001; Kaye, 1996; Ready, 2002). It is clear that these functions tend to be oriented to the more transactional dimensions of leadership, contributing to achieving organisational objectives. Again, naturally occurring workplace discourse has not been a major source of such data; rather, interviews have typically been used to elicit the organisational narratives that provide the basis for this research (Jackson and Parry, 2001).

Narrative discourse as a means of constructing leadership identity has also been explored by the Language in the Workplace Project (LWP) team (Holmes and Marra, 2005; Marra and Holmes, 2005; Marra and Holmes, 2008). Our research has demonstrated that workplace narratives can usefully serve a wide range of both transactional and relational functions. As sociolinguists, however, our investigation of leadership and narratives focuses predominantly on stories embedded in the minutiae of everyday interaction, stories that may appear mundane and unimportant, even to the participants, as in Example 3.1.

Example 3.1

Context: NZ Consultations: Suzanne, the deputy leader of the team, is meeting with two other team members

1	Suzanne:	well that's where my memo comes in
2		um that essentially I've had feedback
3		from secretaries and
4		I'm going to talk to um Cecilia this week too
5		but also my own experience of seeking support
6		and and just not having it available
7		and juniors and me working
8		through the weekend to get things done

Suzanne's story focuses on the need for the organisation to provide more administrative support at times when the demands of the job are high. She describes how she has been given feedback from the organisation's administrative staff, which is supported by her own experience of having to work through weekends to complete jobs. The short narrative articulates her attitude regarding the importance of pitching in when needed, as well as demonstrating her consultative approach to leadership, talking to the secretaries to collect their feedback (lines 2–3). Suzanne commented in a de-briefing interview after the data was collected that she typically prefers a consultative approach to management. Example 3.1 reports an instance of such consultation in her discourse with team members. In terms of our model, this short excerpt also provides an interesting insight into the norms of the organisational culture within which Suzanne is operating. In many white-collar organisations, New Zealand business norms entail long working hours, with what many employees perceive as inadequate administrative support. Suzanne makes this quite explicit by sharing her personal experience and assessment here with her colleagues.

Although such narratives seem relatively insignificant when compared to the stories investigated for organisational myth making, these small anecdotes and accounts in fact provide enormous potential as a workplace communication tool in a leader's repertoire. In particular, they provide a useful discourse strategy for leaders in their ongoing quest to construct and reconstruct an effective leadership identity through talk. Both approaches (big "D" Discourse and little "d" discourse) recognise the significance of discourse strategies such as narrative for exploring leadership. However, our focus is firmly on the micro-level detail of discourse analysis.

Leadership, Language, and Power

Over the last two decades, interest in workplace talk and research using the approaches identified by Fairhurst (2007) to explore little "d" discourse, that is, sociolinguistics, ethnomethodology, conversation analysis, speech act schematics, interaction analysis, and semiotics, has increased dramatically (e.g., Drew and Heritage, 1992; Boden, 1994; Firth, 1995; Bargiela-Chiappini and Harris, 1997a, 1997b; Sarangi and Roberts, 1999; Thornborrow, 2002; Locher, 2004; Richards, 2006). A diverse range of workplaces has been explored in these studies, and many examine contexts in which only some of the participants are "at work", for example, legal settings or medical contexts. Power relationships are important in all such contexts, regardless of whether there are formal leader/follower relationships.[2]

Power is, of course, a central component of leadership, since leaders are people with what has been termed "legitimate power", that is, power due to position (French and Raven, 1959). They may also have "expert power", that is, power derived from expertise and skills (French and Raven, 1959), which has resulted in them being appointed to positions of legitimate power. Early social theories of power, like theories of leadership, did not explore the role of language in power, but more recent theories pay attention to the contribution of language in the construction of power relations.[3] A structural approach regards power as involved in all social action, and this theory has been influential in the area of Critical Discourse Analysis (CDA). One of the fundamental aims of CDA has been to explore social power and the role of language and discourse in maintaining and reinforcing power relationships. This involves not only legitimate power and expert power, but power derived from other social factors, such as gender and ethnicity (Fairclough, 1992; van Dijk, 1993; Holmes, 2004, 2005a; Holmes and Marra, 2002b; Mullany, 2004).

Although the discourse of leaders of different ethnicities has not received much attention to date, gendered discourse has attracted considerable attention in recent research on workplace interaction. Mullany (2007) and Baxter (2010) both focus on the discourse of female leaders in the professional workplace, demonstrating that effective communicators, both female and male, make use of a wide range of discursive strategies to enact power in workplace interaction. Both researchers argue for an integrated analytical approach, drawing on different frameworks, including CDA, interactional sociolinguistics, and pragmatics as appropriate

2. See Holmes (2011) for a review of this material.
3. See Fairclough, 1992, Watts, 2003, Locher, 2004 for further discussion.

(cf. Holmes, Stubbe and Vine, 1999). Both include analyses of the talk of female managers in naturally occurring business meetings, and also draw on data gathered through interviews. Much of this research can be regarded as attempting to reconcile the two types of discourse identified by Gee (1999) i.e., little "d" and big "D" discourse (see also Fairhurst, 2007).

Recent research from the LWP team has also specifically focused on leadership discourse (e.g., Holmes et al., 2009; Vine, Holmes, Marra, Pfeifer and Jackson, 2008), examining the language of both female and male leaders. This has been undertaken within a broader social constructionist approach, which takes account of the influence of dominant institutional norms, social context and cultural values (see our model in chapter 1). Our research falls into the little "d" discourse arena, shifting the emphasis from what people report about leaders' behaviour to observation and analysis of the interactional processes and discourse strategies actually used by effective leaders in their workplaces (Holmes and Stubbe, 2003a; Holmes et al., 2003; Vine, 2004, 2009; Schnurr, 2005, 2008; Holmes, 2006; Marra et al., 2006; Vine et al., 2008). The ways that managers express directives (Vine, 2004, 2009), use humour (Holmes and Marra, 2006; Holmes, 2007b; Schnurr, 2005, 2008), and how they work with others to co-lead (Vine et al., 2008) have all received attention, along with their use of narrative (as mentioned earlier). We have also examined the different leadership identities that female and male leaders construct (Holmes, 2005a; Marra, Vine, and Holmes, 2008). Our detailed discursive analyses support the claims of others (e.g., Dwyer, 1993; Robbins et al., 1998; Sayers, 1997; Fairhurst and Sarr, 1996) that effective leadership evidences a range of diverse competencies, and effective leaders index a wide range of complex stances in constructing a convincing leadership identity.

Discourse analysis provides valuable insights into the way leadership is enacted, and the ways in which different facets of leadership identities are indexed and constructed, since it examines the actual language used by leaders and their teams in their everyday workplace interactions. In the following chapters we focus on a range of micro-level strategies that leaders use to create, maintain, and negotiate their positions as leaders. Transactional and relational considerations are relevant in all interactions, and the way leaders skillfully manage these different facets of workplace talk is evident in the analyses throughout this book. Before focusing on transactional aspects of leadership discourse in particular in chapter 4, however, we first discuss some issues relevant to Māori leadership, setting the scene for further exploration of the interaction between ethnicity, discourse, and leadership in later chapters.

MĀORI LEADERSHIP

As noted in chapter 1, very little research has explored the ways in which indigenous people conceptualise and enact leadership (Baragwanath et al., 2001; Ka'ai and Reilly, 2004; Mahuika, 1992; Nga Tuara, 1992; Sinclair, 2005; Walker, 1993;

Warner and Grint, 2006). Dorfman (2003) calls for leadership researchers not to ignore important differences in leadership norms and practices within countries. This is particularly significant within New Zealand because of the co-existence in a multicultural context of two primary cultures—Māori and Pākehā—characterised in many areas by strikingly divergent value sets (Thomas, 2001). Pākehā leadership has been widely treated as the predominant model for New Zealand leaders (e.g., Elkin, Jackson, and Inkson, 2008; Jackson and Parry, 2001: 25; Trevor-Roberts et al., 2003). However, there is, to date, very little published work that focuses specifically on Māori leaders and leadership outside the world of politics (and, indeed, the term "Māori leaders" tends to be interpreted as meaning "Māori political leaders"). Diamond (2003), for example, provides a set of interviews with one female and five male Māori leaders from different areas of public life. Like others (e.g., Nathan, 1999), he focuses on high-profile leaders, identifying distinguishing characteristics, such as their high level of education and their engagement in public issues and activities. He does, however, acknowledge that his selection of very "public" figures means that Māori leaders (especially women) who work from within communities are omitted from the book. Because our research includes both male and female leaders, it is important to recognise that Māori women leaders are clearly influential, despite cultural barriers that typically downplay their roles and involvement (Henry, 1994; Jones, Pringle, and Shepherd, 2000; Magee, 2001; Te Awekotuku, 1991). Māori women's contribution to the *Kōhanga Reo* ("language nests") movement, an initiative using Maori immersion in preschools, has been documented (Diamond, 2003), but the contribution of Māori women leaders in other workplace contexts has rarely been the focus of research. Māori leadership, male and female, in the setting of the organisation remains largely unexplored.

Māori and Pākehā ways of constructing leadership have much in common. Both cultures value strong, authoritative, and decisive leaders who provide clear direction and behave with integrity. There are also differences, however, and in this section we describe just two characteristics that distinguish to some extent between Māori and Pākehā leadership behaviour. The first is the high value that Māori leaders place on modesty and humility; the second is the equally important value of respect for the dignity of others, illustrated in the following discussion by the tendency for Māori workplace leaders to avoid direct criticism of individuals. Both have their roots in fundamental Māori concepts.

Leadership and *Whakaiti*

> Kaore te kūmara e whaakii ana tana reka
> *The kūmara (sweet potato) does not announce it is tasty*[4]

4. Mead and Grove (2003: 36).

The complementary Māori concepts of *whakaiti,* "being humble, modest",[5] and *whakahīhī,* "boasting, being arrogant, conceited", underpin a good deal of behaviour in Māori workplaces. Metge (1995: 103) characterises whakahīhī as "the wrong sort of pride, pride which focuses on the self separate from the group and involves looking down on others. The fault is not in holding a high opinion of one's status and achievements but in asserting that opinion on an individualistic basis, without waiting for the endorsement of the group or group leaders. The whakahīhī forget that mana cannot be arrogated to oneself but is always delegated by God and by people". Self-deprecation is the preferred Māori norm; self-deprecation is "the way Māori respond when praise is directed at themselves" (Metge, 1995: 160). In line with these values, Māori leaders generally do not self-promote.

By contrast, it is easy to find instances in our data of Pākehā leaders who sing their own praises and provide explicit hero stories or examples illustrating that they provide good leadership (Holmes, 2009). In NZ Productions, for example, Seamus, the managing director, was initially brought into the company as an advisor when the company was close to going under. Example 3.2 is a brief excerpt from Seamus's classic hero story. He describes the state he found the company in.

Example 3.2

Context: NZ Productions: Interview with Seamus, managing director

1	Seamus:	he from what I could see was rearranging
2		the deck chairs on the Titanic
3		they just weren't doing anything about it
4		they were paralysed
5		and heading down hill…
6		I asked all the questions that I needed to ask
7		I pretty quickly got a very good um knowledge
8		of how things were supposed to work…
9		I suddenly had an idea as to
10		how I could um er +
11		get involved and make decisions
12		and make something happen

Seamus tells the story of how he saved what has now become a very successful company through careful planning and hard work. Following a dramatic opening metaphor of devastation, this can be analysed as remarkably self-oriented, as evidenced by the number of instances of *I* (lines 1, 6, 7, 9, 10). We have a number of similar narratives in our database in which a (usually male) leader recounts a

5. Whakaiti can also mean "to belittle". Here we use the meaning "to make small".

typically masculine narrative of contest, describing how he succeeded despite formidable hurdles (cf. Coates, 2003; Johnson, 1997; Holmes, 2009). This is one way in which Seamus constructs himself very positively as a visionary, a decisive business leader.

Another leader in NZ Productions, Rob, the business development manager, provides another example, this time from a discussion during a workplace meeting. Rob constructs an authoritative leadership identity, indexed through the positive and confident stance he adopts in portraying the company's current situation.

Example 3.3

Context: NZ Productions: Seamus, managing director, Jaeson, general manager, and Rob, business development manager, are meeting to discuss how to pitch their services to a potential customer

1	Rob:	if his current perception of a really
2		topnotch production company is [company one]
3		in Napier + this is gonna blow him away
4		I've been through [company one]
5		[company one]'s facility in Auckland
6		is pretty impressive
7		[company two] facility in Napier is
8		this is more impressive than (theirs)

Using a series of laudatory lexical items *topnotch* (line 2), *blow him away* (line 3), *impressive* (lines 6, 8), Rob is here "talking up" the impact that seeing NZ Productions will have on a potential partner (Marra, 2006). Some of their competitors are *pretty impressive* (line 6), but Rob is asserting that NZ Productions is even *more impressive* (line 8).

We can contrast this with the following example from a meeting at the Māori organisation, Kiwi Productions. Taumata, the client services manager, is reporting to a meeting of the whole organisation on the financial results for the previous month.

Example 3.4

Context: Kiwi Productions: Meeting of all staff

1	Taumata:	okay Yvonne did touch on a thing
2		something that has been very positive
3		was the September financial result

4		I must admit when I first put it on my screen
5		and then looked at the printed report I thought
6		there's [laughs]: something: wrong there

Rather than emphasising and basking in the achievement of the company, as reflected in the positive financial report for the month, Taumata's reaction is to suspect an error, indicating his unwillingness to assume that they are doing as well as the figures suggest. He expresses a very different attitude to that of Seamus and Rob from NZ Productions in Examples 3.2 and 3.3. Like others in this Māori workplace, he tends to diffidently underplay the company's achievements, and to avoid boasting and self-promotion.

In a similar fashion, the workplace stories that the Māori leaders told us were often self-deprecatory, and their general demeanour and self-presentation was typically modest and even humble. This was consistently evident in Yvonne's discourse in staff meetings, as illustrated in Example 3.5a.

Example 3.5a

Context: Kiwi Productions: Meeting of all staff. Yvonne, managing director, is providing her monthly report

1	Yvonne:	yesterday I talked I had to give a
2		presentation ( ) conference
3		I was invited by [name]…
4		I felt the presentation wasn't that good
5		because my briefing was about
6		a two-second phone [laughs]: call:
7		[laughter]
8		and so I had no idea who was going to be
9		at the conference and ( ) what's it about
10		I had no program beforehand
11		so I was a bit [unprepared]

Yvonne reports on the fact that, at short notice, she made a brief contribution to a conference in the area of the company's interests. She also reports that she felt the presentation *wasn't that good* (line 4), explaining that she had very little time to prepare *my briefing was about a two-second phone call* (lines 5–6), and that she was not provided with a program in advance (line 10). Yvonne thus constructs herself as responding positively to an opportunity to promote the company's interests, but also as very critical of her own performance; she reports that she felt she had not done as well as she would have wished. Though it is similarly self-oriented (note the recurrence of the pronoun *I*), this story contrasts sharply with Seamus's hero story

(Example 3.2), since Yvonne's orientation serves to take responsibility for a failure rather than a success. This account also contrasts more generally with data from our Pākehā workplaces where, although self-deprecating humour occurs on occasion, we have no examples of a leader negatively evaluating their own performance in a formal, public context. It is probably also worth stating explicitly that this negative self-evaluation should not be interpreted as a sign of insecurity (as it might reasonably be in a Pākehā context). As demonstrated in later chapters, Yvonne is a confident and competent leader who has received a great deal of external recognition for her leadership skills. Rather, her self-deprecation here is typical of her self-critical approach to any task, as well as a culturally appropriate expression of whakaiti.

In Māori contexts, praise appropriately comes not from oneself but from others (Metge, 1995: 160). *Waiho te mihi ma te tangata* or "Leave your praises for someone else", as the Maori proverb says.[6] In relation to the example cited above, it is interesting to note what follows Yvonne's modest report. Sheree had also attended the presentation and she suddenly realises this is what Yvonne is referring to. Example 3.5b is how the discussion continues.

Example 3.5b

Context: Kiwi Productions: Meeting of all staff (continues on from Example 3.5a)

12	Sheree:	is this the one you had yesterday
13	Yvonne:	yeah
14	Sheree:	I loved it
15	Yvonne:	//oh did you\
16		/[laughter]\\
17	Sheree:	(I actually) came home raving
18	Yvonne:	oh that's only because I had a photo of you
19		[loud burst of laughter]
20	Yvonne:	so mm but it's just... anyway so that's me +++
21		next

Sheree is fulsome in praise of Yvonne's contribution *I loved it... I actually came home raving* (lines 14, 17). Yvonne's first reaction is surprise *oh did you* (line 15). When this elicits an upgraded compliment, Yvonne skillfully and humourously refutes it by suggesting Sheree's positive response can be explained because a photograph of Sheree was a component of the presentation (line 18). This occasions general laughter and the humour effectively deflects attention from Yvonne and the compliment Sheree has paid her. Yvonne then passes the baton to the next contributor *so that's me +++ next* (line 20-21).

6. See *http://www.maori.cl/Proverbs.htm.*

In this example, then, Yvonne's leadership behaviour is totally consistent with the Māori value of whakaiti and avoidance of boasting (whakahīhī). She enacts modest and frank stances, and deflects with humour a compliment that draws attention to her oratorical skills. (Chapter 5 provides examples of similar behaviour by Quentin, Yvonne's second-in-command in Kiwi Productions, and Daniel, the Chief Executive Officer (CEO) of Kiwi Consultations). These examples nicely illustrate, then, the ways in which Māori leaders tend to index a humble and self-deprecating stance in constructing themselves as leaders in ways that are consistent with the values of their ethnicised CofPs.

Leadership and *Whakamā*

Another feature that distinguishes between Māori and Pākehā leadership behaviour in some contexts is different preferred ways of indicating respect for the individual. To illustrate this, we discuss how Māori leaders handle criticism of others in the workplace. At least some Pākehā leaders prefer in general to be direct and explicit in identifying behaviour of which they disapprove. Most Māori leaders by contrast tend to avoid direct criticism of individuals, a preference that has its roots in the Māori concept of *whakamā* ("embarrassment", "shame").

Our research has identified a wide variety of strategies for expressing disagreement and criticism in Pākehā workplaces, ranging from very explicit and confrontational linguistic devices through to very indirect and implicit discursive strategies (Holmes and Stubbe, 2003c; Holmes and Marra, 2004a). Strategies range from the blatant imposition of authority, through negotiation and compromise, to avoidance strategies that sideline or divert difficult issues (Holmes and Marra, 2004a). Not surprisingly, we identified many of these strategies for expressing criticisms and managing conflict in the Māori workplaces where we collected data. One noticeable gap, however, was instances illustrating the explicit, confrontational end of the scale. These were used by some Pākehā as strategies for constructing themselves as authoritative and decisive leaders, but they were rarely evident in Māori workplaces.

In an excerpt from a meeting at the Pākehā company, NZ Productions, Rob, a Pākehā manager, interrupts Jaeson, but Jaeson, the general manager (also Pākehā), directly and explicitly insists that Rob let him finish what he is saying.

Example 3.6

Context: NZ Productions: Management meeting

1	Jaeson:	I think the other thing too to note is
2		that we're actually not even already

```
3                    judging these guys we don't
4                    we're not saying that they're doing it wrong
5                    we're saying that they're really that's they're
6                    doing the best they can
7                    //but it's not that no but we no we said=
8     Rob:           /oh no I'm saying they're doing it wrong [laughs]\\
9     Jaeson:        =hear me out we're saying they're\
10                   doing the best they can
11                   but that's not gonna be good enough
12                   when [business name] comes along
13                   because we're gonna be able to offer
14                   such a better system such a better service
15    Seamus:        they just don't know any better do they
16    Jaeson:        they just don't know any better
```

Jaeson asserts that you cannot say that people in other companies are "wrong" for doing things differently (line 4). Rob, however, insists that they are wrong (line 8), but Jaeson has not finished his turn at this point (his intonation clearly indicates that he still wants to hold the floor). When Rob makes his confrontational assertion, *oh no I'm saying they're doing it wrong,* Jaeson does not back off and let Rob take the floor. Instead, he insists that Rob allows him to complete his utterance (*hear me out,* line 9). He assertively insists on his right to the floor at this point, and his right to continue elaborating the point of view he is outlining.[7]

In the same Pākehā company, Seamus, the managing director, frequently challenges his team members quite directly and explicitly about things he disapproves of. Discussing the use of a rusty and dented truck for deliveries, for instance, he asks *who's letting this happen...why wasn't it fixed initially.* In other words, he explicitly demands the name of the person responsible, as well as challenging the decision that led to the unsatisfactory situation. These are very direct and aggressive strategies for expressing disagreement and dissatisfaction, but they are regarded as normal and go unremarked in this rather "masculinist" CofP (Baxter, 2003).

Of course, these confrontational strategies are not used by all Pākehā leaders, nor by these leaders in all discourse contexts. Indeed, the New Zealand norm is generally to avoid direct confrontation and criticism. A common pattern is for a manager to criticise a subordinate very directly in discussion with their team leader, but when actually faced with the recalcitrant staff member, the issue is generally

7. Interestingly, this ultimately involves Jaeson developing a position that is consistent with that of Rob and Seamus, so that the confrontation clearly does not have any longer-term repercussions. Jaeson argues that others are not doing things wrong, and he recognises that they have been doing their best, but significantly *that's not gonna be good enough* (line 10), a position endorsed implicitly by the contribution of the managing director, Seamus, *they just don't know any better do they* (line 14), and echoed by Jaeson in line 15, indicating a harmonious resolution.

presented less directly. So, for example, Jaeson, the general manager in Example 3.3 from NZ Productions, criticises Brendon, another team member, for inefficient and unproductive behaviour when he is talking to Paul, another manager, but the issue is raised in a much more conciliatory manner in his subsequent interview with Brendon. Nevertheless, direct strategies are used relatively frequently by some leaders, especially in more "masculinist" workplace cultures, dominated by relatively contestive norms of interaction, and by normatively masculine attitudes and values (Holmes and Stubbe, 2003c; Holmes, 2006; Baxter, 2003).

Direct confrontation of this kind is much rarer in the Māori workplace data. Traditional Māori formal cultural contexts, such as the marae, provide safe, controlled settings in which people can express their disagreements, criticisms, and complaints. In this context, Māori protocol provides a formal method for containing conflict and managing disagreement (Metge, 2001: 35), with mediation and advice provided by respected elders. Moreover, people who are attacked or criticised in such a context will typically not defend themselves, but rather will leave it to someone else "to speak on their behalf" (Metge and Kinloch, 1978: 29). In less formal contexts, it seems that Māori tend to avoid explicit critical comments, preferring indirect and implicit means for conveying dissatisfaction, such as narrative, humour (Holmes and Hay, 1997; Holmes, 1998a), or sometimes using a third party (Metge, 1995, 2001). Indirectness is an effective means both of self- and other-protection in such contexts.

Overt disagreement and explicit criticism are especially avoided if there is a danger of causing whakamā, which an individual may experience by being explicitly singled out. The concept is very complex as Metge and Kinloch (1978: 24) make clear,[8] but it is useful in understanding the strategies for criticising unsatisfactory work performance, which were favoured in public contexts by Māori leaders in our data. The most common of these was to discuss the general issue rather than focusing on specific unsatisfactory instances. Our analysis of more than 40 meetings identified a strong tendency to focus in Māori meetings on weaknesses in organisational processes rather than discussing specific instances of unsatisfactory performance, a strategy well-designed to protect individuals' face needs (cf. Geyer, 2008).

An example of this from Kiwi Productions, involves Yvonne's dissatisfaction with the performance of one of her employees. She initially expresses her criticisms quite explicitly to the individual's team leader in a one-to-one meeting. However, in the large group meeting context, when she is reporting on the problems arising from the individual's weak performance, she deals with the specific issue very differently. In this context, she mentions the source of her dissatisfaction, but she does

8. Metge and Kinloch (1978: 24) gloss its meaning as "feeling at a disadvantage, being in a lower position morally or socially, whether as a result of your own actions or another's". The sources of whakamā are deeply cultural, as are the behaviours through which it is manifested, and the culturally appropriate responses (Metge, 1995: 284). Bringing shame on one's social group (tribe, subtribe, or family) is one potentially relevant component, especially important because of the way the group is typically privileged over the individual in Māori culture.

not identify the individual concerned in any way. The issue is generalised and the focus is on the processes needed to ensure that the reason for the complaint does not recur. Yvonne's behaviour indicates concern for the health of the group and consideration for the face needs of the individual concerned. She chooses an indirect means of indicating her dissatisfaction and focuses on a constructive response to it. Direct confrontation is avoided and the individual's dignity is taken into account.

Another example from a staff meeting at Kiwi Productions involves one of the section managers who takes the floor to make a complaint about the state of the kitchen. The complaint is embedded in an extended and very amusing performance. Humour is typical of the interactional style at Kiwi Productions (Holmes, 2007b) and is one means by which critical messages are conveyed very indirectly. No particular individual is identified for criticism in such a public context; the comments are directed to the group as a whole, an ethnically acceptable strategy for conveying such a message.

Example 3.7

Context: Kiwi Productions: Meeting of all staff. Quentin has been reporting on what his division has been doing. He assigns the floor to Rangi, his deputy leader, to report on an award ceremony in which the company has been involved. But Rangi begins with a digression about the state of the kitchen. Constant laughter, feedback, background talk, and occasional applause throughout (not noted in transcript)

1	Rangi:	*āe kia ora koutou* ["yes" + greeting]
2		but before we start this is my magic box +
3		*ngaru iti ngaru* meaning wave
4		*iti* meaning in this context microwave +
5		yes it's twelve o'clock by crikey I'm hungry
6		I think I'll shoot down the kitchen
7		and make myself a *kai* ["food"] +
8		grab the plate fill it up put it in the microwave
9		close the lid ring ring ring the bloody phone
10		I'll have to duck down and answer the damn thing
11		ring ring ring ring ring ring
12		pick it up the bugger's gone
13		hang it up in comes a mate yackety yack
14		yackety yack yackety yack yackety yack
15		oh my *kai* I'll race down to the ( ) kitchen
16		[loudly]: open the door bugger me days
17		the damn thing's exploded: +
18		doesn't matter I'll clean it later

19	[sings]: *āe kai* away I go:
20	poor old Yvonne comes down the stairs
21	open the microwave
22	and someone's spewed inside +
23	so [funny voice]: please team when it happens
24	clean it out straight away: +
25	oh it's ten o'clock I'll duck downstairs
26	and have a cuppa +
27	open the cupboard grab the cup
28	open the drawer grab a spoon
29	where has David hidden the coffee
30	bugger me days it's behind the honey +
31	pull it out in it goes open the fridge grab the milk
32	stir stir stir hot water in [whispers]: now:
33	the easiest trick in the world
34	tap on spoon under rinse *mukumuku maroke* ["rinse"]
35	back in the drawer close the drawer
36	[loudly]: spoons for the rest of the day: ++
37	oh bugger (6) *mihini horoi mea paru* ["dishwasher"] +
38	dishwasher finish my *kai* +
39	plate on the bench walk out the door
40	some other bugger will put it inside
41	[loudly]: easy trick: open the door slide it in
42	close the door *haere ra* ["goodbye"] well done

This extended example illustrates many different points. Most relevantly here, Rangi conveys a critical message in a way that is very appropriate in this workplace—indirectly, with humour, and without targeting any individual.

In accomplishing his goal, Rangi plays the part of the forgetful or careless person who leaves the kitchen in a mess. He re-enacts three hypothetical episodes to get his message across while skilfully avoiding pointing the finger at any particular individual. Leaving the microwave in a mess and leaving spoons and plates unwashed is socially unacceptable behaviour. He not only lampoons the unacceptable behaviour but also models the preferred behaviour (e.g., for washing spoons).

There are many features of Rangi's presentation that index his Māori identity and orient it appropriately to his audience in this ethnicised CofP. He begins with a Māori greeting *kia ora koutou*, makes use of a traditional closing phrase *haere ra*, and uses the familar Māori lexical item *kai* for "food" (lines 7, 15, 19, 38). He also teaches, at nicely spaced intervals, three less familiar Māori phrases *ngaru iti* for "microwave" (lines 3–4), *mukumuku maroke* for "rinse" (line 34), and *mihimi horoi mea paru* for "dishwasher" (lines 37–38). This is a common feature in this workplace, where mutual learning and jointly constructed knowledge are the bread and butter of everyday interactions. He uses reporting devices that have been identified as typifying Māori narratives (Holmes, 1998b): for example, the use of direct speech with no explicit quotative signals for immediacy (*by crikey I'm hungry I think I'll shoot down the kitchen and make myself a kai* (lines 5–7)). He uses a good deal of subject elision (e.g., lines 8–9, 27–28, 31, 34–35, 39), emphasising the informality, along with informal lexical items such as *the damn thing* (line 10), *bugger* (lines 12, 37, 40), *bugger me days* (lines 16, 30), *yackety yack* (lines 13, 14), *spewed* (line 22).

Furthermore, the whole monologue is delivered with a steady rhythmic beat that greatly enhances its performance quality, along with his use of special effects such as a whispering voice (line 32), a funny voice (lines 23–24), and high volume and stress at various points (lines 16–17, 36, 41), with the whole performance encouraged and emphasised by audience applause, calls of approval, and laughter throughout.

One other point worth mentioning is the implicit, indirectly expressed respect for Yvonne, the managing director, which is apparent in the reference to her finding a disgusting mess in the microwave (line 20). Māori people are generally very sensitive to status differences, and, unlike Pākehā, who typically deliberately play down differences of rank, Māori often expressly index a respectful stance toward superiors. This is especially characteristic of the politeness norms in this particular CofP. Here Rangi's reference to Yvonne is a subtle reminder of her position, which usefully serves to emphasise his message.

This example thus illustrates some key features of typical Māori ways of doing things, which contrast with normatively Pākehā workplace behaviours. Complaining about the state of the kitchen is a common speech act in many workplaces, but it is usually accomplished by a written reminder from an administrative assistant, which may even be directed specifically to offending individuals when they have been identified. Rangi, handed the floor to make a contribution to workplace business, takes time out to make this point in a very indirect and inexplicit way. His strategic use of the Māori language, and of humour, his teaching strategies, and his concern for protecting people's face are all features that are consistent with Māori values and with Māori ways of doing things.

To sum up, we are not suggesting that criticisms are always accomplished indirectly in Māori culture. Rather we are suggesting that a preference for indirect ways of addressing problematic issues is consistent with fundamental Māori values, such as a commitment to the group, respect for an individual's dignity, and a preference for nonconfrontational ways of dealing with differences. Our analysis demonstrates the omni-relevance of certain shared recognised cultural norms in interaction. The participants clearly orient to these norms and demonstrate their pervasive relevance through their talk.

CONCLUSION

This chapter has explored approaches to the study of leadership. Although language is acknowledged as important within the fields of organisational behaviour and leadership studies, the language of leadership has been largely ignored. Instead, the focus has been mainly on the traits that characterise good leaders, and what others think about them. Interviews and surveys have underpinned much of this research.

In terms of our model, evidence of the pervasive hegemonic ideology of visionary, charismatic, and authoritative leadership that emerges from the standard leadership research literature can also be found in the hero stories of particular leaders in New Zealand organisations. Seamus's story in this chapter provides one example (see also Example 7.10 in chapter 7). Appreciation of the importance of examining the language of leadership through the use of micro-level techniques such as conversation analysis and other forms of discourse analysis is gradually becoming evident in recent work by leadership scholars (Fairhurst, 2007; Jackson et al., 2006), and there has been a call to turn attention to the talk of leaders. The LWP is one of the few research projects that has explicitly examined the language of leadership within specific workplace cultures, taking account of the influence of the norms of the CofP to which leaders belong, although other studies focusing on language and power are beginning to address this gap. In this chapter, we have provided some examples of how discourse analysis of workplace interaction can provide valuable insights into the enactment of leadership and the understanding of leadership behaviour.

As our model suggests, Māori norms are also relevant in accounting for the diverse ways in which leadership is enacted in our focus workplaces. In the last section of this chapter, some distinctive facets of Māori leadership were discussed and illustrated with reference to two concepts that have an important influence on the way leadership is enacted in our Māori workplaces. Whakaiti and the need to avoid causing whakamā are important concepts that help account for some of the ways in which Māori leaders interact with their staff in particular CofPs. The Māori leaders in our data frequently downplay praise or deflect attention that focuses on them, often using humour for this purpose. They prefer to express criticism and disagreement in indirect ways so as not to cause embarrassment or shame to others; nonconfrontational strategies are favoured. Although similar patterns do occur in Pākehā workplaces, there are also occasions when more confrontational strategies are employed by leaders in these organisations, with evidence that these are considered appropriate and normal within particular CofPs.

Having set the scene for our research, we turn now to the main analysis chapters in the book, beginning with a focus on transactional talk, as illustrated by the analysis of workplace meetings in chapter 4.

CHAPTER 4
Business Meetings

Mā pango, mā whero ka oti te mahi[1]
Leaders and workers together achieve the goal

Busines meetings are omnipresent discourse events in workplace communication, which have attracted a good deal of attention from discourse analysts (e.g., Asmuss and Svennevig, 2009; Angouri and Marra, 2009; Barnes, 2007; Bilbow, 1998). They are fully sanctioned "business" talk, and our collaborating participants needed little encouragement to allow us to video record their weekly or monthly meetings. Excerpts from these recorded interactions are used in this chapter to demonstrate how leadership is enacted in the context of business meetings, and to illustrate the ways in which structural constraints at different levels are negotiated by leaders through their meeting talk. We also identify some interesting differences in the ways in which the participants in our Māori and Pākehā workplaces conduct meetings and engage with each other within this discourse context.

It is useful at the outset to define our focus. Even if we confine our consideration to the workplace, the term "meeting" includes a wide range of discourse events, from very informal, small meetings of two or three participants around a desk to large formal meetings in a customised and designated space, with a very clear agenda and speaking rights.[2] We are mainly concerned in this chapter with formal business meetings, defined for our purposes as interactions that focus directly on workplace business, prearranged for a specific and typically regular time, with an agreed agenda, and attended by all relevant, available members of a team. The organisa-

---

1. Mead and Grove (2003: 282).
2. See Holmes and Stubbe (2003a) and Angouri and Marra (2010) for discussion of the features of meetings and criteria for describing and distinguishing different types of meeting. Discussions in relation to specific structural elements can also be found in Chan (2005) and Murata (forthcoming).

tions that are the focus of our research would no doubt contend that their meetings are aimed at getting things done, that is, accomplishing transactional objectives such as planning, reporting, and decision making (the main functions of meetings identified in the relevant literature (e.g., Huisman, 2001; Schwartzman, 1989, and our own work: Holmes and Stubbe, 2003a; Marra, 2003). Important relational goals are also accomplished in meetings, and there is abundant evidence of this in our data. In this chapter, however, our primary focus is the transactional dimension of meeting discourse.

We first identify a number of features that can be considered the unmarked norm for New Zealand business meetings: the basic structure of meetings, as well as the turn-taking norms and strategies used by the chair to manage the meeting. Over the lifetime of the Language in the Workplace Project (LWP), a robust meeting pattern has emerged, and in each of the four workplaces in our current dataset this basic meeting format is again evident. Departures from this pattern, then, become salient and of particular interest. Notable differences from the standard (Pākehā) norm are found in the Māori team meetings, providing a useful warrant for the influence of ethnically distinctive discourse. To demonstrate this, we focus on meeting openings and closings as well as norms for contributions to the floor. In both cases our focus is the role of leaders in meetings and the leadership privileges afforded to the meeting chair.

MEETINGS AND LEADERSHIP

In recent work, Celia Ford defines the leader role as a core component of meeting talk, describing workplace meetings as "institutional events marked by official openings and closings and organised by reference to agreed-upon agendas and persons in *special leadership roles*" (2010: 211 emphasis added). The key role played by the chair as the manager of otherwise potentially chaotic multiparty talk is characteristic of descriptions of meetings in much of the literature, both academic and lay.[3] The chair provides a means of coordinating turns at talk, of operationalising an (agreed) structure, and represents the voice of contextualised authority. Although, as Bargiela-Chiappini and Harris (1997b: 207) note, there is no absolute relationship between the group leader and the chair, there is a strong tendency throughout the data in the wider LWP corpus for the senior members of any team to be those who step into this position, regardless of whether the role of chair is formally assigned. In the case of the dataset used in this book, in all but one organisation it is the designated leaders in the organisational hierarchy who chair the meetings we recorded; the exception, NZ Consultations, is particularly noticeable for its noncompliance with this trend, choosing instead to rotate the role, allowing

3. For further discussion, see Angouri and Marra (2010), Chan (2005), Schwartzman (1989), Murata (forthcoming).

the egalitarian ethos of the particular community to play out in shared leadership.[4] In sum, the chair is conceptualised as a key leadership role in this particular discourse context, qualified with the recognition that this role may be temporary (cf. Onyx, 1999).

In early work on the language of meetings, Cuff and Sharrock (1985) made a somewhat vague, but nevertheless useful, statement that, as participants, we "commonsensically" recognise a meeting. The similarity with which meetings are enacted, in spite of organisational and cultural differences, seems to validate this claim. As documented in our previous research, the tasks of the manager/chair typically include setting the agenda, summarising progress, keeping the discussion on track, and reaching a decision (Holmes and Stubbe, 2003a: chapter 4). Perhaps, the most obvious positions for seeing evidence of the enactment of leadership within the context of meeting discourse is the beginnings and ends of meetings when there is a pre-allocated turn for the chair (Sacks, Schegloff, and Jefferson, 1974). This is the focus of the analysis in the next section.

MEETING OPENINGS AND CLOSINGS AND THE LEADERSHIP ROLE

In most New Zealand workplaces, as argued in earlier chapters, Pākehā interactional norms typically predominate. Although there is variation in the norms of different workplaces, our extensive database of Pākehā meetings supports the view that most Pākehā workplace meetings, including relatively large meetings of up to 20 participants, typically open with the minimum of formality and explicitness, involving a brief and laconic phrase such as *let's go*. The standard pattern, followed in literally hundreds of meetings that we have recorded and observed, is (1) a period of small talk (2) a discourse marker, such as *okay, so, well,* and (3) a "standard marker" (Turner, 1972: 373), such as *we might as well start, time we got underway, okay let's get cracking.*[5]

In a more detailed analysis of the common discourse features of meeting talk in New Zealand workplaces, Marra (2008a) expands on these three parts by describing the typical structure of the meetings in the LWP corpus as consisting of a series of ordered components, realised in recognisable, though often truncated, utterances. Although still reflecting the generalised structure of meetings (opening or introductory section, central development, closing section) proposed by many (e.g., Fisher, 1982; Sollitt-Morris, 1996; Bargiela-Chiappini and Harris, 1997b; Holmes and Stubbe, 2003a), it is argued that the opening components are matched by a set of corresponding steps in the closing section, ordered in reverse. Figure 4.1 depicts these steps diagrammatically.

---

4. See Trevor-Roberts et al. (2003).
5. See also Atkinson and Drew (1979) and Bargiela-Chiappini and Harris (1997b) for relevant discussions of such markers.

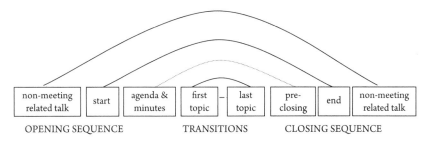

| non-meeting related talk | start | agenda & minutes | first topic | — | last topic | pre-closing | end | non-meeting related talk |

OPENING SEQUENCE   TRANSITIONS   CLOSING SEQUENCE

Figure 4.1
The Typical Structure of a Business Meeting (From Marra, 2008a)

The robustness of this pattern in the LWP corpus is further sustained by the standard way in which the various components of this structure are typically realised: the meeting starts with a simple *okay, let's get started* or *shall we start now?* The preclosing characteristically begins with *anything else?* And the closing with *thanks, that's us* or *thanks everyone.* These succinct phrases encode significant interactional work in orienting the participants to the progress of the meeting and its relevant goals. It is very rare (and consequently marked) for these steps to be performed by a participant other than the chair (or on occasion the most senior member of the team if they are not in the chair), again signaling that these steps are the prerogative of a leader. Interestingly, in the New Zealand context, these steps are frequently expressed as interrogatives (*shall we start?*) or heavily mitigated (*I think we should start now if everyone's here*). These strategies are ways of reducing the power asymmetry, which is particularly apparent when one team member has a right to instigate moves not available to others. This is further evidence of sensitivity to the (Pākehā) egalitarian ethic, which results in pressure to minimise attention to power inequalities among New Zealanders talking together.[6]

The strength of the norm, and its relevance for such a range of teams, is remarkable, especially given our theoretical predisposition to consider that the ways in which individuals construct their community membership is highly contextualised. Nonetheless, evidence for the pattern abounds. Example 4.1 nicely illustrates this by drawing attention to a departure from the norm. Failure to attend to the standard opening steps of a meeting is noticeable to the participants and becomes a source of humour.

6. An international culture and leadership survey of 62 nations reported that New Zealand was characterised by a particularly egalitarian style of leadership, and also that "New Zealanders respect achievement, but at the same time resent overt displays of power" (Trevor-Roberts et al., 2003: 524).

Example 4.1

Context: NZ Productions: Jaeson, the general manager, is having a catch up meeting with another senior manager, Rob. This is the very start of the interaction

1	Jaeson:	yeah I'm talking to Rob Bellinger
2	Rob:	I broke it down [coughs] to
3		what I thought was the most logical
4	Jaeson:	what happened to the small talk?
5	Rob:	[laughs] I love the col-
6		I love what you're doing
7		with your hair these days
8	Jaeson:	[laughs] oh you're just
9		so straight into it you know [laughs]
10	Rob:	[laughs] um when we talked about
11		[sighs] the style of operation...

The interaction begins with "verbal labeling" for the benefit of the researchers, a practice we encourage to help us understand who is interacting in an extract when there will be no associated video recording available. At this point, Rob starts with his report, the first agenda item for the catch up meeting (lines 2–3). Jaeson's meta-discoursal comment about the lack of small talk, albeit humourous (line 4), suggests that the participants themselves are aware of their normal interactional patterns that dictate that they begin their transactional talk with some attention to relational goals, the typical content of the non-meeting related talk referred to in Figure 4.1. Rob quickly plays along with the humour and introduces a stereotypical, and noticeably gendered, topic for small talk, a compliment about Jaeson's hair. Joyce Fletcher (1999) contends that this relational talk often "disappears" in business contexts, and is considered women's work, which is arguably reflected in Rob's humourous response (lines 5–7). However, the interchange in Example 4.1 indicates that, if relational talk is totally missing, this is a noticeable and unacceptable absence. Jaeson teases Rob that he is *just so straight into it* (lines 8–9), a comment on the directness and explicitness that typifies Rob's interactional style generally. Although just a brief example of the significance of the routine structure of meetings, this humourous extract is nonetheless a telling indication of the strength of standard meeting conventions. The various steps in the structure of meeting openings and closings are well illustrated in our earlier research (Marra, 2003, 2008a; Holmes and Stubbe, 2003a). In this chapter, we illustrate how the particular communities in the current dataset open and close meetings, drawing on strategies from their shared repertoires.

Meeting Openings

Within the sales team at NZ Productions, the pattern of meeting openings was so well established that the "start" component (according to Figure 4.1) was astonishingly similar in each. The distinctive falling intonation and phrasing of the realisations of the opening move (*fire away Rog, let's fire into it eh, shoot Rog*), as well as its enactment by the same chair, resulted in a series of remarkably parallel utterances.

Example 4.2

Context: NZ Productions: Opening sequences from six regular sales meetings chaired by Paul, sales manager

Sales Meeting 1:	fire away Rog
Sales Meeting 2:	right guys?
	[24 sec of no talk and paper shuffling]
	yeah er Jaeson and Sharon should
	come through soon [inhales]
	um + fire away Rog
Sales Meeting 3:	[inhales] oh let's fire into it eh
Sales Meeting 4:	okay we'll fire into it eh
Sales Meeting 5:	oh okay
	right let's fire into it eh
Sales Meeting 6:	shoot Rog

In this set of meeting openings, then, the shared repertoire of the community is particularly evident. There is an interesting repetition of a battle metaphor in the form of *fire away/into it* (meetings 1–5) and *shoot* (meeting 6), each of which signals the official start of the meeting for the group.[7] The pragmatic tag *eh,* which occurs in three openings, is a distinctively New Zealand discourse feature, which has its origins in informal Māori English interaction, but which is steadily spreading through New Zealand society (Vine and Marra, 2008; Vine and Marsden, forthcoming). Here it indexes informality and CofP membership. The naming of Rog(er) within this move is also structurally meaningful to team members. Roger's duties as a team member include providing the weekly administration report, which takes the first agenda slot in each of the meetings. By naming Roger as next speaker, Paul is simultaneously calling the group to order, drawing attention to the implicit and understood routine agenda, and starting the reporting turns, which the recurring agenda requires.

---

7. Interestingly, we discovered in a feedback session that the team members were not particularly aware of the fact that these phrases regularly recurred to open their meetings. The prevalence of war metaphors in business discourse is discussed by Koller (2004).

As is characteristic of Pākehā teams more widely, the opening sequences here are very brief. Typically, there is enough shared knowledge to warrant a minimum of preparation for the "start" utterance. In most instances, *okay* or *right* or *oh* serve as standard utterance initial discourse markers. As the most elaborated of the opening sequences, the longer section in meeting 2 deserves comment. Paul checks everyone is ready, *right guys?* (line 1), and pauses to note explicitly who is missing (lines 3–4); then, using their standard start phrase, *fire away Rog* (line 5), he assigns the first turn to Roger to deal with the opening agenda item.

The very truncated nature of these meeting openings and their obvious informality is quite representative of meetings in the majority of the Pākehā workplaces in our LWP database. The fact that a team has worked together for some time obviously helps account for such verbal shorthand. However, the overall preference for informality in New Zealand workplaces also makes a contribution. Even the most formal Pākehā meeting opening in our large dataset is very brief, and formality is conveyed through lexical choices, for example, *well formally let me open the [laughs]: meeting:* (with the laugh suggesting that even this briefly formal utterance is perceived as somewhat marked).

In the opening to this chapter we noted that the team at NZ Consultations has a slightly different pattern in terms of meeting management. Rather than a fixed chair for the meetings, the team rotates the chair role among its members. This behaviour sits well with both their business goals and industry, in which team members need to work closely together, and in which they make use of shared industry-specific expertise. It also matches the spirit of equality that pervades their everyday interaction, as described in chapter 2. Interestingly, however, although rotating the chair goes some way to reducing the appearance of status differences between the senior managers and the rest of the team, the significance of Angelina, as the division manager, is nonetheless subtly acknowledged as illustrated in Example 4.3.

Example 4.3

Context: NZ Consultations: Team meeting. Jared and Frances chat while waiting for Kate, the chair, to start the meeting

1	Jared:	how are you Frances?
2	Frances:	I'm good and you? how's your family? ...
3	Kate:	so Angelina's away
4		is Rowan back today?

In this example the task of chairing the meeting is taken up by team member Kate. After a period of small talk (including the discussion between Jared and Frances about their respective family members, which begins in lines 1 and 2), Kate commences the meeting start with a "verbal headcount", a frequent feature of these sequences (Marra, 2008a). Most interestingly, she begins with a comment on the whereabouts of the division manager (*so Angelina's away*) followed by mention of another senior team member, Rowan. The fact that the absence of these leaders is noticeable enough to deserve explicit mention highlights the temporary nature of the leadership assigned to the chair role; despite Kate being the avowed "leader" in this meeting context, the leadership of Angelina is still highly salient.

Meeting Closings

Just as the meeting opening sequence is routinised around the tasks of the chair, the enactment of the meeting closing sequence is similarly assigned to the chair. As argued in Marra (2008a), and illustrated in Figure 4.1 earlier, each element of the meeting opening has a parallel element in the closing sequence as the participants move out of the meeting talk.

The examples of meeting openings have demonstrated the preference for exceedingly short opening sequences. In the case of the closing sequence of meetings, this tendency can be taken to an extreme, relying heavily on the shared knowledge of the group for its accomplishment. This could be a shared understanding that the team has moved through the entire agenda, through the allocated time, or indicated by nonverbal behaviour, such as people leaving the room. Examples 4.4, 4.5, and 4.6 provide illustrations of typical meeting closing patterns found in the data.

Example 4.4

Context: NZ Productions: Management meeting chaired by Jaeson, general manager

1	Jaeson:	okay any general business?
2		( ) point people want to bring up
3	Harry:	er Marshall when when was the [equipment]…
4		[discussion of various sundry topics]
5	Paul:	…I'm pretty sure they'll go with it
6		she's basically sent me an email saying
7		she wants to order fifty thousand more sets
8		but she needs to get prices
9		but I also need to talk with her about timing
10		on it and then it's a three month project really
11		is knowing what we know now so (11)
12	Jaeson:	okay + thanks everybody
13		[several overlapping conversations as people leave]

In Example 4.4, Jaeson begins the closing sequence by asking if the others have *any general business* or issues to raise, a typical preclosing marker signaling the meeting is nearing an end. At this stage, Harry begins discussion about a piece of equipment (line 3) and there is subsequent talk around related topics, ending with Paul's extra information about potential sales (lines 5–11). At the end of Paul's report, there is a lengthy pause of 11 seconds. When no one takes up the opportunity to raise any more general business topics, Jaeson closes the meeting with the discourse marker *okay* and the frequently used meeting close *thanks everybody* (line 12). The team recognises this as the implicit formal close to the meeting as indicated by the various non-meeting related conversations that begin.

In this instance, Harry and Paul had some general business issues to discuss, but in many cases there are none, with the entire closing section consisting of simply *okay*, or *thanks*, often with associated pausing, as exemplified here. An extract from a meeting at New Zealand Consultations illustrates such a case.

Example 4.5

Context: NZ Consultations: Team meeting chaired by Angelina, division manager

1	Kate:	basically no surprise as policy is the …
2	Frances:	yeah ++
3	Angelina:	okay + thank you
4		[meeting ends, small talk in background]

The closing seems abrupt from an outsider's perspective, but the meeting participants are clearly comfortable with it. Frances contribution *yeah* is followed by a pause, which is sufficient to cue Angelina's closing moves, *okay* and *thank you*.

An excerpt from a smaller meeting at Kiwi Productions provides another example.

Example 4.6

Context: Kiwi Productions: Yvonne, managing director, is meeting with Jorjia. They are talking about an invoice that needs to be paid

1	Yvonne:	and um +
2		and we don't suppose we're gonna dispute it
3		but I just wanted Taumata to know
4		how much it was for
5	Jorjia:	oh okay well I can show it to him if you like
6	Yvonne:	okay yeah maybe do that +++
7	Jorjia:	okay //well I'll\ show it to him
8		when he gets back
9	Yvonne:	/okay\\
10	Yvonne:	okay + thank you

In line 1 Yvonne begins summarising the decision that has been made about how they will deal with a particular invoice, the issue under discussion in the meeting. She gives Jorjia instructions about what to do about the invoice, expressed as a hint (lines 3–4), but one that Jorjia understands as a directive (to tell Taumata about Yvonne's decision) and somewhat reluctantly agrees to carry out (lines 5 and 7). Once the action is agreed we find a clustering of utterance-initial *okays* (lines 7, 9, and 10), reminiscent of the preclosing sequences of a telephone conversation (cf. Schegloff, 1979). The topic that Yvonne and Jorjia have met to discuss has come to an end, and, like Angelina, Yvonne closes the meeting with the customary thanks to her co-participant (line 10).

The opening and closing sequences serve to move participants in and out of meeting talk (cf. Button, 1987 on moving in and out of conversation). The Pākehā norm, which dominates the meetings in our data, favours the briefest and most informal enactment of these sequences. Much is left implicit, with accurate interpretation dependent on familiarity with the standard meeting structure in the particular community of practice (CofP). More formal Māori meetings contrast in a number of ways.

MEETING STRUCTURE IN MĀORI WORKPLACES

For the Māori teams, in addition to their role in opening and closing meetings, the opening and closing discourse sequences also serve to move the discussion in and out of Māori space (Salmond, 1975). Although the opening and closings of one-to-one meetings in these organisations share the brevity and simplicity associated with Pākehā meetings (as illustrated in Example 4.6), larger meetings in our Māori organisations contrast markedly with the corresponding Pākehā meetings. In formal meetings, the meeting opening (and to a lesser extent closing) is the place where we see the most overt differences in the discourse of the Māori and Pākehā organisations in our dataset. The influence of culturally significant protocols is particularly apparent in this context, and they derive their structure from traditional Māori greeting protocols.

When Māori from different areas or tribes meet on a marae, proceedings open with a formal "ritual of encounter" or welcome ceremony, usually referred to as a *pōwhiri*, which first emphasises and then closes the physical and emotional distance between hosts and guests (Salmond, 1974, 1975; Metge, 1976; Metge and Kinloch, 1978). Likewise, any get-together that involves Māori people, and that is organised by Māori, typically begins with some formal element involving an explicit greeting and welcome. It frequently includes a karakia, often in the form of a "prayer" or traditional chant reflecting the ways in which spirituality, *taha wairua* ("the spiritual dimension"), imbues all aspects of traditional Māori life and activity (Metge, 1995: 82–88; Henare, 2003). This contrasts markedly with many Pākehā gatherings where informality is valued as a sign of friendliness and solidarity.

Evidence of the influence of these communicative norms can be found to different degrees at both Kiwi Productions and Kiwi Consultations.[8] Depending on the size and formality of the meeting, the openings vary in length and complexity. At the informal end of the continuum, openings are most similar to the short opening formulas that characterise Pākehā meetings, though it is rare that there is not at least a minimal Māori *mihi* ("greeting") from the chair, such as the informal *kia ora* (*tātou*) ("hi (to you all)") or the more formal *tēnā koutou katoa* ("greetings to you all") at the meeting opening.[9] At the formal end of the spectrum, mihi or meeting openings in Māori organisations comprise a number of ritualistic and culturally significant components. Although the general structure is relatively fixed and predictable, the precise length and the specific content of the opening mihi is usually shaped by and adapted to the precise participants in the specific context in which it occurs. Two examples, one from each of our focus workplaces, must suffice to illustrate this.

Example 4.7 is taken from a meeting of Quentin's team in Kiwi Productions. As described in earlier chapters, Quentin is the most senior Māori male in the organisation, and he is highly respected for his knowledge of Māori cultural matters, his tikanga Māori, or expertise in all matters relating to Māori customs and matters of protocol, and his fluency in Māori. More Māori language is used in meetings of Quentin's team than in any other team in this organisation, though English nonetheless predominates in their meetings. Example 4.7 is quite typical of his meeting openings. Quentin opens the meeting with a karakia.

Example 4.7

Context: Kiwi Productions: Team meeting

1	Quentin:	*kia ora tātou*
		["hello everyone"]
2		*me huaki e tātou tā tātou hui*
		["let's open our hui/meeting"]
3		*i runga i te karakia*
		["with a prayer"]
4		*nā reira kia inoi tātou*
		["therefore, let us pray"]
5		*e pā tēnei anō mātou tēnei whānau*
		["Father, here we are, this family"]

8. See Schnurr, Marra, and Holmes (2008) for a fuller discussion of the features of the openings of Māori business meetings.
9. The Māori politician, Pita Sharples, comments that, in his view, meeting openings are typically much more perfunctory in modern times: "[as a kid] the mihimihis would take hours, and we'd expect them to—that's how it was. Nowadays [...] quick prayer, one mihi, one answer, into work". (Diamond, 2003: 191–192).

6	e noho tahi ana i raro i te maru
	["gathered (sitting) together under the
	shelter/protection"]
7	o tēnei whare
	["of this building"]
8	nā reira i tēnei wā
	["therefore, at this time"]
9	ka tukua ō mātou inoi ki a koe
	["we send our prayers to you"]
10	māu tonu mātou katoa e manaaki
	["for you to treat us well"]
11	e tiaki i roto i tēnei ata
	["and care for us all this morning"]
12	i roto anō i tā mātou hui
	["during our meeting"]
13	kia haere pai ā mātou kōrero e pā
	["so that our discussions go well"]
14	i raro i ō manaakitanga
	["under your kind favour"]
15	i runga anō i te tika te pono
	["and in correct behaviour, truth"]
16	me te māramatanga
	["and clarity"]
17	me te aroha anō o tētahi ki tētahi
	["and the love of one for another"]
18	tēnei mātou e inoi hoki
	["here we are also praying"]
19	māu e manaaki nei
	["that you look after"]
20	ō mātou whanaunga
	["our relatives"]
21	ahakoa kei hea e pā
	["no matter where they are Father"]
22	ko rātou kei raro i te kapua pōuri
	["those under the cloud of sadness"]
23	me ērā anō kei roto i te māuiuitanga
	["those, too, who are unwell"]
24	māu tonu e tiaki e manaaki i a rātou
	["look after them, care for them"]
25	kia piki tonu te kaha me
	["so that they get stronger"]
26	te ora hoki ki runga i a rātou
	["and healthier"]

27	*tēnei ō mātou inoi i tēnei wā e pā*
	["this we pray at this time Father"]
28	*i runga i te ingoa o tāu tama*
	["in the name of your son"]
29	*tō mātou kaiwhakaora a Ihu Karaiti*
	["our saviour Jesus Christ"]
30	*āmene*
	["amen"]
31	*āe*
	["yes"]
32	now I um + I did up an agenda
33	which I thought at the time had all the information
34	there may be some other things that people have got
35	but that's really the main things that I come through
36	with er for er our *hui* ["meeting"] today um

This mihi or opening sequence, including the karakia, follows a standard structure which is summarised in Table 4.1.

Quentin opens with a greeting followed by a karakia, a very explicit indication of the orientation to Māori ways of doing things in this organisation.[10] Though the exact wording differs slightly, these components recur routinely and usually in this

---

Table 4.1. STRUCTURE OF THE OPENING OF A MEETING IN A MĀORI WORKPLACE

(This standard structure was described by Paranihia Walker and Mary Boyce, members of our research team to whom we express our appreciation.)

- Opening greeting to team members present [line 1]
- Pre-opening signal [line 2]
- Karakia opening (*e pā* signals this is not a traditional karakia, but a "religious" one) [lines 5–12]
- Reference to the purpose of the gathering and proper behaviour in this context [lines 13–17]
- Reference to extended family and especially those who are sick or dying and to any recent deaths [lines 18–26]
- Signal of the beginning of the closing [line 27]
- Closing [line 28–30]
- Transition marker from karakia to business [line 31–32]

---

10. Christianity is just one possible vehicle for Māori spirituality; hence the karakia may take a variety of forms, including, for instance, a traditional chant rather than a Christian prayer. So, although in many areas of Māoridom, Christian formalities and protocols have been seamlessly integrated into traditional ceremonies, their function, as here, is fundamentally cultural rather than religious.

order in the karakia that opens the meetings of this team, even when Quentin is away and his deputy leader, Rangi, chairs the meeting. They are also standard components of the rituals of encounter that occur in more elaborate form on more formal occasions in Māori culture (Salmond, 1975).[11] This illustrates the very formal and most Māori end of the spectrum of meeting openings in Māori organisations in which we have observed or recorded. Every meeting except one of the 10 consecutive recorded meetings of Quentin's team at Kiwi Productions opened in this way.[12]

Example 4.8 is an excerpt from a formal meeting opening at our other Māori workplace, Kiwi Consultations. In this mihi or meeting opening, Daniel, the Chief Executive Officer (CEO), mentions the recent death of the sister of one of the members of the organisation. Again, the whole sequence is in Māori and Example 4.8 is an abbreviated version. We have provided just the opening and closing lines in Māori, with the rest in translation, since our focus here is the content.

Example 4.8

Context: Kiwi Consultations: Meeting of all staff

1	Daniel:	oh *kia ora ano tātou* +
		["hello again everyone"]
2		*um tēnā tātou i huihui mai nei i tēnei ata + um +*
		["greetings to us all who have gathered here this morning"]
3		*er he tuku i roto i tēnei āhuatanga*
		["let me mention respectfully"]
4		*me maumahara ki tā tātou nei tuahine a Mere*
		["let us all remember our sister Mere
5		who has just buried her younger sister in Hukatai
6		our thoughts are with her
7		and everybody else who is under this cloud of darkness"]
8		…
9		["our thoughts are with her and the children of her

11. It is interesting to note similarities to components of the formal rituals described by Kotthoff (2007): for example, positive mention of families, expression of respect for deceased members of families.

12. The one exception occurred when the company director, Yvonne, came in to talk to Quentin's team. Yvonne arrived and was welcomed very briefly, and then Quentin stated the reason for her presence. There was no formal meeting opening and no karakia. Subsequent discussion indicated that Yvonne assumed the meeting had already been formally opened, since Quentin welcomed her when she walked in, and immediately mentioned the issue she was there to discuss. Yvonne responded to this as a cue to proceed with the issue. Thus the arrival of Yvonne apparently precipitated a move to the first item on the agenda

10		younger sibling…"]
11		*he tika tēnei kia tīmata i roto*
12		*i te whakawhetai ki te atua*
		["it is right that we begin with a prayer to the lord…"]
13	All:	*āmine*
		["amen"]
14	Daniel:	*kia ora* everyone

Clearly, Daniel's formal mihi or Māori meeting opening includes similar components to those used by Quentin, illustrated in this example by a reference to the death of a colleague's sister, and the inclusion of a karakia. Using the dimensions for analysing intercultural interaction outlined in chapter 1, Māori norms can here be characterised as involving ad hoc formulations and innovative expressions, "created anew for the occasion" (House, 2005: 21), rather than the formulaic tokens (*let's go, let's start, let's get underway*) preferred for Pākehā meeting openings. It is also obvious that Māori openings, which refer directly to matters of relevance to the particular participants, can be described as more oriented to addressees, than to content, another of the dimensions we have identified as useful for analysing cross-cultural difference.

As noted earlier, this pattern clearly derives from the much more elaborate and formal rituals of encounter on the marae, but even in its truncated and briefer forms, it serves as an important affirmation of Māori culture and the importance of Māori values by the participants in the midst of their normal working day. Furthermore, and importantly, the specific form that an opening takes is strongly influenced by a number of dynamic and fluid aspects of the specific context in which it occurs— precisely who is present, where the meeting is taking place, and what the purpose of the meeting is, are among the most obvious of these. Another important point illustrated by these formal and structured openings is the evidence they provide of explicit commitment to Māori values, such as spirituality (*taha wairua*), respect for the dead (*he whakaaro nui ki te hunga mate*), concern for family and relationships (*whanaungatanga*), and so on. These Māori communicative norms are relatively explicit, direct, and very self-referential compared to Pākehā. As indicated in the previous section, there is no evidence of this kind of extended, formal creative opening component in meetings in Pākehā workplaces where we have recorded. Personal and family issues are rarely raised in Pākehā meetings other than in small talk preceding the meeting, as in Example 4.3, and certainly not in formal sections of meetings.

Meeting openings provide a point of contrast between the two Māori workplaces as well as a point of similarity. In Kiwi Productions, the more explicit commitment to tikanga Māori is evident in the fact that even some small team meetings open and close with a formal Māori component, however brief, sometimes involving a karakia, and typically personalised to the interests and identities of those present. There was no evidence of this in Kiwi Consultations, where it was mainly the large meetings which included the more formal opening structure. It is important to emphasise that there is no one-size-fits-all, even in workplaces where Māori tikanga is respected, a point elaborated in chapter 7.

The meeting opening (and the correspondingly mirrored closing) in both workplaces is an opportunity for an extended stretch of talk in Māori, an opportunity generally welcomed by members of both Māori workplaces. Because the structure of the sequences is routine, it can be followed even by those with limited competence in the language. An interesting exception occurred in the data collected at Kiwi Consultations. In this case, Caleb a young and rising Māori leader (who was standing in for Daniel, the CEO, who was away from the city on a business trip) performed a meeting opening and karakia unusually in English.

Example 4.9

Context: Kiwi Consultations: Management meeting

1	Caleb:	oh okay *kia ora anō tātou katoa*
		["hello again everyone"]
2		first of all it's good to have a welcome
3		for a new staff member
4		and um I'm certain that you'll look after her here Hari
5		but also too in your um *whakatau* ["welcome"] to her
6		and I also acknowledge it to er passing of [name]'s father
7		and um so it was good that that was acknowledged
8		so welcome here today
9		and I hope everything's going well f- with you too Albert
10		and the *whānau* ["family"]
11		so um *kia kaha e hoa* ["be strong my friend"]
12		okay moving into it we've got two agenda items so far...

Example 4.9 largely follows the structure in the opening sequences illustrated in Examples 4.7 and 4.8: there is a greeting (line 1), and acknowledgment of events relevant to the participants, including the formal welcome to a new staff member (line 5) and a death in the wider workplace community (line 7). The reference to Albert's family and their current concerns (line 9–11) gives a potential clue about why Caleb chooses to use English here. It becomes apparent that the opening has been designed for Albert, one of the few Pākehā members of the team and a monolingual English speaker. The use of English ensures that Albert understands the support he is being offered by his colleagues.

Although Caleb uses English in this meeting opening, the amount of codeswitching is noteworthy. Lines 1 and 11 are phrases that are understood by many Pākehā, and would certainly be understood by Albert, and the use of the lexical items *whakatau* and *whānau*, representing their respective Māori concepts, also adds a Māori "flavour" to the English while being common loanwords. Caleb also uses a somewhat stilted style of English, which perhaps reflects his attempt to translate the components of a standard Māori opening: for example, *it's good to have a welcome* (line 2), *I'm certain you'll look after her* (line 4), *I acknowledge [the] passing...* (line 6). As a whole, the effect clearly signals that the group is entering Māori space. In the process, Caleb performs leadership appropriately in this Māori workplace, while taking account of the needs of his co-participants.

These examples illustrate what some non-Māori speakers perceive to be unnecessarily long and "merely" ritualistic meeting openings. The closings in many of the meetings of Quentin's team in particular at Kiwi Productions are similarly formally structured and ritualistic.[13] Because Pākehā meeting participants appear to prize brevity and informality, as suggested by the patterns in Pākehā workplaces, then it is easy to see that they might misconstrue the elaborate Māori openings as simply a "waste of time". Similarly, for Māori participants in a Pākehā meeting, lack of attention to the concerns and relationships of the participants as well as the protocols that establish both equilibrium and a joint goal can make subsequent discussion appear inadequately introduced and unimportant. This is one particular feature of meeting discourse that seems open to misunderstanding by outsiders.

The meeting opening and closing are the most obvious examples of meeting management by the chair. Less obvious, but equally significant, is the localised management of talk between the opening and closing sequence, including the coordination of the contributions of various team members. Patterns of verbal interaction, including the role of the chair in managing this interaction, is the focus of the next section.

INTERACTION IN MEETINGS

As noted in the introduction to this chapter, meetings are a prime example of multiparty talk, and one of the roles of the chair is to monitor the ways in which participants contribute to the group interaction. Formal allocation of turns is one aspect of this management; the meeting chair typically designates a speaker to report on their team's work, for example, or assigns the introduction of specific topics to individual speakers. In the discussion that follows, our focus is on the ways in which the participants organise their turns at talk within these macro-topics.

In most Pākehā workplace meetings, the basic turn-taking rules involve one speaker at a time, with the expectation that others will listen silently. Paying attention means not interrupting, not providing audible comments beyond appropriately placed signals of listenership in the form of minimal feedback, and not

13. See also Example 6.20, for a closing in a meeting of all staff at Kiwi Consultations, which is chaired by Daniel.

holding side conversations while the speaker holds the floor. This one-at-a-time (OAAT) style (Coates, 1989: 120) is illustrated in Example 4.10, which is typical of the interactions at NZ Consultations.

Example 4.10

Context: NZ Consultations: Team meeting

1	Jared:	Angelina what was the trigger for the um reports
2		being sent to the client in the first place?
3		when I say in the first place I think it was
4		after the meeting the reports were sent to the client
5	Rowan:	there was a instruction from the client
6		which identified two or three um documents
7		that had been referred to elsewhere in another report
8		and things like that //+ and they\
9	Jared:	/right so\\ during the course of the meeting
10	Rowan:	well yeah they said um it was their business
11		that had identified these um
12		and then they also asked for any other
13		potentially relevant documents um n-
14		the internal documents that we created

Although there are many more participants present at this meeting, this extract includes contributions from only two participants, Jared and Rowan, each of whom produces comparatively long turns. Interestingly, despite specifically naming Angelina as the appropriate respondent (line 1), Jared's question is answered by Rowan who holds the expert knowledge on this particular client. When Rowan takes up the question, Angelina remains silent. Notably there is no interruption or even audible feedback other than in lines 8–9 where Jared begins his turn at an obvious transition relevance place, as indicated by the pause in Rowan's turn, although it would seem that Rowan has not quite finished. Once Jared begins, Rowan quickly gives up the floor for Jared to ask for further detail (i.e., the possibility of a potential "trigger" *during the course of the meeting*). This classic OAAT turn taking with a "tightly organised" floor (Jones and Thornborrow, 2004: 403) is typical of Pākehā formal meetings, but less so for Māori meetings, as Example 4.11 illustrates.

Before discussing Example 4.11, however, it is important to consider another area where Māori interactional norms differ from those of Pākehā, namely in the provision of feedback and signals of attention in formal meetings. Describing the norms of etiquette at Māori public meetings, Metge and Kinloch (1978: 20–21) note that Māori people "accept a certain amount of noise—low-voiced chatter and movement—as normal in public gatherings, expressive of approval, support, and trust in the speaker or activity in progress". (See also Metge, 2005: 85). So, providing frequent affirmatory feedback (e.g., *āe, kia ora*) while someone is speaking is considered positive and appropriate behaviour (see Kell, Marra, Holmes, and Vine, 2007). This pattern of supportive feedback while someone is talking can be described as the "conversationalization" of the meeting discourse (cf. Fairclough and Mauranen, 1998); it creates an atmosphere of informality, engagement, and involvement.

As one component of our comparison of Māori and Pākehā meeting norms, Kell et al. (2007) analysed two separate meetings with the same agenda in the same workplace, a government department, where one meeting involved a Pākehā group and the other a Māori group. The Māori meeting was characterised by much more overlapping talk, explicit verbal feedback, and collaborative all-together-now (ATN) interaction (Coates, 1989) than the Pākehā meeting. This active style of attending to a speaker is very evident in meetings in Māori workspaces, but it is almost completely absent from Pākehā workplace meetings. Contributions often overlap and could be misinterpreted as disruptive attempts to take over the floor by those who adhere to the more tightly constructed floor typical of many Pākehā formal meetings. The frequent verbal feedback and on-topic side conversations, which Metge and Kinloch (1978) indicate are evidence of engagement, are often misinterpreted by Pākehā as signals of inattention and lack of respect. Pākehā audiences expect silence from the audience while someone speaks in a formal context (cf. Spencer-Oatey, 2000; Jaworski, 1993), and, hence, Pākehā listening to the interaction in Māori meetings often feel that the audience is not demonstrating sufficient respect toward the speaker. This is illustrated perfectly in an explicit discussion at Kiwi Consultations involving Steve, a Pākehā member of the organisation. As the industry match for NZ Consultations, the contrast in interactive style is particularly remarkable.

Example 4.11

Context: Kiwi Consultations: Meeting of all staff (Ants is Frank's in-house nickname)

1	Steve:	we have capability development um
2		the g m oversight here //is from Ants with Caleb\
3	Frank:	/[quietly to Daniel]: and what's maraetai mean?:\\
4	Steve:	the manager in charge budget of a hundred
5		and //eighty\ seven k
6	Daniel:	/[quietly]: mm?:\\
7	Frank:	[quietly]: what's maraetai mean?:
8	Steve:	obviously key area

9		//we want to ensure that um\
10	Daniel:	/[quietly]: it's by your left\\ eye:
11	Frank:	[quietly]: mm?:
12	Daniel:	[quietly]: it's by your left eye:
13	Frank:	[quietly]: by your left eye:
14	Daniel:	//[quietly]: mm my right eye:\
15	Steve:	/one of the important\\ things in communication is
16		not to talk when others are talking
17		[laughter]
18	Steve:	I hope that the cameras picked up (that)
19		[laughter]
20	Frank:	Steve this indicates a need for you to be out in *hui*
21		[laughter]
22	Frank:	one of the things that you learn very quickly
23		is that a sign of respect is that other people are
24		talking about what //you're saying while you're
25		saying it\
26		/[laughter]\\ [laughter]
27	Steve:	I see I see
28	Caleb:	//good recovery Ants good recovery\
29	Daniel:	/that's right Steve Ants is\\ bicultural
30		[laughter] [other indecipherable comments]
31	Daniel:	he was just enquiring about who this Johnny
32		Maraetai //guy was\
33	Steve:	/oh I see\\ I see okay
34	Frank:	Daniel says it's right beside your left eye [laughs]

During Steve's extended contribution to the meeting, many participants make quiet remarks to each other, but when Frank (Ants) makes a comment to Daniel, Steve reacts by humourously reprimanding them: *one of the important things in communication is not to talk when others are talking* (lines 15–16). This is amusing on several levels. First, Steve is reprimanding his superiors. Daniel is the CEO and Frank is a very senior manager. Secondly, it draws attention to the fact that effective communication is the averred focus of the LWP research in which they are participating, and suggests that Steve is here identifying an example of bad or inappropriate communication for our benefit. Third, and relatedly, Steve is inappropriately asserting the Pākehā communicative norm in a workplace where Māori ways of speaking obviously prevail, as is evident from the fact that others have been talking quietly during Steve's contribution.

Frank responds (line 20) by challenging Steve's rebuke as inappropriate, implying that Steve is not yet familiar enough with Māori interactional norms *Steve this indicates a need for you to be out in hui* (i.e., to attend more Māori meetings). Frank then spells out the Māori norm: *a sign of respect is that other people are talking about what you're saying while you're saying it* (lines 23–25). Caleb laughingly compliments Frank on his riposte to Steve's scold *good recovery Ants good recovery*, and Daniel adds *that's right Steve, Ants is bicultural* (line 29), a comment that is almost certainly contestively ironic, since Frank's very self-conscious Pākehā identity is something Daniel is very aware of, as he has indicated in interview. Because our recorders picked up Frank and Daniel's conversation, we know that Frank's comment was, in fact, on topic and that Daniel accurately subsequently summarises its content (lines 31–32). Ironically, as a result of drawing attention to the quiet side conversation, Steve causes an even bigger interruption to his presentation and attracts (good-humoured) critical attention to his own cultural ignorance and insensitivity.

Māori ways of providing feedback and signaling attention and engagement with a speaker in a formal meeting are, thus, rather different from those of Pākehā. Furthermore, it is worth noting, with reference to House's (2005) analytical dimensions, that, again, it is the Māori communicative norm that involves explicit and direct signals of interest, approval, or agreement, as opposed to the Pākehā implicit and indirect norm of conveying attention. For Pākehā, "silence indicates consent", whereas, for Māori, silence often signals disapproval or dissent (Metge and Kinloch, 1978; Metge, 2005). These contradictory norms draw stark attention to the fact that, in most organisations, it is the Pākehā "norms" that predominate. As Example 4.11 illustrates, Pākehā employees in Māori workplaces find themselves in the unusual position, for majority group members, of being expected to be bicultural. Ethnicity is suddenly a workplace issue influencing what is considered effective and appropriate communication. This point is elaborated in chapter 8.

By Pākehā standards, ongoing background talk gives the impression of a disorganised and unfocussed discussion. Moreover, to those unfamiliar with this Māori norm, there is a danger it might also be judged as less productive in large workplace meetings. As we have noted elsewhere, "An observer of the Māori meeting who is not conversant with Māori cultural protocol might well misinterpret the level of effectiveness with which the Māori meeting produces a range of high-quality work-related outcomes" (Kell et al., 2007: 326). Without extensive exposure, it is difficult to develop an understanding of how the deeper-level processes of discussion and inclusion, and the fostering of a collaborative and involved style of discussion both unites and educates the group by creating jointly constructed knowledge for everyone to share.

As Example 4.11 suggests, the collaborative floor preferred by the Māori team is not only ratified by the leader, but the simultaneous side conversation is instigated by leaders. In Example 4.10, by contrast, the absence of overlapping is this team's standard and unmarked norm, and the chair's lack of intervention supports this interpretation, a pattern also reflected more widely in the dataset and the literature. Once again, there is evidence of cultural norms playing an influential role in the enactment of meeting talk.

CONCLUSION

The data described in this chapter provides evidence of the ways in which various layers of context (as presented in our model in chapter 1) influence the ways in which team members engage in meeting talk. In particular, the influence of western norms is especially apparent in the discourse of meetings. Recent research, comparing European workplace data (collected from non-native speakers of English in a consortium of multinational corporations in Europe) with our New Zealand Pākehā dataset, demonstrates wide-ranging similarities in the co-constructed sequencing and enactment of meeting discourse (Angouri and Marra, 2009). In datasets that should, on the basis of reasonable assumptions about the pervasive influence of contextual factors, be distinct, the analysis suggests a dominant meeting genre to which all participants orient, suggesting that a type of business or even "management speak" hegemony prevails, regardless of the country, business, or nationality of the speakers (Angouri and Marra, 2010).

At a more specific level, the particular CofP plays a recognisable and significant role in the form of talk that enacts the functions of the meeting. The analysis of the data from NZ Productions and NZ Consultations, the two Pākehā organisations, illustrates this clearly. In both cases, the teams have their own idiosyncrasies (e.g., Paul's *fire away Rog* versus the equitable allocation of the chair role by NZ Consultations). What they share is the brevity and minimal formality of meeting management sequences, which is reasonably consistent across all the Pākehā teams with which we have worked, where a simple *okay* can often do significant work as a means of calling a group to order, cementing the authority of the chair, and simultaneously beginning or ending the business of the meeting.

It is at this level that we see the most significant differences in features of the meetings in our Pākehā and Māori datasets. The Māori CofPs paid attention to formal protocols in the opening and closing sequences of regular meetings, reflecting behaviour transferred from the marae setting. The significance of the ritual openings and closings could easily be misconstrued as window dressing added to an otherwise recognisably Pākehā meeting structure. However, this would be a naïve underestimation of the significance of these meeting components. Language choice is another important point of contrast. For the majority of participants at both Kiwi Productions and Kiwi Consultations this is an extended stretch of Māori, with a recognisable and ritual structure to support the understanding of those with limited competence in the language. Beyond the code choice, the components are of particular significance to the tikanga followed by both organisations, setting up Māori space and establishing equilibrium. Caleb's enactment of the opening in English (a rare but telling example from the dataset) demonstrates the discourse significance of this aspect of meeting management for leaders; the leaders use ritual openings and closings to move in and out of productive interactional space, space that is ethnically salient.

In this chapter, we have demonstrated how leadership is enacted within the normative constraints of the meeting as a discourse event. Business meetings emerged as a rich site for exploring the influence of ethnicity in Māori and Pākehā workplaces. Although there are many similarities in the way business meetings are structured and conducted in all four workplaces, our analyses have also identified a number of explicit and significant ways in which they differ. Each organisation conducts meetings in ways that are consistent with the ethnic orientation of the team, and, thus, the influence of the norms and values of an ethnicised CofP is evident in meetings at Kiwi Consultations and Kiwi Productions. These differences have the potential to cause miscommunication if their significance goes unrecognised by outsiders, a point discussed further in chapter 8.

The essence of a meeting is multiple participants gathered together to achieve a particular goal. The management of the contributions of these participants, although negotiated in interaction, is typically handled by the meeting chair. In the Pākehā meetings, brief, succinct utterances accomplished considerable interactional work in opening and closing meetings. In the Māori workplaces, by contrast, the opening and closing sections provided an opportunity for the enactment of the ethnic orientation of the workplaces, incorporating ritual components from interaction patterns observable in formal contexts, as well as an opportunity for the use of the Māori language. These events served to signal and set up Māori space, further constructing the ethnic orientation of the teams. Similarly, alongside the formal management of the opening and closing sequences, the ways in which the teams gave audible feedback and organised their turns revealed pragmatic differences, the Pākehā organisations preferring a single floor with limited overlapping, the Māori organisations tolerating and expecting far more overlapping and audible feedback. These differences, although subtle, play a significant role in constituting the shared repertoire of the communities and the (re)production of the ethnic orientation.

At the outset to the chapter, we noted that meetings were considered by our participants as sanctioned talk at work. They are overt and recognised demonstrations of transactional, task-focused business talk. Throughout the chapter, however, the analysis has indicated that it is impossible to divorce transactional talk from the simultaneous people-oriented work in which participants are inevitably engaged. In the next chapter, we turn the focus explicitly to relational talk at work, examining, in particular, some ways in which the relational dimension of leadership is enacted in our Māori workplaces.

CHAPTER 5
Relational Talk at Work

"...[ko] te tohu o te rangatira, he manaaki"
the sign of a leader is being able to look after others, generosity[1]

hapter 4 focused on meetings as quintessential examples of on-task sanctioned leadership talk. In this chapter, we focus on how leadership talk contributes to the construction of positive interpersonal workplace relationships. Effective leaders devote considerable effort to establishing, developing, and fostering strong collegial relationships among their team members, recognising that this is an important component in the overall mix that contributes to the achievement of workplace goals. This "relational work" (Locher and Watts, 2005: 10) is accomplished in many different ways as we will illustrate, highlighting, in particular, the distinctive approach of Māori leaders to fostering harmonious relations in Māori workplaces.

Relational work refers very broadly to all the ways in which people attend to the face needs of others. It is "the 'work' individuals invest in negotiating relationships with others" (Locher and Watts, 2005: 10).[2] Although such negotiations may include contesting, challenging, disagreeing with, and insulting others, the focus in this chapter is on ways in which people use language to construct and maintain rapport, index collegiality, and develop solidarity in the workplace. As illustrated in our earlier research, there are many ways to accomplish relational work (Holmes and Stubbe, 2003a; Holmes and Marra, 2004b). The discursive strategies available for

---

1. Whata Winiata in Diamond (2003: 67).
2. Locher makes the point that "relational work" is a more useful term than "facework" because facework is often assumed to be confined to mitigating behaviour, whereas the term *relational work* more obviously "covers the entire spectrum of behaviour, from rude and impolite, via normal, appropriate and unmarked, to marked and polite" (Locher, 2006: 250). Spencer-Oatey's concept of *rapport management* covers similar territory, referring to the use of language to "promote, maintain, or threaten harmonious social relations" (2008: 4).

this purpose include a wide range of ways of attending to others' "face" needs, including social talk, supportive humour, compliments, and expressions of admiration and approval. This chapter focuses on social talk and humour.

We also make use of the more specialised concept of "relational practice" (Fletcher, 1999; Holmes and Marra, 2004b). Relational practice (RP) is relational work that is not only oriented to the face needs of others but that also has an identifiable transactional function. It is relational, backstage work intended to ensure that workplace objectives are achieved.[3] RP is a particularly useful term when considering how leaders use social talk and humour in workplace interaction, since their motives are often more obviously strategic.

We begin by considering social talk as a component of effective leadership in the New Zealand workplaces in this study, with particular attention to features that distinguished small talk in the Māori organisations we have researched.

SOCIAL TALK AS RELATIONAL PRACTICE

Small talk and, more generally, social talk at work is one obvious means by which people establish and nurture collegial relationships. Social talk is face-oriented, explicitly addressing people's social needs, and it is widely regarded as peripheral and irrelevant to serious workplace business.[4] Much of it is also, strictly speaking, irrelevant to the transactional objectives of the workplace. However, social talk undoubtedly makes an important indirect contribution to achieving organisational objectives. Although discussions about how people spent their weekend, what movies they have seen, what sport they are currently involved with, and so on, typically have little direct relevance to the workplace business at hand, they are by no means irrelevant in the overall context of an organisation's goals. Interestingly, our extensive database indicates that workplace leaders are often centrally involved in encouraging and even introducing social talk at appropriate points in workplace interaction (Holmes and Stubbe, 2003a; Holmes, 2007b). Even more interestingly in relation to the theme of this book, there were fascinating contrasts in the underlying values reflected in the social talk recorded in our focus Pākehā and Māori workplaces.

Example 5.1 is an excerpt from a meeting between two managers, Jaeson and Brendon, at NZ Productions. The excerpt is from the beginning of their meeting before they have begun the business at hand they are discussing a comedy workshop that Brendon attended on the weekend. Improvisational comedy is an area in which Brendon is very interested.

---

3. Fletcher (1999: ix, 32–33, 47–48) defines it as the wide range of off-line, backstage, or collaborative work that people do, which goes largely unrecognised in the workplace, but which makes an important contribution to the smooth running of the organisation.

4. Holmes (2000) explores in some detail the distribution, content, and complex functions of small talk and social talk in Pākeha workplaces. See also Coupland (2000).

Example 5.1

Context: NZ Productions: Jaeson, general manager, is meeting with Brendon, an account manager

1	Brendon:-	and like it was a really big warmup and ++
2		this um + the second term was actually more
3		on singing and stuff like that
4	Jaeson:	oh like hoedowns?
5	Brendon:	like ho- yeah yeah we actually did a a er um
6		irish drinking song la di da di
7	Jaeson:	[laughs]…
8		so so how- when you say you came second
9		how do you get how do you get //scored on this?\
10	Brendon:	/well we had\\ a lot of um + er you know
11		like different skits and then the audience would +
12		score everybody on the skits ++
13		and you'd (just) like a er eliminate people
14		(you know) skits and songs…
15		er and then we got it it was down to two of us
16		me and Wendy Wendy who's a very good singer…
17		they he asked the audience okay
18		what's Wendy going to sing ++
19		somebody yelled out fuzzy cows
20		so she had to song a sing a song on fuzzy cows
21		//and\ it was fantastic
22	Jaeson:	/[laughs]\\
23	Brendon:	and I knew I couldn't //beat that\
24	Jaeson:	/[laughs]\\ [laughs] what was your song on?
25	Brendon:	and then um okay what's Brendon going to sing +
26		embarrassing gas
27	Jaeson:	[laughs]
28	Brendon:	so I had I sang a song on embarrassing gas
29	Jaeson:	[laughs]
30	Brendon:	Ryan played the music
31	Jaeson:	awesome
32	Brendon:	yeah so it's not second's not too bad
33	Jaeson:	no that's very good +
34		and and how you going to use this skill at work? +
35	Brendon:	[exhales]
36	Jaeson:	I guess it comes as as good you know
37		at relieving awkward moments ++
38		the amusing gas anyway //[laughs] [voc]\

39	Brendon:	/[laughs]\\ no I reckon relieving my stress
40		at work what it can do is I'm really going to
41		concentrate on this skill and in about
42		twenty five years I'll be able to have a
43		I'll be able to leave here and take up a job
44		on the stage I'll be able to make enough money
45	Jaeson:	oh well done
46	Brendon:	it's good you see so there's light
47		at the end of the tunnel ++
48	Jaeson:	[exhales]
49	Brendon:	now Company R&P

The conversation moves from social talk to work talk: it begins with a discussion of Brendon's experience at a comedy workshop that he has attended on the weekend (lines 1–3, 5–6), and moves on to a discussion of the relevance of the workshop to Brendon's contribution in the organisation (lines 34–39). The exchange suggests that Jaeson, the general manager, is very aware of the boundary between social talk and business talk. In line 34, he explicitly draws Brendon's attention to the distinction, albeit humourously, by first asking about the relevance of Brendon's social talk to their meeting agenda, *and how you going to use this skill at work*, and then suggesting a humourous potential application, *I guess it comes as as good you know at relieving awkward moments* (lines 36–37). Brendon responds by taking the jocular comment semiseriously, *no I reckon relieving my stress at work* (lines 39–40), and then elaborates by saying that it might also provide him with a means to exit the organisation in the long term (lines 41–44). He appears to recognise, however, that Jaeson's comment could be a signal that it is time to switch to business. When Jaeson does not respond verbally to Brendon's comment, *it's good you see so there's light at the end of the tunnel*, as indicated by the two-second pause followed by a long exhalation from Jaeson (lines 47–48), Brendon switches explicitly to the business topic that they have met to discuss, *now Company R&P* (line 49).

This example illustrates how social talk can be adroitly segued into business talk, thus simultaneously serving both relational and transactional goals. Jaeson's skillful use of contestive humour does valuable relational work to effect a smooth transition to work-related talk. This social talk serves, then, not just as relational work in general, but more specifically as RP, since it relates to more than purely interpersonal objectives such as building rapport. Although the topics of singing and drama in Example 5.1 clearly comprise nonwork-related social talk, Jaeson's challenging question (line 31), and Brendon's response, which mentions stress relief (line 35), suggests how they can be considered as relevant to Brendon's work situation.

Similar examples occur in all the organisations in which we have collected data.[5] Discussions of holidays, for instance, frequently move very subtly from plans for

5. See Holmes (2006: 87–92), and Holmes and Stubbe (2003a: chapter 5) for a number of further examples of social talk at work.

how the recreational time will be spent to a consideration of how the organisation will cope with the person's absence, talk that manifestly serves both interpersonal and transactional goals. It seems that off-topic, social talk often functions as a means of addressing an issue of direct concern to the progress of a project, or the smooth running of a department. In Pākehā workplaces, these conversations are consistently located at the boundaries of workplace business: they typically occur at the beginnings and ends of meetings, as in Example 5.1, often as people are walking into or out of a room, and during social breaks. In other words, they usually occur backstage and "off the record"; the transactional goal is achieved "by the way" during a conversation that participants would consider as primarily involving social talk, thus illustrating the subtle ways in which effective leaders can use apparently rapport-oriented discourse to serve organisational goals.

Background social information about clients or professional contacts is another area in which small talk and transactional talk intersect, and the boundaries may be difficult to draw. Meeting participants often introduce amusing anecdotes or personal information in the context of discussing particular business contacts. This is common in many of the organisations in which we recorded as illustrated in Example 5.2.[6]

Example 5.2

Context: NZ Productions: Management meeting

1	Seamus:	I mean he's a Rotary club person I you know
2		don't want him Dennis involved
3		who knows what Dennis is telling him
4	Jaeson:	you wanna hear this do you wanna the the
5		I forgot to tell you this Dennis said
6		look don't worry I'll put it right
7		I'll put some pressure on Maxwell's
8		to give you more work
9	M1:	[laughs]
10	Seamus:	//don't tell him to do anything like that\
11		/[laughter]\\
12	Paul?:	gee thanks
13	Jaeson:	[laughs]: gee thanks:
14	Seamus:	[with disbelief]: put some pressure on Maxwell's:
15	Paul?:	[laughs]
16	Jaeson:	I've got a lot of pull down there he said +

6. See also Holmes (2006: 133).

17	Paul:	that's probably what he told Maxwell's
18		I gotta lot of pull down at NZ Productions
19	M2:	[laughs] (20)
20	Jaeson:	well welcome everyone to the meeting
21		thanks for coming along ++

This pre-meeting talk is more obviously business related than the chat between Jaeson and Brendon in Example 5.1, but it is nonetheless off-record, light-hearted chat about the potential behaviour of the company's business contacts. Seamus, the managing director, first expresses concern that, because two of their contacts are both members of the Rotary club, they may be sharing information about NZ Productions (lines 1–3). He is concerned in particular about what one of the men, Dennis, might say. Jaeson, the general manager, then relates how Dennis told him that he has influence with the other man's company and can use this to get more work for NZ Productions (lines 5–8, 16). Seamus is horrified that Dennis has said this. Paul, a section manager, then constructs a fantasy scenario, suggesting that Dennis makes the same claims to the other man about his relationship with NZ Productions (*I gotta lot of pull at NZ Productions*).

Humourous banter is frequent in the pre-meeting talk at NZ Productions. The main function is to fill in time in a socially acceptable way while people arrive and before Jaeson starts the meeting (lines 20–21), *well welcome everyone to the meeting thanks for coming along,* although, as in this example, transactional goals may also be achieved. There is a potentially pertinent underlying message that you should never take a client's position for granted nor assume that clients are not in touch with one another. This is particularly true for New Zealand where close-knit, multiplex networks are common, especially in the business community.

As noted earlier, social talk in Pākehā workplaces typically occurs at the beginnings and ends of meetings, and occasionally at topic boundaries. Although social exchanges may be quite lengthy as the chair waits for everyone to arrive, once the meeting is underway, any social talk at topic boundaries is generally very brief indeed. The meeting opening is generally clear-cut, often following a relatively long pause, as in Example 5.2. When there is no significant pause, the shift from social talk to business talk may appear particularly abrupt to nonparticipants.

In our Māori workplaces too, every meeting was preceded by social talk, which often extended for a considerable time, and, as in Example 5.2, the talk often provided subtle information of potential relevance to transactional objectives. However, some additional features also distinguished relational talk in Māori meetings. First, there was overall simply more social talk in Māori organisations, and second, social talk was much more common *within* Māori meetings than in Pākehā meetings. In particular, seamless segueing between social talk and transactional talk was frequent and often very subtly accomplished in Māori contexts. Stories told by the managing director of Kiwi Productions, Yvonne, and the Chief Executive Officer (CEO) of Kiwi Consultations, Daniel, about their personal experiences frequently served to illustrate points of relevance to the addressees' work (see, for instance, Marra and Holmes 2005). As in Māori culture more generally (Thornton, 1985; Metge, 1995; Benton, 1996), metaphor was a common indirect means of conveying a message, and meanings were typically expressed implicitly rather than spelled out. Kiwi Productions' senior managers, Quentin and Rangi, in particular, moved smoothly in and out of personal anecdotes about their organisational contacts so that it was very difficult to draw boundaries between what was purely social information, and what was useful background for those who would be contacting or working with the people to whom they referred Example 5.3 illustrates this in a meeting at Kiwi Productions.

Example 5.3

Context: Kiwi Productions: Team meeting

1	Quentin:	Yvonne had a meeting with Rawiri Thomas
2		who was actually //I don't know if you all heard\
3	Irihapeti?:	/mm mm\\
4	Quentin:	that he was in hospital he had a heart attack
5	Irihapeti?:	//mm\
6	Paula:	/oh\\
7	Quentin:	Rawiri so um he's now at home convalescing
8		and um on restricted duties
9	Irihapeti:	mm
10	Quentin:	but um he's using the time because +
11		he's actually in the process of preparing a screenplay
12		for a film for Kiwi Productions to produce
13	Paula:	mm
14	Quentin:	um not sure exactly what the title is but er or the topic
15		but Yvonne went out to have lunch with him yesterday
16		and he made her cheese scones and + er
17	Irihapeti:	yeah he's a very //domesticated\ man
18	Quentin:	/yeah\\
19	Rangi:	mm
20	Quentin:	but just he just passes on his regards to everyone
21	Irihapeti:	oh
22	Quentin:	um he's still not allowed to have visitors
23		and //things\ like that
24	Irihapeti:	/mm mm\\
25	Quentin:	but he is out of hospital seems to be okay
26		so that yeah that's just on those ones um
27		just an update on the project

In this excerpt, Quentin reports transactional information of relevance to the team: first he notes that Yvonne, the managing director, has met with Rawiri Thomas, who has been contracted to do some work for them, and second, he reports on how the work is progressing (lines 11–12, 14). Then providing more detail about Yvonne's visit (lines 15–16), Quentin reports that Rawiri sends regards and he provides further information on Rawiri's condition (lines 20, 22, 25). He then ends the topic (line 26), and moves on to the next topic (line 27).

The line between what the team needs to know and what is non-work related additional personal information is not very clear, but it is safe to say that the information about Rawiri's domestic skills (lines 16–17) is not strictly essential to the work being reported to the team. It is likely that the information about the embargo on visitors (line 22) is also not strictly relevant to the team, though it could be an implicit warning in case any other team member had ideas of following up Yvonne's visit. In this Māori context, such information is quite unmarked; Quentin's personalisation of the topic is entirely appropriate and normal in a Māori organisation such as Kiwi Productions.

The boundaries between social talk and transactional talk are thus often treated as fluid in both Pākehā and Māori organisations, and this fluidity is regularly exploited by leaders to neatly integrate relational and transactional goals. Example 5.3 illustrates that these boundaries may be particularly subtle and permeable in Māori organisations, and the precise point of shift between transactional and personal information may be hard to determine, and indeed such a distinction may be considered irrelevant or puzzling to those engaged in such interactions in a Māori context.

Interestingly, the permeability of discourse boundaries in Māori meetings (from a Pākehā perspective) is also evident in the personalisation of the formal opening of meetings. As discussed in chapter 4, personal information about workmates is a typical component of the opening mihi. Information about the condition of team mates who have been sick, or about illness or a death in the family of an employee, is typically woven into the formal meeting opening. This was illustrated in Example 4.8, where Daniel, the CEO, refers, in his opening mihi for a meeting of all staff, to the recent bereavement of a colleague, who is attending the *tangihanga* ("funeral") of her younger sister, and expresses sympathy for her and the children of her sister.

This is yet another instance of the extent to which matters that Pākehā would consider personal, and even private, are explicitly integrated into the work routines of Māori workplaces. All those present consider this quite appropriate, and, indeed, failure to refer to Mere's loss at this point in the proceedings would be considered reprehensible in the context of this Māori organisation. As noted in earlier chapters, concern for the welfare of members of the organisation extends well beyond the strict boundaries adhered to by many Pākehā organisations, and automatically includes employees' whānau ("extended family"). These formal meeting openings, which explicitly acknowledge those present and their family concerns, are further important components of relational work in Māori workplaces.

To sum up, social talk always occurs before meetings, and often after meetings, in both Pākehā and Māori organisations, and it may be quite prolonged, especially if it is filling a gap while people arrive. However, social talk *within* meetings occurs much more frequently in the Māori workplaces than in the Pākehā organisations where we recorded. Apparent social talk "digressions" often last for a considerable time in Māori meetings without any evidence that participants find this problematic or feel pressure to return to the official meeting agenda.

Moreover, as the discussion has indicated, drawing boundaries between social talk and work talk is not always straightforward. Information gleaned through social talk (e.g., someone's state of health, aspects of personality) might well prove directly or indirectly relevant to a company's business. This fluidity was especially prevalent in Māori meetings where apparent digressions on social and personal topics regularly recurred throughout. In other words, the distinction between what qualified as social talk and what should be considered business talk was often difficult to maintain. Furthermore, it became apparent, drawing on the expertise of our Māori researchers, that a Pākehā researcher's analytical lens on what was "relevant" to the business at hand, versus what was purely "social" talk was often different from a Māori researcher's culturally informed lens. A passing reference to a Māori participant's relative, for example, might serve as a hint that the speaker considered the relative a source of useful advice on the topic under discussion. What was considered a legitimate contribution to the agenda as opposed to a digression was a very culturally influenced evaluation. And subtle references to shared cultural knowledge meant that there were often layers of meaning available to Māori participants that were not at all obvious to outsiders.

This suggests a very interesting area of potential miscommunication. What is regarded as central and what is considered peripheral to the business at hand may well be perceived differently by Māori and Pākehā meeting participants. Topic boundaries seem more permeable in Māori meetings, and social talk is often regarded as relevant in some way, if one knows the "code". In other words, social talk should never be dismissed as irrelevant; it may contain a wealth of implicit meaning for those who are alert to its potential significance.

In concluding this section, it is also worth emphasising that the commitment of Māori to family values, and the priority given in both our Māori workplaces to the claims of whānau, mean that the introduction of social concerns, including family concerns, is not experienced as uncomfortable, inappropriate, or problematic in any way. By contrast, in NZ Consultations and NZ Productions, although matters relating to leave and holidays are discussed, and social activities outside of work are mentioned, as in Example 5.1, there is little explicit discussion of family concerns. This observation is supported by our analyses of data from the larger Language in the Workplace corpus. In the most "masculinist" workplaces (Baxter, 2003), there was relatively little conventional small talk focused on personal or social topics, even before and after meetings, the prototypical positions for such talk in most workplaces (Marra, 2008a; Holmes and Marra, 2004b). Rather, the participants in these workplaces used the times around the edges of the meeting to catch up on work-related topics that were typically outside the scope of the meeting's ratified business. It appears, then, that appropriate topics of pre-and postmeeting talk, as well as what is considered peripheral as opposed to relevant in such contexts, differ between different workplaces, including Pākehā and Māori workplaces, reflecting different priorities and cultural values.

Social talk is an obvious strategy for enhancing workplace relationships. In this section we have identified features that characterise social talk as RP in both Māori and Pākehā workplaces, and then we discussed some features that appear to distinguish the Māori workplaces in our dataset. The extensive imbrication of work and personal concerns emerges as a very distinctive feature of the ethnicised Māori organisations in our research corpus. We turn now to a consideration of humour, another aspect of workplace interaction that is a key component of an effective leader's repertoire in doing relational work.

HUMOUR AS RELATIONAL PRACTICE

Like social talk, humour is a valuable communicative resource for reconciling the competing transactional and relational demands that face leaders in different workplaces. There is a large amount of earlier research investigating humour in the workplace from different perspectives and across a range of disciplines.[7] This research encompasses many different aspects of workplace humour, including how it benefits employment relationships, job satisfaction, creativity, and even productivity (e.g., Caudron, 1992; Clouse and Spurgeon, 1995; Morreall, 1991), how it may serve as a control mechanism, encouraging conformity to group norms (e.g., Collinson, 1988), as well as its function as a strategy for expressing resistance to management (e.g., Rodrigues and Collinson, 1995). Here, we focus on the relational functions of humour and, specifically, its role in assisting leaders to construct good workplace relationships and to facilitate team work.

As a multifunctional discourse strategy, humour is a very versatile means of doing RP in any context. In the workplace, it is invaluable to those managers who can use it with skill. By definition humour is aimed at providing amusement, and, hence, it is often perceived as dispensable and peripheral and even distracting in workplace interaction. It is quintessentially off record. In other words, no matter how work focused an utterance is, it can be argued that the injection or addition of a component of humour is always, strictly speaking, an extraneous element. Witty comments illustrate this well: the content is often clearly transactional, but the clever concise formulation in the context of a workplace discussion generates amusement, as in Example 5.4. Daniel, the CEO of Kiwi Consultations, is discussing with his finance manager, Frank, the naïve belief of one of their staff that if he aims to become a manager he will not need to devote much time to developing his writing skills.

---

7. See Schnurr (2008) for a thorough review.

Example 5.4

Context: Kiwi Consultations: Daniel, CEO, is meeting with Frank, finance manager

1	Daniel:	yeah you have to show people
2		that you know what you're doing
3		before they'll let you stop [laughs] + mm

Daniel's witty aphorism succinctly captures an interesting distilment of his experience as CEO. It is amusing because it expresses an apparent contradiction or illogicality. He points out that, typically, one must demonstrate certain skills before being appointed to a position, but that once in the position, ironically, those skills may no longer be required. The humour helps make the point more effectively and more memorably. The example illustrates how, like small talk, workplace humour may qualify as RP by simultaneously addressing both relational and transactional goals; it is, thus, an invaluable resource for team leaders.

Our previous research in Pākehā workplaces has demonstrated that leaders in different communities of practice (CofPs) tend to use a range of rather different styles of humour.[8] Some workplaces, for instance, tend to favour predominantly supportive and collaborative humour, sharing amused attitudes to issues, and commenting entertainingly on workplace behaviour (see Example 5.8 below). In these CofPs, leaders often used self-deprecating humour in subtle, low key, and off-record ways, especially to reestablish good relations after being particularly directive. In a government department, at the end of a tense and difficult meeting, for instance, a senior manager claimed she would not get a job in another department because she could not even make good coffee (Holmes and Stubbe, 2003b). The self-deprecating remark generated laughter and eased tension. In Example 5.5, Suzanne, the deputy leader of the team, describes to a less senior member of the team an incident in which she was treated disparagingly in a public context by a consultant from another organisation.

Example 5.5

Context: NZ Consultations: Suzanne, deputy leader of the team is meeting with Rowan, team member

1	Suzanne:	it was also terrible because of conflicts
2		with other enquiries

8. See Holmes and Stubbe (2003a: chapter 6) and Holmes (2006: chapter 4) for exemplification. See also Schnurr (2008).

3	Rowan:	mm
4	Suzanne:	[laughs] particularly with the consultant
5		who kept calling me what was I called [laughs] madam

The use of the term *madam* in a context in which Suzanne expected the consultant to use her first name is a skilful distancing device. It appears respectful and so provides no grounds for complaint, but it denies the relationship that Suzanne thought she had established, and potentially implies she is being impertinent in this context. Suzanne tells this story against herself to a sympathetic Rowan. Self-deprecating humour of this kind is a good way of "creating team" (Fletcher, 1999: 48) and downplaying power differentials.

Other workplaces appear to prefer more contestive, challenging, and even jocularly insulting humour to create team and maintain good workplace relationships. Leaders in these workplaces need to be quick-witted and even ebullient in their style of humour in order to maintain their position. NZ Productions provides many examples of this kind of humour, often instigated by Jaeson, the leader who is second in command to Seamus, the managing director. In Example 5.6, Jaeson teases Rob about the fact that he has time available for a meeting, despite the fact that he always gives the impression he is very busy.

Example 5.6

Context: NZ Productions: Jaeson, general manager, is meeting with Rob, business development manager

1	Jaeson:	okay so we shall make it um + um tomorrow?
2	Rob:	okay well I'll tell you what I've got tomorrow
3	Jaeson:	yep
4	Rob:	I've got a one o'clock and a three o'clock
5	Jaeson:	it'll have to be three o'clock then
6	Rob:	no I mean I'm committed at three
7	Jaeson:	oh //[laughs]\ [laughs]
8	Rob:	/and at one\\
9	Jaeson:	[laughs]: I thought you were really important
10		for a minute then: [laughs]

The two men are trying to find a time for a meeting the next day and when Rob says *I've got a one o'clock and a three o'clock* (line 4), Jaeson mistakenly assumes these are the only gaps in Rob's calendar for the day. When it turns out these are in fact his only appointments for the day, Jaeson teases him with the comment *I thought you were really important for a minute then* (lines 9–10), implying that, since he has plenty of time available, Rob is in fact *not* very important after all. This kind of friendly jibing is very common in this workplace, and serves to construct and maintain rapport between team members.

But Jaeson is a skilled leader and on other occasions he uses a different style of humour to achieve his workplace objectives. An example of RP illustrates the skill with which he uses self-deprecating humour as a relational strategy to achieve what he regards as the most desirable outcome of a meeting discussing the entertainment at a party planned for NZ Productions staff and clients. His co-participants in the meeting want to add a poetry reading as well as music, but he skillfully steers the discussion so that they finally decide that just music will be a satisfactory source of entertainment. A burst of humour occurs at a typical point for humour, that is, when a contentious point has been resolved. They all contribute ideas about the kind of music that could be appropriate, and Jaeson sings some possible tunes.

Example 5.7

Context: NZ Productions: Jaeson, general manager, is meeting with two members of the sales team to organise a social event

1	Anna:	well maybe we could use you
2		as back up you know [laughs]
3		and a special guest appearance
4	Jaeson:	I could be the wind section

When Anna laughingly suggests they could use Jaeson as entertainment if their plans fall through, he wittily responds with a self-deprecating remark (line 4). He has achieved his goal; he can afford to be humourously self-denigrating. It will also be apparent that, in his leadership role, Jaeson makes a strong contribution to nurturing collegial relations, a point developed in chapter 6.

Styles of humourous interaction in different workplaces and in different contexts within workplaces tend to differ, often quite markedly. In our workplace corpus as a whole, we found that there were some workplaces in which explicitly negative instances of humour were rare, whereas in others the great majority of humourous comments comprised sarcastic and challenging jibes, apparently intended to deflate the addressee.[9] Effective leadership in such different workplace CofPs requires skilful management of humour as RP. In the dataset considered here, Kiwi Productions and NZ Consultations (i.e., one Māori and one Pākehā company) tended to use more supportive and collaborative styles of humour, whereas Kiwi Consultations and NZ Productions (the other Māori and Pākehā organisations) tended to prefer a more contestive and challenging

9. See Holmes and Marra (2002a, 2002b) for a range of examples. See also Kuiper (1991) and Kiesling (2001) for instances of this kind of "masculine" discourse among New Zealand rugby players and U.S. fraternity members, respectively, and Bell and Major (2004) for an analysis of the exploitation of this kind of humour in billboard advertisements for New Zealand beer.

style of humour with a good deal of teasing and jocular insult. In terms of style of humour, then, ethnicity did not seem to lead to the favouring of a particular style. When ethnicity did appear to be relevant was in motivating or contributing to understanding particular instances of humour. In the next section, we explore the relevance of ethnicity in understanding the humour in the Māori workplaces, focusing, in particular, on the use of humour by leaders in these ethnicised CofPs.

HUMOUR IN MĀORI WORKPLACES

He rongoā anō tō te kata
Laughter is the best medicine[10]

Both Māori organisations use a wide range of different styles and types of humour (Holmes, 2007a). The humour at Kiwi Productions included both supportive and collaborative humour as well as contestive and challenging humour. However, as mentioned earlier, collaborative humour was decidedly the predominant style in this workplace. This was apparent in many different contexts, from one-to-one discussions and small team meetings, to larger team meetings and full staff meetings, as illustrated in Example 5.8.

Example 5.8

Context: Kiwi Productions: Meeting of all staff. The topic is a recent media awards ceremony. Whitney is describing the event. General laughter throughout this section— not notedin the transcript

1	Whitney:	[numerous people talking over top of her]:
2		um most of these here
3		when they had to um receive their awards ( )
4		um: Rua another university prof- professor on the list
5	Keith:	yeah from our university professors series
6	Whitney:	[laughs] the name dropping series
7	Keith:	significant New Zealanders of the twentieth
8		century series
9		[laughter]
10	Whitney:	[drawls]: and: still //selling (well)\
11	Keith:	/and porno documentaries\\
12		[laughter]

10. This apt saying with its English equivalent was suggested by one of our Māori advisors.

This brief excerpt is typical of the collaborative humour that characterises many of the meetings at Kiwi Productions, and it is valued and fostered by the managing director of the company, Yvonne. There is a great deal of simultaneous talk, and it is clear that the humour is jointly constructed and supportive in orientation. Each contribution adds another amusing component to the banter. With a good deal of overlapping talk, the group pokes fun at a university professor who was given an award in a public awards ceremony they are discussing. Keith refers sarcastically to *our university professors series* (line 5), and then Whitney joins in, even more explicitly ridiculing the proponents by referring to the series as *the name dropping series* (line 6). Keith extends the humour further, *the significant New Zealanders of the twentieth century series* (line 7–8) and then refers to *porno documentaries* (line 11) (definitely NOT something this company actually produces!), thus beginning a humourous fantasy about how the company might make more money. This idea is then extensively developed (not included here for space reasons), with collaborative contributions from a range of people. The participants enthusiastically embrace a play frame (Coates, forthcoming), and sustain it for a considerable period of mutual entertainment.

This kind of humour contributes to team spirit, reinforces solidarity, and is consistent with the collectivist Māori values that characterise this workplace. Although something similar could have occurred in many workplaces in which team spirit is fostered, and value is placed on collegiality and supportive attitudes, the managing director, Yvonne, commented in interview that the amount and type of humour characterising Kiwi Productions was an important component of what made their workplace distinctive. She remarked explicitly and positively on how much laughter and joking went on at the company, especially in their staff meetings, and we observed that she actively nurtured this in the interests of maintaining a good organisational ethos.

In Kiwi Consultations, on the other hand, the humour was typically contestive and challenging, with a great deal of teasing and jocular abuse, often instigated by Daniel, the CEO, as illustrated in Examples 5.9 and 5.10.

Example 5.9

Context: Kiwi Consultations: Management meeting. Hinerau's mobile rings with a loud musical tone

1	Hinerau:	oh sorry
2	Daniel:	well turn it up
3	Hinerau:	[indignantly]: sorry:

[Hinerau leaves the room to answer the call]

Daniel here comments sarcastically on the disruptive noise created by Hinerau's cell phone, while in Example 5.10, Hari makes fun of Daniel's claim that he put on only a hundred grams of weight while away on a business trip.

Example 5.10

Context: Kiwi Consultations: Management meeting

1	Daniel:	I'll have you know I only put on a hundred grams
2		while I was away
3	Hari:	is that the facial hair? //[laughs]\
4	Daniel:	/that's probably it if I have a shave and a haircut\\
5		I'll be right back to where I was +

Hari's quip *is that the facial hair?* (line 3) refers to Daniel's new beard. Never one to passively accept a verbal put down, Daniel responds wittily by suggesting that *a shave and a haircut* will exactly restore him to his former weight (lines 4–5).

As the CEO of Kiwi Consultations, it is clear that Daniel's style of humour is quite consistent with that of the wider team. He uses a great deal of humour, with frequent witty but good-humoured quips, often directed at his colleagues, as illustrated in Example 5.9, as well as by this quip from another meeting: *Catherine will get everyone back awake after Steve's had a go on the accounting side.* Example 5.11 provides a further illustration, with the organisation's security procedures as the butt of Daniel's humour.

Example 5.11

Context: Kiwi Consultations: Management meeting

1	Albert:	we just need to watch security things
2		for instance on Friday when everybody left here
3		the two doors alongside the lifts were still
4		propped open so the whole place was wide open
5		I mean there's not much point closing off the lifts
6		if we have er [laughs] all the access ways
7		wide open
8	Daniel:	yeah cos those doors are only blocked off
9		because of the cumbersome security cards
10		we have to carry all the way to the bathroom eh
11	Albert:	as far as I'm aware
12	Daniel:	and they weigh two or three grams

13	Albert:	well that's right it's weight training
14		weight training //so we don't have to go\
15		to the gym [laughs]
16	Daniel:	/[laughs]\\
17	Frank:	by the time I've got my cup of coffee
18		and my cellphone and all the papers
19		that I'm working on I can't get to it + [laughs]

Albert, who is in charge of security, reminds the team about the importance of security measures within the organisation (lines 1–7). Endorsing his comments, Daniel adopts an ironic stance expressing sympathy with staff members over the demand that they carry their *cumbersome security cards* (line 9) which weigh *two or three grams* (line 12) with them at all times. This is a nice example of RP, illustrating the dry sense of humour that pervades much of Daniel's discourse. Albert, in typical Kiwi Consultations fashion, retaliates with a humourous rejoinder, *it's weight training weight training so we don't have to go to the gym* (line 13–15), and Frank adds a further humourous comment (lines 17–19) expanding the theme.

Although these contrasting styles of humour distinguished the two Māori workplaces, there was also a good deal of culturally distinctive humour that characterised both of these ethnicised CofPs. Example 5.12 below is one of many that could be used to illustrate the fact that familiarity with Māori cultural values and beliefs is important in interpreting the rich and complex meanings being conveyed in these workplaces. It illustrates, in particular, the complementary Māori concepts of *whakahīhī* and *whakaiti,* which were introduced in chapter 3.

Yvonne, the managing director of Kiwi Productions, regularly refers to this Māori value as the basis for a humourous comment. Example 5.11 is from the first meeting that we video recorded in this workplace and, unsurprisingly, some members of the team play up to the cameras. Yvonne comments that she predicted the room would divide into those who "performed" for the cameras, showing off and boasting (whakahīhī), and those who took a back seat and kept a low profile (whakaiti).

Example 5.12

Context: Kiwi Productions: Meeting of all staff (first video recorded regular staff meeting). Gretel, a manager, is about to deliver her monthly report. Laughter throughout this section from the participants

1	Gretel:	do you want me to read it?
2	Lillian:	yeah
3		[laughter]

4	David:	are you shy?
5	Zara:	talk to the camera babe
6	Gretel:	talk to the camera
7		[laughter]
8	Lillian:	I'm Lillian by the way
9		[laughter]
10	Gretel:	I'm ready for my closeup now ( ) um
11	Yvonne:	[smiling broadly]: I told them beforehand
12		the room will divide easily into the *whakahīhī*
13		the *whakaiti*:

In this excerpt, David and Zara tease Gretel (who is Pākehā, and one of the senior managers) about appearing on the video camera: *are you shy, talk to the camera babe* (lines 4, 5). Gretel is about to deliver her regular report to the staff meeting and realises she will be filmed doing this. She first reacts with mock horror saying *talk to the camera* (line 6) in an appalled tone. Then she adjusts and declares audaciously *I'm ready for my closeup now* (line 10). Meanwhile, Lillian (another Pākehā) is also performing for the camera, stating clearly who she is (line 8)—so the talent spotters won't miss her! Yvonne comments at this point that she foresaw this would happen, and she categorises the performers as *whakahīhī*, whereas the quiet observers are the modest *whakaiti*. This could be interpreted as a mild reproof since self-promotion is not encouraged in this organisation, but since the whole of this interaction is so much of tongue-in-cheek "performance", Yvonne's wry comment fits well into the general atmosphere of mocking humour. The excerpt nicely illustrates that Māori values are a constant background to behaviour at Kiwi Productions, as well as demonstrating the generally positive atmosphere of solidarity and good humour that characterises this organisation, as noted earlier.

A similar example from Quentin, a senior manager in Kiwi Productions, is also worth examining for the light it throws on the tension between doing leadership and being appropriately self-deprecating in a Māori context. Quentin is leader of a production team. He is valued not only for his wide practical experience in areas of the organisation's business but, as noted in chapter 1, also for his outstanding expertise in Māori tikanga and the Māori language. Indeed, Yvonne seeks his advice in this area and defers to him in all matters relating to appropriate cultural behaviour. Quentin is the undoubted leader in matters relating to Māori tikanga at Kiwi Productions. Quentin's team members all understand Māori and many are fluent speakers; the team members "code switch" between Māori and English during their meetings, with whole turns often in Māori from some team members. This is important background for understanding why Example 5.13 occasions laughter and is regarded as so amusing by his team members.

Example 5.13

Context: Kiwi Productions: Team meeting. Quentin is checking future commitments

1	Quentin:	[we] are at the [technician's office]
2		through this weekend
3		have I got that day right for you to see Paula?
4	Paula:	yeah the it's the Tuesday //the\
5	Quentin:	/yeah\\ yeah
6	Paula:	not Wednes- you had Tuesday the twenty second
7	Quentin:	yeah I know Matariki pointed that out to me
8		and it's my it's my calendar
9		I still don't know those days
10		the Māori names for days of the week
11		[laughter]
12		so I look up and it's the third and I think
13		oh let's move

Quentin here acknowledges that he does not know the (new official) Māori names for the days of the week. To interpret accurately the significance of this admission, it is important to know that fluent Māori speakers such as Quentin learned a version of the days of the week that was a transliteration from English (e.g., *Mane, Tūrei, Wenerei*). In recent years, *Te Taura Whiri i te Reo Māori* (the Māori Language Commission) has been promoting new names for the days of the week, based on diverse and complex sources, both Māori and European (e.g., *Rāhina, Rātū, Rāapa*), and these are now the "official" versions for use in formal contexts. Hence, fluent Māori speakers who learned their Māori many decades ago find themselves wrong-footed by newer learners who are familiar with the currently prescribed "official" names. So Quentin is here being self-deprecating in line with Māori values relating to acknowledging fault and being modest. However, ironically, the root cause of the need for modesty is in fact his highly valued and respected cultural expertise and his exceptional fluency in Māori. Indeed the laughter that his admission occasions derives precisely from the fact that his team appreciates his outstanding linguistic skills and the humourous irony of his admission. As illustrated in chapter 3, Yvonne, the managing director, also consistently uses humourous self-deprecation, indexing basic Māori values while doing effective relational work.

In Kiwi Consultations, even the ebullient Daniel uses self-mockery on occasion. He comments, for instance, that after participating in a speed-reading course, he has nothing but an attendance certificate to show for it: *this is just terrible am I gonna put this on the wall certificate of attendance.* And he manages to combine both self-mockery and jocular abuse in a comment to Hari that he should accompany Daniel to a formal meeting with an external group: *so I don't look like the dumbest guy there.* These self-directed jibes reflect the underlying Māori values that those working at

Kiwi Consultations subscribe to no less than those at Kiwi Productions, though they are expressed in a somewhat more robust style.

It is important to reiterate that we are not claiming that self-deprecating humour does not occur in Pākehā workplaces. See earlier Example 5.7, for instance. There are certainly examples of self-denigrating humour in a number of workplaces, particularly among women leaders, and in "feminine" CofPs (see, for example, Holmes and Schnurr, 2005).[11] The "tall poppy" syndrome, referred to in chapter 1, means New Zealanders generally view blatant self-promotion as unacceptable. However, that is not quite the same as a culture that positively values humility and encourages explicit recognition of the contribution of others. Certainly, our analyses indicate that instances of humour based on self-deprecation occur more frequently in the Māori workplaces, and it is clear that such humour is consistent with and instantiates fundamental Māori cultural values. Further research will be valuable to indicate whether this suggestion finds support in the analysis of interaction in other Māori workplaces.

Although the overall style of humour in each of the Māori organisations contrasted in many respects, there was also a good deal of humour in both organisations, which indicated awareness of the pervasive significance of ethnicity and ethnic boundaries, and signaled sensitivity regarding interethnic relations. Example 5.14 illustrates Māori members of Kiwi Consultations, encouraged by Daniel, poking fun at Pākehā who, in the current political climate, see strategic advantage in siding with Māori, and specifically with their new Māori neighbors in well-to-do suburbs.

Example 5.14

Context: Kiwi Consultations: Management meeting

1	Caleb:	multimillion dollar properties up //( )\
2	Daniel:	/[laughs]\\ oh they'll have a happy weekend
3		then won't they
4	Hari:	yeah
5	Daniel:	[laughs]: the neighbors hey:
6	Caleb:	//[laughs]\
7	Hari:	/that's good\\ they love it eh
8	Daniel:	[laughs]: yeah: I bet they love it
9	Hari:	they love they love that stuff
10		//that Māori dynamic\
11	Daniel:	/that cultural colour\\
12	Hari:	yeah
13	Hinerau:	[name] was //saying that they've been\

11. Interestingly, however, the areas that are denigrated are never crucial in relation to work expertise, and the self-deprecation often occurs at meeting boundaries and in less transactionally oriented sections of talk.

14	Hari:	/the property values go up\\
15	Hinerau:	coming round to offer offer what they can do
16		whether they can bake or
17	Daniel:	//[laughs] [laughs]: yeah yeah choice:\
18	Hari:	/yeah oh yeah yeah straight up eh\\
19		Māori is the new black eh Caleb?
20	Caleb:	yeah it is
21		[laughter]
22		it is it is the new black bro [laughs]
23		[laughter]

This interesting excerpt clearly illustrates collaborative humour at Kiwi Consultations with hypocritical Pākehā as the target. Daniel makes explicit fun of rich Pākehā who find they have new Māori neighbors *they'll have a happy weekend then...I bet they love it...that cultural colour* (lines 2–3, 8, 11). Hari's comment that *the property values go up* (line 14) is especially telling since the traditional cultural stereotype entails depressed house prices in Māori neighborhoods. Hari follows this up with another witty comment, using a rich metaphor, *Māori is the new black eh Caleb* (line 19). The metaphor conveys many levels of meaning: using a well-known phrase referring to the current fashionability of the colour black in the clothing industry, it also subtly references black-power movements, and ironically satirises the fact that Māori people, with skin colour ranging from light to dark brown, are nonetheless perceived and labeled as "black" by many Pākehā. The contributors in this example are all Māori, with Daniel leading the humour and encouraging his team in mocking Pākehā hypocrisy.[12] The example is marked discursively as in-group Māori interaction through features such as the pragmatic tag *eh* (lines 7, 18, 19), a rapidly spreading feature of New Zealand English, which has its origins in Māori interaction, and which is strongly associated with Māori ethnicity (Stubbe and Holmes, 2000; Meyerhoff, 1994; Vine and Marra, 2008; Vine and Marsden, forthcoming), as well as the address term *bro*, which is also associated with Polynesian identity (Bell, 2000). Repetition (evident in lines 7–9 and lines 19, 22) is another feature that has been identified as characterising Māori discourse (Metge, 1995). The syntactic apposition evident in Daniel's comment, *they'll have a happy weekend then won't they...the neighbors*, also tends to characterise Māori English discourse.

This kind of boundary-marking humour served to construct and maintain solidarity between members of the organisation, including, in some cases, both Māori and Pākehā participants. So, for instance, both Māori and Pākehā staff at Kiwi Productions condemn Pākehā who mispronounce Māori words, especially in public

12. The boundaries are drawn differently in Example 8.6, where those Pākehā who are sympathetic and knowledgeable line up with Māori to make fun of those Pākehā who are ignorant of Māori ways of doing things.

contexts (see chapter 8, Example 8.6). Lillian, a Pākehā staff member says witheringly of the announcer at an awards ceremony *she could say Versace but she can't say kia kaha*.

This section has illustrated the ways in which leaders in the focus organisations use humour to construct and maintain positive workplace relationships and, especially in Māori workplaces, to reinforce fundamental cultural values and emphasise significant cultural boundaries. Humour is an effective means of identifying transgressions of Māori values, a means that maintains the pleasant and amusing tone that typifies interactions in this workplace and avoids indexing a teacherly identity through an overly pedantic stance. The leaders also often use self-deprecatory humour, instantiating the Māori value of whakaiti, which is fundamental to their ways of constructing leadership in this Māori organisation. They avoid explicit self-promotion, finding other means to index authority and convey the message that they are effectively meeting the challenges of leadership. Humour is a useful strategy for integrating these competing demands. Moreover, a general culture of support and collaboration, as opposed to one of challenge and contestation, is apparent in all the data discussed in this section. We have illustrated how effective leaders make use of strategies such as humour in accomplishing relational work, which not only contributes to the quality of collegial relationships but may also contribute in more effectively achieving transactional goals.

CONCLUSION

Most current discussions of effective leadership recognise the importance of attending to relational aspects of workplace interaction (Jackson and Parry, 2008). Relational talk is regarded as an important means of constructing and maintaining harmonious and productive workplace relationships. In this chapter, we have illustrated two important strategies through which leaders attended to workplace relationships, namely, social talk and humour, both discourse strategies that generally contribute to creating team and strengthening rapport and solidarity between workplace participants.

The analysis in this chapter has again drawn on our theoretical model in illuminating how these different strategies manifest themselves in our focus workplaces. At the institutional level, we are often unaware of the sociocultural constraints that operate in our society; they just seem "normal". So, for instance, the occurrence of small talk before and after meetings seems natural in many western societies, but there is no expectation of small talk before Japanese business meetings, for example (Murata, forthcoming). Although acceptable and appropriate patterns and types of humour clearly differ from one workplace culture and CofP to another, there are few constraints on who can contribute humour in meetings in New Zealand society. In Japan, by contrast, there are many society-wide, institutionally recognised constraints based on relative status that influence acceptable behaviour, including who can appropriately initiate humour in business meetings.

Within New Zealand society, our data clearly indicates that different workplace cultures and CofPs develop different norms and different styles of interaction. In some CofPs, the topics of small talk tend to revolve around personal and family concerns, whereas, in others, business preoccupations intrude even into social talk. In some CofPs, a more contestive style of humour predominates, whereas a more supportive, collaborative style is preferred in others. Different CofPs contrast in the frequency, length, positioning, topics, and style of humour that typify their interactions. In Māori organisations, meanings are more likely to be implicit and understated, and often metaphorical; Māori cultural values constitute a presupposed underpinning or foundation for understanding within any interaction. The relevance of societal and institutional norms was also apparent in the analysis. The paramount importance of whānau loyalty, a value common to all Māori, in relation to loyalty to the organisation per se, was frequently evident in social talk in Māori workplaces, whereas in Pākehā workplaces, institutional norms prescribe that family loyalties take second place to work demands. Furthermore, institutionalised ethnic boundaries and the prescribed social norms of appropriate workplace interaction are a more frequent target of explicit humour in Māori interactions than in Pākehā.

Constructing oneself as an effective leader involves making use of relational skills. We have examined some of the ways in which the more technical concept of RP is instantiated in our focus workplaces, exploring in some detail its use by Māori leaders and its particular manifestations in Māori workplace contexts. The analysis of social talk and its often complex relationship to business talk in workplace interactions throws up some interestingly different patterns between our Māori and Pākehā workplaces. In particular, it seems that the boundaries between what counts as social talk and business talk appear to differ depending on which cultural perspective dominates.

Humour is another way of doing RP, which provides particularly illuminating insights into distinctively Māori ways of constructing leadership. Māori leaders face a conflict between, on the one hand, the need to index leadership by adopting an authoritative and decisive stance, and, on the other, the Māori cultural expectation that the individual is appropriately subordinated to the group, reinforced by the cultural unacceptability of self-promotion and the associated expectation that a modest stance is appropriate for leaders. In this context, humour provides a useful indirect strategy for negotiating these areas of potential conflict, especially areas where mainstream expectations regarding appropriate leadership behaviour conflict with traditional Māori cultural values. The examples discussed in this chapter illustrate a range of ways in which leaders, together with their team members, use humour to negotiate appropriate ways of doing leadership, ways that take account of the cultural requirements of an ethnicised workplace.

Relational talk is thus another area that illustrates the extent to which ethnicity acts as a constant implicit backdrop for workplace communication, providing a set of guiding norms that influence how people interact and the ways in which they construct their leadership identity. This chapter has illustrated just some of the discursive resources available for managing the competing demands of the transactional and interpersonal aspects of doing leadership, while indicating the extent to which the relational significance of workplace discourse is often deeply embedded within ethnic cultural constraints.

CHAPTER 6
Co-Leadership

Nāu te rourou, nāku te rourou, ka ora ai te iwi
With your food basket and my food basket the people will be satisfied[1]

Our previous chapters have explored the importance of discourse in enacting transactional and relational aspects of leadership. In this chapter, we illustrate how leaders in the four workplaces share different facets of the leadership role and work together to successfully "co-lead" in each organisation.[2] The concept of co-leadership was first developed and discussed by Heenan and Bennis (1999) in their book *Co-leadership: The Power of Great Partnerships*. They define co-leadership as two leaders in vertically contiguous positions who share the responsibilities of leadership, and they describe co-leaders as "truly exceptional deputies—extremely talented men and women, often more capable than their more highly acclaimed superiors" (Heenan and Bennis, 1999: 6). Co-leadership has not been extensively researched, but several scholars suggest that when implemented intelligently, it improves leadership effectiveness (Heenan and Bennis, 1999; Huxham and Vangen, 2000; O'Toole, Galbraith, and Lawler, 2002; Sally, 2002; Alvarez and Svejenova, 2005), allowing top managers adequate attention for different aspects of leadership (Bass, 1990).

Leaders may cooperate in a range of different ways. To capture this diversity, Jackson and Parry (2008: 55–56) suggest the relationship between leaders is best conceptualised as a continuum, with Heenan and Bennis's notion of co-leadership at the more conservative end, see Figure 6.1. Further along the continuum is shared leadership, where the responsibility for leading a group can rotate among its members, depending on the demands of the situation and the particular skills and resources required at that moment (Raelin, 2003). Even

1. One version of a well-known Māori proverb. Cf. Mead and Grove (2003: 259).
2. This chapter draws on Vine et al. (2008).

further along the continuum is the concept of distributed leadership in which the team leads its work collectively, as a group, and independently of formal leaders, by creating norms of behaviour, contribution, and performance and by supporting one another and maintaining the morale of the group (Day, Gronn, and Salas, 2004; Nielsen, 2004).

The analysis in this chapter demonstrates how successful co-leaders cooperate within our four focus organisations, dynamically shifting roles and integrating their leadership performance to encompass different aspects of leadership through their discourse in different workplace contexts. In each organisation, we consider how transactional and relational aspects of leadership are enacted, and we examine who takes responsibility for these, particularly in interactional contexts. The visionary role is also examined. In other words, we consider who provides the big-picture view and who takes responsibility for inspiring and motivating employees in each company. Our analyses clearly indicated that no single person took sole responsibility for all aspects of leadership in any particular workplace. Furthermore, it was clear that the specific organisational contexts within which different leaders operated was a very important influence on the different kinds of co-leadership partnerships that were co-constructed through discourse in the different organisations.

CO-LEADERSHIP AT NZ CONSULTATIONS

The team recorded at NZ Consultations belonged to an important and core department within a large organisation. The management style of the team leader, together with the nature of the team's work, and the skills and expertise of the individual team members, resulted in a type of leadership that, using the model referred to earlier, can best be described in some respects as "shared" leadership (Raelin, 2003). The senior members of the team clearly respected one another's areas of expertise and experience, and they looked for leadership from different team members according to the issues being discussed.

Nevertheless, within this context of shared leadership, the division manager provided a constant reference point for staff. In the staff meetings, she was the one from whom team members sought clarification and direction, and specific questions were frequently addressed directly to her, as illustrated in Example 6.1.

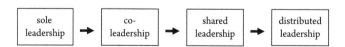

Figure 6.1
Leadership Continuum

EXAMPLE 6.1

Context: NZ Consultations: Team meetings

a.	Candice:	so Angelina does this matter call for
		some immediate response from the commission
		or do we have to do something?...
b.	Jared:	Angelina what was the trigger for the um
		reports being sent to the review panel
		in the first place ?...

Angelina also takes great care to make sure that everyone fully understands the issues and has the information they need to be able to do their jobs. In Example 6.2, Angelina asks if the team wants more information from her on an issue.

EXAMPLE 6.2

Context: NZ Consultations: Team meeting

1	Angelina:	um I just wondered if people were um
2		felt like they had enough information
3		about the [topic] issues
4		that um emerged over the [work project]
5		there's been a circulation of
6		some of the relevant memoranda
7		but if not I could briefly summarise that

This is a very collaborative way of indicating that she has special background knowledge in this area. Rather than simply launching into a monologue, Angelina thoughtfully checks whether her team members feel they have enough information already, or if they wish her to provide a summary. Hedging devices such as *I just wondered* (line 1), and the modal *could* (line 7) index her considerate stance.

Then, responding to the team's indication that they would value more information, Angelina proceeds to outline the background to the issue, demonstrating her knowledge of the broader context and the implications for the work the company is doing. She talks for approximately nine minutes on the issues, while the others listen attentively with no interruptions. This turn-taking pattern, which is typical of formal Pākehā meetings, as discussed in chapter 4, provides clear evidence of her authority in this team (Fairclough, 1989; Vine, 2004). After her monologue, another member of the team, Candice, says she has the latest version of a document relating to this issue if anyone is interested. Suzanne, Angelina's deputy leader in this team, asks a question about the document, and Angelina sits back and lets Candice answer. Jared then directly asks Angelina a question about the situation (Example 6.1b, see also Example 4.10), but it is Rowan who answers. He looks at Angelina as he begins to answer and she nods her head and allows him to lead the next section of discussion on the issue. It is another few minutes before Angelina makes a further contribution. As the discussion continues, Kate asks a question, provided in Example 6.3.

EXAMPLE 6.3

Context: NZ Consultations: Team meeting

1	Kate:	does that have anything to do with the allocation
2		of resources to the contract?
3		cos I know it was from the o- office perspective
4		it was just Aasha that was in house
5		does that does that make a a difference to how
6		the process occurred? or are we looking at
7		allocating more consultants for urgent inquiries
8		in the future to make sure we've got coverage
9		on some of the stuff? or do we know?
10	Suzanne:	I'm not sure we have those plans
11		but surely I think in this case
12		we probably it is an issue that we need to um identify
13		coming out of the contract
14		whether we actually did need to have a bigger team
15		working on it
16	Angelina:	I think that's an ingredient that you know
17		has to do with a lot of our work
18		that um this is a permanent issue to address

Again Angelina allows another senior staff member to answer Kate's query, in this case, her second in command, Suzanne, and then Angelina adds a more general comment (lines 16–18), indexing her leadership identity by pointing out the wider implications of the issue that Kate has identified. At different points throughout this discussion, different members of the team have taken a lead role. Angelina, Candice, Rowan, and Suzanne all contribute to the discussion. These people are all senior members of the team. The turn taking in this meeting clearly enacts the authority and roles of the various individuals, and their different contributions to team leadership (Jackson et al., 2006).

Team members frequently had work commitments that took them outside the organisation, and, thus, inevitably, their attendance at meetings was irregular. Of the six meetings we recorded, for example, Angelina attended only three, and in only one of these did she chair the meeting. The role of chair was shared, a different person taking on this role at each meeting. Suzanne, the second leader we recorded, attended four of these meetings, but she did not chair any of them. Of the 16 people on the team, only two attended all six of the team meetings that we recorded. In such a context, the fluidity of roles and the construction of shared leadership makes good sense.

Similarly, because of the nature of the work in which the team was engaged, each person needed to self-manage to a certain extent. They were not creating a product, as in Kiwi Productions and NZ Productions, and this had implications at a practical level. Team members needed to be able to conduct the day-to-day aspects of their work independently of other team members in a wide range of outside contexts.

The nature of the organisation's work also has implications for the analysis of leadership construction at a relational level. As demonstrated in detail in Vine et al. (2008), and illustrated in a number of excerpts in chapter 5, the second most senior leaders in Kiwi Productions (Quentin) and NZ Productions (Jaeson) take major responsibility for relational aspects of leadership, initiating and maintaining small talk and humour, for example, in ways that construct solidarity, and nurture team relationships. By contrast, the most senior leaders in these organisations (Yvonne and Seamus) tended not to engage in so much small talk, or to instigate as much humour, and this was also true for Angelina. The shared nature of the leadership at NZ Consultations was again evident, as other senior members of the team made a considerable contribution to this aspect of team building. An analysis of the humour that occurred during the first team meeting recorded in this workplace, for instance, indicates how the senior team members jointly "create team" (Fletcher, 1999), and others also join in. In Example 6.4, Jared, a senior team member, is reporting back on a meeting that he attended with Suzanne and Kate outside the organisation.

EXAMPLE 6.4

Context: NZ Consultations: Team meeting

1	Jared:	they're very keen to have [group] being in control
2		of what is going to happen whatever happens um
3		they very much disliked us
4		they dislike consultants with an intensity
5		and one wonders why //( )\ yeah [laughs]
6	Suzanne:	/including their own [laughs]\\
7		[Jared continues to outline the issue]
8	Jared:	John mentioned that these *kaumātua*
9		didn't have any protection from the facilitators
10		in fact it was the other way around
11		[laughter]

Suzanne and Jared both joke during the discussion of this issue, making fun first of the fact that people often express dislike of people in their profession, even though many organisations employ people from it (lines 4–6). Jared then generates laughter by noting that concern to protect Māori elders from the professionals proved to be misplaced and that it was the professionals who needed the protection (lines 8–10). The humour depends on shared implicit knowledge among the group that Māori *kaumātua* ("respected Māori elders") involved in such discussions are generally intelligent, skillful, and extremely experienced in negotiation.

In Example 6.5, several people contribute to the humour.

EXAMPLE 6.5

Context: NZ Consultations: Team meeting

1	Angelina:	...the team um the function which is
2		this Thursday at three o'clock in (the) um
3	Candice:	I didn't get an invitation to that in the end
4	Frances:	[quietly]: didn't you?: +
5	Candice:	no + I'll come though
6	Frances:	excellent
7		[laughter]//[laughter]\
8	Rowan:	/you speaking\\ well you- you're speaking actually so
9		[laughter]
10	Suzanne:	//who is speaking? [laughs]\
11	Rowan:	/no no really [laughs]\\
12		[laughter]
13	Brina:	no they usually make all the new people
14		(give a blurb about themselves)
15	Angelina:	yeah Frances what's the deal? it's um
16	Frances:	exactly that
17		[laughter]
18	Brina:	sorry [laughs] just spoilt the surprise
19		[laughter]

Angelina introduces the topic of an organisation-wide function that is coming up (line 1), and Candice comments that she has not received an invitation (line 3). She jokes that she will attend regardless (line 5), and the others add a number of humourous and teasing comments, indicating that she will be required to speak as a new team member (lines 8–18). Rowan, Frances, and Brina all contribute to the humour that is very collaborative in both content and style (Holmes, 2006; Vine, Kell, Marra, and Holmes, 2009).

To sum up, although Angelina, the division manager, constructs the big-picture view and is a source of advice and guidance to all team members, she rarely enacts facets of practical or relational leadership at NZ Consultations. Team members are expected to self-lead to a certain extent at a practical level due to their skills and expertise, and the nature of the work they are engaged in (Raelin, 2003), whereas relational aspects of leadership are shared by several of the senior members of the team, including Angelina's second-in-command, Suzanne. In the next section, we examine the rather different kind of co-leadership partnership identified in our second Pākehā workplace.

CO-LEADERSHIP AT NZ PRODUCTIONS

As indicated in chapter 2, we focused on two or three leaders when collecting data in each of the four organisations. At NZ Productions the target leaders were Jaeson, the general manager, and Paul, the sales manager, but two other leaders present in the management meetings also enacted particular facets of leadership in the company. These were the managing director of the company, Seamus, and the business development manager, Rob (see Jackson et al., 2006; Vine et al., 2008).

In each organisation, the highest-level leader typically took responsibility for providing vision and passion, for inspiring and motivating the staff, but, interestingly, at NZ Productions two leaders shared this role. Both Seamus and Rob were energetically involved in enacting this aspect of leadership. At the time of recording, the company was planning to expand, and, hence, they were about to go through some major changes. As the business development manager, Rob was employed to help plan and push the changes through. Given his expertise in the area, his job responsibilities involved helping plan and strategise the new direction for the company. This involved him in many meetings in which his role was to outline the anticipated changes for the benefit of different groups. In one senior management meeting, for example, he spent 30 minutes talking about the changes, motivating the management team, and highlighting the positive impact that the proposed changes would have. During this time, his discourse indexed his leadership role through a range of relevant stances, including an authoritative, an expert, and a visionary stance.

Rob's section of this meeting was then followed by 30 minutes where Seamus, the managing director, took the lead in discussing the changes. Highly energetic and motivated to succeed, Seamus had high expectations of his staff in relation to the proposed changes, as illustrated in Example 6.6, an excerpt from his contribution.

EXAMPLE 6.6

Context: NZ Productions: Management meeting

1	Seamus:	you guys are managing all areas
2		which are gonna be affected...
3		you've got to own your own areas
4		and the change within them...
5		promoting and embracing the change within our teams...
6		the ones that want to do well
7		the ones that want to embrace the change
8		they'll be jumping out of their skins to be part of it...
9		nothing's gonna hold us back here
10		and if er if it does we're gonna remove it
11		we can't get somewhere great
12		without having everyone on board
13		everyone doing their best
14		and without removing obstacles

Seamus uses strong, persuasive, and emotive language. He addresses the team very directly *you've got to own your own areas and the change within them* (lines 3–4). He talks about *promoting* (line 5), and *embracing* change (lines 5, 7), with the aim of getting somewhere *great* (line 11). Any obstacles will be removed (lines 10, 14). His metaphors are striking, including *they'll be jumping out of their skins to be part of it* (line 8). His expectations for his management team, and for the whole organisation, are expressed in very direct language and are very explicitly spelled out.

On the practical side of task accomplishment, Jaeson is the senior manager who most regularly steps into the implementation role at NZ Productions. As general manager, Jaeson is responsible for making sure things happen. His questions during meetings anticipate problems and identify potential issues to be resolved. In Example 6.7, the senior management team have been discussing a technical problem. Jaeson makes his philosophy and practical orientation quite explicit.

EXAMPLE 6.7

Context: NZ Productions: Management meeting

1	Jaeson:	but what you're saying Ivo um
2		just confirms what Rob's team came up with you know
3		and that is shunt these problems
4		get them sorted as soon as possible
5		get them out of the system

6		don't go all the way down the system
7		and then discover that you gotta change it you know…
8		um so and (I mean) we've talked about it for ages
9		we know that we've gotta do this

In this example, Jaeson clearly signals his view that it is very important to anticipate ways in which things might not run as smoothly as planned. Jaeson interprets Ivo's previous comments (*what you're saying Ivo*), and links them constructively to the analysis provided by Rob's team (line 2), skillfully providing an indirect compliment to Ivo in the process, as well as reinforcing the analysis undertaken by Rob's team. Jaeson's clear, direct summary is expressed in bald imperative clauses (*shunt these problems, get them sorted as soon as possible, get them out of the system*), simple grammatical structures that serve to emphasise his meaning. His personal position is equally clearly stated in simple direct language: *we know that we've gotta do this* (line 9). This decisive, authoritative stance indexes a very clear-cut, practically oriented style of leadership.

Illustrating the point that effective leaders typically adopt a range of different styles at different times and in different contexts (Baxter, 2010; Holmes, 2006; Schnurr, 2008; Vine, 2009), Seamus also gets engaged in the nitty-gritty of implementation at times, and becomes absorbed by the practical issues relevant to getting things done, as illustrated in Example 6.8 (see Holmes and Chiles, 2010). During a management meeting Jaeson, the chair, introduces the topic of selling off old photocopiers and purchasing new ones. Seamus first expresses surprise (*is that all*) at the price Jaeson is expecting for selling an old photocopier, and then begins asking specific questions (highlighted in bold for ease of identification) about the purchase of a new one.

EXAMPLE 6.8

Context: NZ Productions: Management meeting

1	Seamus:	Tommy that's **did you buy that photocopier?**
2	Tom:	no
3	M1:	[voc]
4	Tom:	oh the
5	Seamus:	we were talking about buying a photocopier
6	Tom:	we are buying it ( ) oh we have bought one
7	Seamus:	**you have bought one?**
8	Tom:	yep
9	Seamus:	okay **it's about fourteen wasn't it?** …
10	Evan:	are we leasing it or are we buying it?
11	Tom:	I don't know you and Deb sorted that out
12	Seamus:	**has that deal been done?**

13	Tom:	pretty much //( )\
14	Seamus:	/okay so\\ **is it a programmable photocopier?**
15		**does it have?**
16	Tom:	yeah
17	Seamus:	okay **so it's got a movable back gauge**
18		**and all of that?**
19	Tom:	yeah
20	Seamus:	okay **how physically big is it?**
21	Tom:	oh it wouldn't be more than a meter square
22	Seamus:	**and how much did it cost?**
23	Tom:	probably about I thought I thought it was about twelve

In this example, Seamus's questions about the photocopier become increasingly demanding, proceeding from a general question, *did you buy that photocopier*, through to more challenging and detailed questions about its capabilities: *is it a programmable photocopier* (line 14), and its price, *how much did it cost* (line 22). The extent of Seamus's engagement in this exchange about a routine nuts-and-bolts issue illustrates that, although he is at times the big-picture, visionary leader, at others he can become totally engrossed by the details of making things work within the organisation.

In terms of addressing people-oriented goals and relational behaviour, Jaeson is clearly the frontrunner at NZ Productions. He is frequently the instigator of humour, a discourse strategy that takes account of the relational needs of the team by enhancing solidarity and smoothing out tensions (Holmes and Marra, 2006; Holmes, 2007a). In Example 6.9 he uses humour to diffuse a situation in which Veronica is getting frustrated at the attitude of other members of the team to health and safety issues. She is in charge of making sure all health and safety regulations are followed.

EXAMPLE 6.9

Context: NZ Productions: Management meeting

1	Sharon:	it's just a logo
2		I don't imagine anything in the health and safety
3		//we\ (could) actually change
4	Veronica:	/yeah\\
5	Sharon:	for the few offices //+ upstairs\
6	Veronica:	/oh you have to for the powers that\\ be though
7		to have all the paper work for the powers that be
8		we have to go in and do your monthly inspections
9		and all that stuff + no idea
10	Jaeson:	you think it's easy Sharon? [laughs]
11	Sharon:	no it's crazy

Jaeson's comment here, *you think it's easy Sharon?* (line 10), sums up how Veronica is feeling. As a senior manager, Jaeson's contributions carry weight. The effect of this comment, uttered in a sympathetic but humourous tone of voice and followed with a laugh, is to lighten the atmosphere. This allows Sharon to acknowledge the difficulty of the situation, and she then expresses sympathy with the unreasonable demands on Veronica, *it's crazy* (line 11). The health and safety regulations are outside their control but must be adhered to.

In summary, in NZ Productions, Seamus, the managing director, takes on the role of inspiring and motivating, and co-leads in this respect with Rob, the business development manager. In terms of the practical and relational aspects of leadership, Jaeson, the general manager and second-in-command, steps up for these roles. Although Seamus at times takes an interest in practical issues, he mostly leaves this aspect of leadership to Jaeson. Thus, through their discourse, the NZ Productions team provides a range of evidence of the advantages of flexibility in enacting diverse aspects of leadership through different co-leadership combinations.

CO-LEADERSHIP AT KIWI PRODUCTIONS

At Kiwi Productions, there are two main leaders who take responsibility for different aspects of leadership, Yvonne, the managing director, and her second-in-command, Quentin. Yvonne provides the bigger picture and vision for the company's future direction, and through her talk she inspires and motivates her staff. In Example 6.10, we see evidence of this in Yvonne's discourse when she addresses a meeting attended by all staff.

EXAMPLE 6.10

Context: Kiwi Productions: Meeting of all staff

1	Yvonne:	but the best news of all actually this month
2		is the financials …
3		the most exciting part …
4		our sales to date are just above budget
5		which is amazing

Yvonne's utterances are rich with positive exclamations when talking about the company's achievements and her team's performance, as demonstrated in her use of strong positively evaluative adjectives (*best, exciting, amazing*), and the intensifying adverb *actually*. (This provides an interesting contrast to her self-deprecatory style when describing her own performance as illustrated in chapter 3).

There is abundant evidence that Yvonne's staff admire her rhetorical skills, and respect her visionary leadership. When, for example, Yvonne describes a conference presentation, which, as noted in chapter 3 (Example 3.5), she thought was not as good as it should have been, Sheree, a junior staff member who was at the conference says how much she enjoyed it.

EXAMPLE 6.11

Context: Kiwi Productions: Meeting of all staff

1	Sheree:	is this the one you had yesterday?
2	Yvonne:	yeah
3	Sheree:	(I) loved it
4	Yvonne:	//oh did you?\
5		/[laughter]\\
6	Sheree:	(I actually) came home raving

Sheree's comments are clearly spontaneous and complimentary.

Yvonne's leadership style is generous and appreciative. She inspires and motivates through the use of compliments, consistently expressing approval of the actions taken by her employees, as illustrated in Example 6.12. During a regular meeting of all staff, Yvonne is updating everyone on what has been happening since the last meeting.

EXAMPLE 6.12

Context: Kiwi Productions: Meeting of all staff

1	Yvonne:	we had a [subject] workshop in Māori
2		that was taken by Sheree and Pat
3		that was amazing…
4		all credit to them they were just fantastic I thought

Yvonne here makes a public statement about her positive evaluation of the work done by Sheree and others as she goes through her summary of the company's recent activities. In short, Yvonne habitually adopts an appreciative stance, indexing a very positive and inspirational leadership style.

When it comes to practical aspects of leadership, Yvonne takes a back seat, and Quentin picks up the reins. Quentin is involved in the day-to-day implementation of policy in order to achieve the company's goals. He takes primary responsibility for task accomplishment (Yukl, 2002). His focus on the practical side of things is illustrated in Example 6.13.

EXAMPLE 6.13

Context: Kiwi Productions: Team meeting

1	Quentin:	that was something that I was thinking of
2		for instance you know you wanted to
3		like say we wanted money to do
4		get a survey on children about [product] you know
5		you could send that ahead of time
6		and it could be something that they do
7		so that when we get there
8		it's actually has been done and completed
9		it just saves time you know
10		and and it doesn't less interruption or you know
11		if we wanted to talk to maybe a a group of children
12		then you could still do that um
13		but it's just a way of thinking ahead

In this example, Quentin suggests a practical way of obtaining feedback on some of the items that the company produces for children: conducting a survey with these children (line 4). Moreover, he proposes that they save time and money and disruption to the schools (lines 9–10) by sending the survey item to the schools *ahead of time* so that the teachers can have it completed by the time they get there (lines 5–8). This is just one representative instance of Quentin's practical orientation to the tasks they must undertake, and his focus on ways to help them achieve their goals effectively and efficiently. His attention is consistently on how to get things done efficiently yet within the spirit of the company's ethos and orientation to Māori values.

Attention to relational aspects of leadership at Kiwi Productions is also very evident in Quentin's discourse. He takes a leading role in "creating team", nurturing good relations among staff, mentoring and supporting them. To a much greater extent than Yvonne, he readily engages in small talk and jokes, classic relational behaviours (Laver, 1975; Morreall, 1991; Coupland, 2000), especially before and after his team meetings. Quentin's attention to relationships is also apparent when he attends the general staff meetings. In Example 6.14, Quentin is reporting back on what has been happening in his unit to a meeting of all the staff. In a humourous way, he relates a phone conversation he had with a person from outside the company.

EXAMPLE 6.14

Context: Kiwi Productions: Meeting of all staff

1	Quentin:	when I spoke to er their manager on the phone
2		we were we're talking away and then she said

3		um oh I might tell you a secret Quentin
4		and so I thought oh oh this is good +
5		um I won't tell anyone else
6		[laughter]
7		and she said um + we prefer to work with
8		[Kiwi Productions products]
9		we can't work with [other company's products]
10		so we we decided
11		well that's not actually their secret
12		[laughter]
13		that [Kiwi Productions products] are better than
14		better for them to work with
15		(so) they tried working with the other [products]
16		and they just can't work with them
17		so I think you know that's a credit
18		to the work that er Rangi and [the team] have done

Everyone laughs in response to Quentin's humourous recounting of this story, and the humour contributes to the group cohesion. Quentin also uses his humourous narrative as a lead-in to an explicit expression of approval of the team responsible for producing the products in question, and the complete story reflects positively on the whole company.

In this Māori workplace, Quentin is also the "cultural leader", the expert in matters relating to tikanga Māori (as discussed further in chapter 7). In their own words, when asked to describe their roles in interview, Yvonne and Quentin both agree that Yvonne's responsibility is to provide the vision and the direction, and Quentin's role involves ensuring that it is achieved in a culturally appropriate way. Quentin has strong Māori language skills, and Yvonne explained that Quentin's control of the Māori language means he can speak for the organisation in Māori contexts, and that he can give occasions a "sense of moment" (see Holmes, 2007b). Example 6.15 is an excerpt from an interview with Yvonne in which she makes quite explicit her awareness that they have complementary skills.

EXAMPLE 6.15

Context: Kiwi Productions: Interview with Yvonne, managing director

1	Yvonne:	why we work together well is he can um
2		you know pick up on where I'm weak you see
3		um so I guess that's probably why
4		when I think about it that we work so well together
5		we have different strengths and different weaknesses
6		and his is definitely in *te reo Māori*
7		cos mine's not nearly as strong as his
8		and he has and his sense of ceremony

9	I am much more direct and and he has a lovely way of um
10	and this happens we have this I have said this a lot
11	whenever we go somewhere to a Māori group
12	I'd always let Quentin speak
13	partly because he speaks in Māori
14	but partly because he has a
15	he can make a sense of making a a thing about it
16	rather than just say well thanks for inviting me
17	now today I want to talk about bang bang bang
18	whereas he is he can give it
19	a real sense of moment you know

Yvonne expresses her admiration for Quentin's cultural knowledge, linguistic proficiency, and relational skills, while also, in line with the Māori cultural value of whakaiti, adopting a modest and self-deprecating stance regarding areas where she claims she is weak (line 2). There is no doubt that Quentin's proficiency in the Māori language is greater than Yvonne's; but she also points out that her more direct approach—*well thanks for inviting me now today I want to talk about bang bang bang* (lines 16–17)—which is, of course, very appropriate and effective in majority group Pākehā business contexts, is experienced as inappropriately brief and unsubtle in Māori cultural contexts where skill in conveying meaning through metaphorical allusions, and indirect implication, is valued.

It is also worth noting, however, that, in addition to a relative language proficiency issue, there is also a gender issue here. This is a Māori organisation, operating according to Māori values and tikanga. In most Māori tribal areas, overt leadership on many occasions is exercised by men (Metge, 1995). On these two counts, then, it is appropriate for Quentin to take the lead in matters relating to Māori *kawa* ("formal discourse rules") or protocol. He is a skilled speaker of Māori and he is recognised as the cultural leader by all those who work at Kiwi Productions. As noted in chapter 4, he opens his team meetings with a karakia, and he ensures that Māori protocol is respected and followed as appropriate in all the organisation's activities. One interpretation is that, like a traditional Māori chief or *rangatira*, Quentin "weaves people together" (the literal meaning of rangatira) at Kiwi Productions, paying attention to their spiritual, relational, and material needs. As Example 6.15 illustrates, this also goes beyond the company's walls, enabling them to operate effectively within the wider context of the products and services they provide to the community.

In summary, at Kiwi Productions, two leaders work effectively together in a co-leadership partnership, a relationship that they openly acknowledge and appreciate. Yvonne, the managing director of the company, enacts the visionary facets of leadership, whereas Quentin, her second-in-command, takes on the practical aspects of leadership. The relational dimension of workplace interaction is one of Quentin's areas of particular strength, with an important component of this involving his universally acknowledged role as cultural leader at Kiwi Productions.

CO-LEADERSHIP AT KIWI CONSULTATIONS

At Kiwi Consultations, the Chief Executive Officer (CEO), Daniel, takes on the role of providing vision and direction. This is consistently evident in his contributions to meetings, as illustrated in Example 6.16, where he clearly identifies the direction in which he thinks the organisation should be moving and the importance of looking beyond the immediate goals to the bigger picture.

EXAMPLE 6.16

Context: Kiwi Consultations: Meeting of all staff

1	Daniel:	if you think back a couple of meetings
2		I said that er I was trying to turn turn our minds
3		to the process management issues in front of us
4		because we've er got a pretty good handle on allocation
5		and we've got to start turning our mind toward the things
6		we're gonna be doing in the long term

Daniel reminds people that he has signaled earlier that they would need to start paying attention to the issue of how to manage the new process, and he indicates that he wants to develop a longer term view: *we've got to start turning our mind toward the things we're gonna be doing in the long term* (lines 5–6). He presents the big picture view, the classic responsibility of a visionary leader.

The main practical aspects of leadership—implementing policy and following up on decision—fall to Daniel's second-in-command, Frank. Like Yvonne, Daniel prefers to be less involved in these day-to-day, practical aspects of leadership. He does not attend meetings of the individual teams within the organisation and he encourages the team leaders to step up and take a leadership role within their teams. It is evident both from what he says in interview and, more importantly, from the evidence in his workplace discourse, that he believes in open communication and in empowering his staff. This philosophy of encouraging others to develop leadership skills is evident in Example 6.17 where he comments on a new financial procedure.

EXAMPLE 6.17

Context: Kiwi Consultations: Meeting of all staff. Daniel is in the chair and the finance manager has just completed an outline of the budgeting process

1	Daniel:	look the thing with this budgeting is
2		that it's not designed to make it harder

3	it's designed to do a number of things
4	(it's) supposed to make things easier for everybody
5	but it's also a chance for the managers
6	to learn how to run their own budgets
7	rather than having them run for them
8	so that when they become general managers
9	in some big outfit all that stuff'll be a piece of cake

Daniel's stance here is consultative and encouraging as he points to the benefits of the new system for the company's managers. First, it will increase autonomy, a point designed to appeal to team members: *a chance for the managers to learn how to run their own budgets rather than having them run for them* (lines 5–7). Second, using this new system will provide experience, which can be usefully transferred to future positions: *when they become general managers in some big outfit all that stuff'll be a piece of cake* (lines 8–9). Daniel constructs himself as an empowering leader who wants his managers to learn and develop their skills.

In interview, Daniel explicitly comments that delegation was an issue with the previous CEO who had about eight managers reporting directly to him, rather than allowing a middle level of management who would deal with staff further down and who were encouraged to take on leadership roles. A restructuring of the organisation to endorse a middle-management level involving three key managers was one of the first changes that he instigated in coming into the organisation and taking over the CEO role. (See Example 7.10 in chapter 7). As a result, most of Daniel's managers now report to Frank. It is Frank's responsibility to supervise the implementation of the company's policy decisions, and he firmly sets out his expectations for his staff in terms of practical goals. In team meetings, for example, he makes it clear that they need to meet their targets, as Example 6.18 illustrates.

EXAMPLE 6.18

Context: Kiwi Consultations: Team meeting

1	Frank:	as I said to you guys last time about us
2		making certain that we are clear
3		about what targets
4		we want to get to by Christmas
5		so we can then go and have a well earned break
6		and not have to rush madly when we get back

Frank has a firm idea of goals and the need to achieve these in a timely fashion. He repeatedly brings this up to make sure that the team keeps on track. His stance is authoritative, and even "teacherly", as he enacts a decisive style of leadership.

Unlike the leaders who take the second-in-command position in the other three organisations, Frank does not take a large role when it comes to relational aspects of leadership. He does make some efforts in this area, including contributions to small talk and humour in the management meetings we recorded. Before one meeting starts, for instance, he talks about a new house he has recently moved into, and when one of his staff asks how formally they need to dress for a meeting outside the organisation, he humourously replies, *it's not walk shorts or jandals*. His role in this area, however, is overshadowed by Daniel, who makes a much larger contribution to developing and maintaining collegiality among company members. This is due in part to Frank's more introverted nature, but it can also be accounted for by Daniel's deliberate focus on providing an informal working environment (as discussed in chapter 7). Relational practices such as small talk and humour make a large contribution to creating this atmosphere, which Daniel actively and explicitly encourages (Marra et al., 2008). In Example 6.19 we see him joking at a meeting of all the staff.

EXAMPLE 6.19

Context: Kiwi Consultations: Meeting of all staff

1	Daniel:	so you're all welcome to come to that
2		if you'd like to bring um someone with you
3		you can do that but please let Maureen know
4		so we can make sure we've got enough
5		for the catering and things eh
6		get an extra sausage roll
7		if you can't get a date um come and see me
8		I'll see what I can do

Daniel has just been informing everyone about an upcoming Christmas function that all staff are welcome to attend. He indicates that they can also bring a guest (lines 2–3), and asks them to make sure they let Maureen know if there will be extras for the catering. He jokes that they will then add *an extra sausage roll* to the catering order (line 6). He goes on to joke that he can also help get dates for people who do not have anyone to bring. Daniel frequently makes amusing and witty comments such as these, as illustrated in chapter 5.

A third relevant factor when it comes to relational aspects in this Māori workplace is Frank's ethnicity. Frank, who is Pākehā, cannot fill the cultural leadership role that is such an important aspect of the relational role at Kiwi Productions, as discussed earlier and in chapter 8. Again, it is Daniel who takes on this role. As illustrated in chapter 4, he consistently opens staff meetings with a karakia, for example.

Daniel also encourages others to share this role, once again indicating his attention to developing the skills of his staff. Example 6.20 is an excerpt from the end of a meeting of all staff. (See discussion of ritualistic closings in chapter 4). Daniel began the meeting with a karakia, and he asks another member of his management team, Hari, to lead the closing karakia.

EXAMPLE 6.20

Context: Kiwi Consultations: Meeting of all staff

1	Daniel:	we started with a *karakia* we'll finish with one eh um
2		... Hari ++
3	Hari:	*kia ora mai tātou ...*
4		["hello/thank you everyone"]

Here Daniel actively encourages Hari, the youngest member of the management team, to take on this cultural role. In keeping with Māori values and the concept of whakaiti, Hari will not volunteer himself, and Daniel recognises this, and makes a point of explicitly asking him to lead the closing.

At Kiwi Consultations, then, the co-leadership responsibilities are again divided somewhat differently. Daniel, the CEO, takes on the main responsibility for both visionary and relational aspects of leadership, whereas Frank, his second-in-command, looks after the practical side of implementing company policy decisions. Daniel's philosophy of developing the leadership skills of his staff entails a strong mentoring role; he encourages others to step up and take responsibility for aspects of leadership within their own teams, and at times he calls on others to take a role for the whole organisation.

CONCLUSION

The concept of co-leadership provides a means of accounting for the ways in which a successful organisation benefits from the range of skills available in its senior management team (Avolio, Sivasubramaniam, Murry, Jung, and Garger, 2003). The four case studies provided in this chapter demonstrate how the particular leaders and organisations involved discursively shape and influence the nature of effective leadership partnerships. Just as there is no one way to lead, there is no one way to co-lead. Each co-leadership partnership reflects the relationship between individual leaders, their particular skills and experience, and the influence of the workplaces and CofPs within which they are operating.

The higher-level managers in each organisation consistently take the visionary role, whereas practical aspects tend to fall to the second most senior leader in each case. This seems to be a pattern that operates at the level of New Zealand society as a whole, that is, at the societal level in terms of our model. A global survey of 62 nations, involving 17,000 questionnaire responses, concluded not only that New Zealand leadership included "an important component based on egalitarian principles" (Trevor-Roberts et al., 2003: 536), but also that this egalitarianism manifested itself through team leadership rather than individual leadership; team leadership is identified as "a key dimension" of New Zealand leadership (2003: 535). Our detailed analyses of leaders' discourse provides unique evidence of how this dimension plays out in workplace interaction. Other NZ workplaces at which we have undertaken research tend to have similar co-leadership partnerships in relation to these aspects of leadership, providing further support for this analysis. NZ Productions offers a variation on this pattern that was particular to their CofP, with two leaders sharing the visionary and motivational role during the period we were recording. This situation was the result of the specific environment of change that the company was undergoing at that time, which entailed the managing director bringing in another manager at the top level to help supervise and drive the changes and to take on a co-leadership role.

The role that the managing director took in relation to practical aspects of leadership at NZ Productions also provided a variation on the general pattern. Seamus was often relatively "hands on" and involved in aspects of practical implementation in comparison to Angelina, Yvonne, and Daniel who were happy to delegate this responsibility. Some leaders are more able than others to take a backseat when it comes to this aspect of leadership. Although Seamus clearly trusted Jaeson to manage the implementation of policy decisions and the practical aspects of managing the company's work, his abiding interest in the day-to-day running of the organisation, deriving from his previous experience in Jaeson's role, still sometimes came to the fore. Angelina, Yvonne, and Daniel were more willing to leave these aspects of leadership to others. Angelina simply could not always be around because of the demands of the particular organisation for which she worked, whereas Yvonne and Daniel consciously adopted a policy of encouraging others to take responsibility for themselves and their work, and to self-lead. Both stated that they did not mind if people made mistakes, as long as they learned from them.

Relational aspects of leadership also tend to be the explicit responsibility of the second-in-command in most organisations, although this role was shared among several senior members of the team at NZ Consultations, while at Kiwi Consultations the most senior leader took on this role. The nature of the work that the team at NZ Consultations is involved in is relevant in accounting for the variation observed in this workplace; each team member must work independently to a certain extent, and they frequently work outside the organisation. In this context, the relationship between the group of senior staff and the group of more-junior staff becomes important, rather than one-on-one relationships with individuals. On the other hand, the switch between the expected responsibilities in terms of relational practice for the CEO and his second at Kiwi Consultations reflects a number of aspects particular to the individuals and to the CofP in which they operate. Frank, the second-in-command, is much more introverted than any of the other leaders we recorded. He is also a Pākehā working in a Māori workplace (see chapter 8 for further discussion of this issue). Therefore, Daniel, the CEO, took on relational aspects of leadership that we would otherwise expect Frank to enact. As illustrated in chapter 5, as well as in the next chapter, Daniel makes jokes throughout meetings and engages in small talk much more often than Frank.

At Kiwi Productions and Kiwi Consultations, the backdrop of the minority cultural norms that permeate the workplace culture add an interesting dimension to the relational responsibilities of the leaders. Given his ethnic background, it is not appropriate for Frank to take on a cultural leadership role at Kiwi Consultations in the way that Quentin does at Kiwi Productions. Hence, Daniel enacts these aspects of leadership, albeit in a rather different way from Quentin, as discussed in the next chapter. Daniel also adopts a mentoring role in relation to others, which is very consistent with Māori values, nurturing the younger Māori managers, in particular, to step up and take on some leadership responsibilities, especially in the area of cultural leadership.

To summarise, societal norms are at work in the way roles are taken on and shared, but organisational and CofP norms interact in each case in the way the co-leadership partnerships are discursively enacted. Furthermore, leaders dynamically shift roles at different times and in different contexts, and they skillfully integrate different facets of leadership into their performance, as appropriate. This has important implications for organisations, as Kerfoot (2003: 91) comments: "organizations can easily raise their collective IQ by tapping into many more collective brains who have the intelligence to build excellent outcomes for the organization". Successful co-leadership, then, entails all aspects of leadership being enacted effectively, but not necessarily by the same person all of the time. Different leaders complement each other's strengths and jointly accomplish leadership in ways that are appropriate to the CofP in which they are operating.

In the next chapter, we begin to draw together the threads of our exploration of leadership, discourse, and ethnicity, by identifying some of the distinctive features of discourse in ethnicised CofPs, while also recognising the importance of variation in the ways in which particular Māori leaders construct their leadership identity in different social and discourse contexts.

CHAPTER 7

Māori Leadership at Work

"The things I learnt from those Māori leaders—respect, knowing who you are, who they are and acknowledging them"[1]

T his quotation from the Māori political leader, Pita Sharples, indicates the importance for an aspiring leader to recognise the distinctive qualities of Māori leadership, the focus of this chapter. The chapter draws together some of the threads identified in our exploration of the relationship between leadership and ethnicity as instantiated in workplace discourse. We focus, particularly, on features of ethnicised communities of practice (CofPs), highlighting those that seem to distinguish the discourse of Māori from Pākehā leaders in workplace contexts, as well as the varied ways in which particular leaders construct their leadership identity in different social and discourse contexts.

The chapter begins by illustrating, in more detail, the concept of the ethnicised CofP on which we have drawn throughout the book—a concept in which minority-group ethnic values pervade all aspects of interaction. The second and longer section develops and illustrates the important point that, although there are a number of identifiable discursive patterns that characterise Māori ways of enacting leadership, there is also considerable variation and diversity in the ways Māori leaders construct their leadership role, within the broad dimensions analysed. This chapter, thus, explores some of the contrasts as well as the similarities in Māori ways of performing leadership at work.

ETHNICISED COMMUNITIES OF PRACTICE

As this book has consistently argued, ethnicity permeates interactional behaviour in New Zealand workplaces, enacted and negotiated through talk. For most Māori New

1. Pita Sharples in Diamond (2003: 200)

Zealanders, however urbanised, Māori ethnicity and its associated values are constantly relevant, pervasive, dynamic components of their interactional behaviour, including their discourse. Anthropologists have emphasised, for instance, the extent to which spirituality permeates all aspects of traditional Māori life and activity (Metge, 1995: 82–88, 2001; Salmond, 1974, 1975; Metge and Kinloch, 1978). Māori culture is deeply spiritual and, for many Māori, all aspects of life are imbued with spiritual significance (Henare, 2003). Ruwhiu and Wolfgramm (2006: 4) note that "the spiritual dimension is preeminent in the Māori social order... the natural, spiritual and social worlds are interrelated and interconnected". This orientation accounts for the deep respect among Māori for the individual's dignity, for the predominance of the whānau's claims on an individual's loyalty, and for the expectation that leaders will be decisive but modest (Metge, 1995), all characteristics discussed in this chapter. Although many Pākehā do not fully understand these values, there is no doubt that Pākehā New Zealanders are generally conscious that Māori priorities and approaches are rather different from their own in many areas of everyday life.

Pākehā ethnicity is generally unmarked, and, as illustrated in every chapter, Pākehā ways of doing things serve as the norm in most New Zealand workplaces. But there is also a pervasive awareness of Māori culture that often subtly influences social interaction; Māori culture is always there in the background, whether acknowledged or not. Even in extremely "masculinist" (Baxter, 2003) Pākehā-oriented workplaces, there is evidence of awareness of Māori ways of doing things. This sometimes takes the form of mockery and resistance (as illustrated in Example 5.14), but these are strong signals that cannot be ignored in New Zealand workplaces, even though Māori values may not be embraced by all. At the other end of the spectrum, a deep and whole-hearted commitment to Māori values is precisely what distinguishes the Māori workplaces that have been one focus of this study. Earlier chapters have made it clear that, it is not simply the ethnic identity of employees that is relevant, but rather the distinctive values, beliefs, orientations, and ways of doing things that characterise distinctively ethnicised CofPs.

In Kiwi Productions and Kiwi Consultations, ethnic issues constitute the heart of their transactional objectives. Their kaupapa is Māori-oriented, and the organisations are committed to promoting Māori values and Māori issues within Pākehā-dominated industries. This is evident in Example 7.1, taken from a discussion in a meeting of Quentin's team in Kiwi Productions. The team is discussing the production of educational materials and, in particular, products such as DVDs. This leads into a discussion of the pros and cons of translation in relation to Māori resources and the need to be constantly developing their own proficiency in the Māori language.

EXAMPLE 7.1

Context: Kiwi Productions: Team meeting. Quentin's team is discussing progress with transactional objectives

1	Paula:	think about it what we should be doing
2		for our own language development +
3	Quentin:	yeah yeah no yeah I think
4	Rangi:	( ) and to help ( )
5	Quentin:	yeah + well I- I I sort of saw it
6		cos it's in the other notes
7		and you'll see it about a language policy +
8		for the company + //you know\
9	F1:	/that's what we\\ want
10	Quentin:	where for each employee there is a
11		expectation but there is also a way
12	Paula:	an opportunity yeah
13	Quentin:	yeah that a person could develop
14		their proficiency eh
15	Carissa:	we want I sort of take the point about translation
16		but to me one of the things that um you know
17		makes what I do meaningful
18		is that that i- it's for *te reo Māori* ["the Māori language"]
19	Quentin:	//yeah yeah\
20	F2:	/mm mm\\ ...
21	Quentin:	first and foremost yeah
22	Carissa:	so that's a way of strengthening *te reo*
23		as well as ( ) commercial opportunities ...
24	Quentin:	like for me it's sort of working out
25		where your priority lies
26		and you know I'm here to do stuff for Māori

Here the members of Quentin's team discuss their motivations for the work they do. Paula suggests that, as part of their professional development, they should be attending to their language development (lines 1–2), by which she means their Māori language development. Quentin supports her point, noting that this has been suggested as a component of the organisation's language policy. Carissa then declares quite explicitly that it is precisely the fact that her work is contributing to strengthening *te reo,* that makes it meaningful (lines 16–18). A few minutes later Quentin reinforces and extends this point, *I'm here to do stuff for Māori* (line 26), directly stating the kaupapa of the organisation as a personal motivation for his work.

There is also evidence that the company's commitment to Māori issues is apparent beyond the walls of the organisation, in the wider community of which they are a part. Example 7.2 illustrates this, as Yvonne reports on feedback she has received on a presentation she gave.

EXAMPLE 7.2

Context: Kiwi Productions: Meeting of all staff. Yvonne, managing director, reads out a letter from a member of the public who has written to her after hearing her speak about Kiwi Productions at a public event

1	Yvonne:	I was very impressed with the *kaupapa*
2		that is driving you to succeed +
3		for more Māori to hear their story...
4		the Māori experience...
5		good luck Yvonne with what you're doing
6		I believe in what you're about...
7		and you know the unlimited potential we can achieve
8		as Māori as people

This "fan letter", as Yvonne laughingly describes it, is interesting evidence that Kiwi Productions is successfully achieving its goal of promoting Māori interests and values in the wider community, and that their efforts are appreciated by Māori in particular.

Similarly in Kiwi Consultations, there is a fundamental commitment to Māori values; again the core business in this organisation involves looking after Māori interests. In general, and typically for this organisation, Māori are perceived and referred to as *iwi*, that is, in terms of separate tribal groupings, rather than as an undifferentiated ethnic group of Māori, a point made in chapter 1. Example 7.3 is an excerpt from a discussion between Daniel, the Chief Executive Officer (CEO) of Kiwi Consultations, and Frank, the finance manager, about the need to keep the different tribal groups with and for whom they are working informed of their activities and progress.

EXAMPLE 7.3

Context: Kiwi Consultations: Daniel, CEO, is meeting with Frank, finance manager

1	Frank:	so that's we're gonna sort out +
2		er as part of um all of them
3		and our need to sort of work with *iwi* ["tribes"]
4		um you know in our budget each part...
5		management and capability
6		they wanted to have sort of

| 7 | regular communication |
| 8 | newsletter type things with *iwi* |

In this brief excerpt Frank makes explicit the organisation's need to work with Māori iwi as part of the core business, and he explains how his team has identified a regular newsletter as one way of keeping their Māori partners up-to-date.

Ethnicity is clearly a fundamental dimension in relation to the core transactional goals of these organisations. However, as the analyses throughout this book have illustrated, ethnic values permeate much further than this; they are evident in many aspects of interaction in these Māori workplaces. Communication in both workplaces is influenced by Māori beliefs about appropriate ways of treating others: for example, with respect for each individual and for their whānau responsibilities and concerns, which are typically well known to members of the CofP. Commitment to whānau is a taken-for-granted fundamental value in both Māori workplaces. So, for example, leave to fulfill family obligations is an unquestioned right, team members are always aware when someone is under stress and are ready to provide support, and the regular presence of babies at meetings and young children around the place at different times provokes no comment, apology or "excuse" in either workplace. A bereavement, a serious illness, or an accident involving someone's family, elicits an immediate and supportive response. At Kiwi Productions, for instance, we saw evidence that in a number of such situations, team members visited and provided practical support; and the whole company was aware of the progress of the affected person (see Example 7.7 below). At Kiwi Consultations, Daniel looks after his sick son at work for a period while his wife meets a commitment. In both organisations, celebrations are arranged for achievements and special occasions. Organisational life does not stop at the office door, and the boundaries between personal and company business are fluid. Again, although this may also characterise other companies, it is a deep-rooted and ethnically based component of the Māori workplace culture that was evident to some degree in almost every interaction in these workplaces.

There are other more subtle indications of the underlying attitudes and values in these ethnicised workplaces. Example 7.4 is one such piece of evidence. Complimentary remarks on the beauty of a woman with a *moko* ("chin tattoo") are unlikely in Pākehā workplaces.

EXAMPLE 7.4

Context: Kiwi Consultations: Daniel, CEO, is meeting with Hinerau, a senior (female) manager. He goes out to get a file and passes a baby in the foyer on his way back

| 1 | Daniel: | there you go +++ [to baby]: hello beautiful: + |
| 2 | Hinerau: | she awake? |

3	Daniel:	yep (15) I ran into Hemi yesterday +
4	Hinerau:	mm
5	Daniel:	Hemi's the big fella eh?
6		he's big he's about forty years old +
7	Hinerau:	yep
8	Daniel:	his wife's got a *moko*
9	Hinerau:	yeah yeah
10	Daniel:	she's beautiful
11	Hinerau:	she is
12	Daniel:	and her *moko* makes her look really you know
13		it's really striking you know
14		like it's + it's really fine
15		and oh I just thought man I mean
16		it was all I could you know like
17		wow you look beautiful I didn't say that //[laughs]\
18	Hinerau:	/yeah\\ she does she looks beautiful //with it\++
19	Daniel:	/yeah\\
20	Hinerau:	is he alright? I haven't heard from him for a while
21	Daniel:	I don't know what he's doing
22	Hinerau:	yeah haven't heard from him
23		since he finished working for the er + that the ( )
24	Daniel:	oh yeah
25	Hinerau:	the education thing [clears throat]

Both Hinerau and Daniel clearly admire the moko and consider that it adds to the woman's beauty. This excerpt occurs toward the end of their meeting and illustrates a number of additional features of Māori interaction, particularly tolerance for long silences (Stubbe and Holmes, 2000), as illustrated here by the 15-second pause (line 3), which is remarkable compared to similar interactions in Pākehā workplaces. Note, too, the presence of the baby in the workplace (lines 1–3), something that, as noted, is treated as entirely acceptable. Furthermore, the ease with which Daniel identifies Hinerau's referent as Hemi (line 20), despite the fact that his name has not been mentioned for some time, exemplifies another feature of Māori discourse, a tendency to leave meanings implicit and to rely on tacit, shared knowledge for comprehension (Holmes, 1998b; Stubbe, 1998b).

In this section, we have briefly discussed and exemplified some of the characteristics that led us to describe Kiwi Productions and Kiwi Consultations as ethnicised workplaces. In the next section, we turn to the important issue of diversity and difference within Māori leadership styles. We have illustrated in earlier chapters some of the features that distinguish the construction of leadership in Māori and Pākehā workplaces, focusing in the process on similarities in the approaches and discursive behaviours of leaders from each ethnic group, and especially on the discourse patterns characterising Māori leadership. In what follows, we turn the telescope around to focus on diversity and variation.

MĀORI LEADERSHIP: NO "ONE SIZE FITS ALL"

> *Ka ketekete te kākā, ka koekoe te tūī, ka kūkū te kererū.*
> *'The kākā chatters, the tūī sings, the kererū coos.'*
> Each bird has its own voice and way of expressing itself.[2]

This proverb, used in chapter 2 to highlight the advantages of methodological diversity, is equally appropriate for this section in which we examine diversity in leadership styles. As described in chapter 3, Māori and Pākehā ways of constructing leadership have much in common. Both cultures value strong, authoritative, and decisive leaders who provide clear direction and behave with integrity. Chapters 4 and 5 described both similarities and differences in aspects of leadership construction in Māori and Pākehā organisations, instantiating both shared and contrasting values and beliefs. The high value that Māori leaders place on modesty, for example, and on avoiding self-promotion contrasts with the expectation in Pākehā organisations that leaders will be prepared to assert their strengths and present their achievements in a positive light when appropriate. Another interesting contrast is the tendency for Māori leaders to avoid direct criticism of individuals, an indication of the high value that Māori place on respect for the dignity of others. Such criticism is normal and expected in many Pākehā workplaces, especially in more masculinist Pākehā organisations, where being able to "take criticism" is regarded as a strength. These observations have emerged from our analyses in the form of broad patterns identifiable in the Māori and Pākehā workplaces where we have recorded. In this section, we focus instead on some of the variation we have observed, illustrating, in particular, the different ways in which the Māori leaders in our sample construct their professional identity as leaders, while also appropriately indexing their ethnicity.

Our two Māori organisations are similar in many respects, as outlined in chapter 1. However, there are also differences that reflect their somewhat different orientations to the wider community, and these are also evident to some extent in the communicative norms that prevail in each CofP. In Kiwi Productions, for example, as described in chapter 2, tikanga Māori plays a significant and explicit role in the day-to-day operations of the organisation, but this is not so obviously the case in Kiwi Consultations. Māori greetings and lexical items are heard frequently in both workplaces. However, as noted in chapter 4, the Māori language is used for more extended communication and more often in Kiwi Productions. Professional relationships in Kiwi Productions appear to be expressed more formally than in Kiwi

---

2. Proverb provided by one of our Māori participants.

Consultations, whereas a more contestive and aggressively challenging style of interaction, including style of humour, prevails in Kiwi Consultations.

This diversity is especially apparent in contrasting features of the leadership styles of Yvonne and Quentin on the one hand, and Daniel on the other. Put simply, Quentin and Yvonne subscribe to a more traditional model of Māori leadership: they enact leadership in a dignified and culturally conservative way. Both referred in interview to the distinctive "cultural" leadership that Quentin provides for Kiwi Productions. Examples 7.5a and 7.5b are excerpts from an interview in which Yvonne gives a specific example of what she means by this.

EXAMPLE 7.5A

Context: Kiwi Productions: Interview with Yvonne, managing director. Yvonne comments on how Quentin stepped up as leader when she was sick

1	Yvonne:	when I got sick when I um injured my leg
2		um Quentin just stood up and said I'll run this...
3		Quentin stood right up and led the company
4		I think not just in a business sense
5		but in a more in a real leadership sense

As Yvonne expands on what she means by "a real leadership sense", it is clear that she is commenting on Quentin's deep commitment to Māori cultural values, which put people and whānau first. In particular, she points out how he looked after people's emotional needs with great sensitivity when the child of a team member died while Yvonne was away.

EXAMPLE 7.5B

Context: Kiwi Productions: Interview with Yvonne, managing director

1	Yvonne:	everybody was devastated
2		we had to everyone had to carry on with their work
3		and meet all their commitments to clients and things
4		um but you know there was a lot of personal
5		sort of soul searching inside the company
6		but I think Quentin he you know
7		we had formal like little karakia sessions and things
8		and and um yeah and he sort of got people through that
9		because I mean I wasn't here to do it

As indicated in chapter 1, Quentin is very aware of his responsibility to provide "cultural leadership" for the organisation. When asked about it directly, he commented as follows:

EXAMPLE 7.6

Context: Kiwi Productions: Interview with Quentin, senior manager

1	Quentin:	it is a it is a leadership role
2		of a different kind
3		in terms that it's er it's cultural leadership
4		and er but also knowing is that
5		I'm really doing that on her behalf
6		and on the company's behalf um
7		and and and being aware also that the things
8		that should be done and need to be done
9		given the sphere that we are working in
10		and and so the cultural practices
11		and and and things like that
12		I just see those things are important
13		in terms of relationship development
14		maintenance of relationships
15		and um really helping Kiwi Productions walk the talk...
16		and also you know providing er
17		some guide for the staff as well...
18		one of our s- er colleagues
19		lost her b- er young daughter
20		and um so we've worked through a lot of things...
21		I mean I see that as part and parcel of us being we are
22		while we are staff we're also a family
23		and these things happen in families you know

As these comments indicate, Quentin and Yvonne demonstrate deep respect for each other, as well as for other staff members and clients, and this is evident both in their face-to-face interactions, and when discussing staff or clients who are not present. The culture of respect and appreciation they nurture is enacted in their discourse, and it is equally evident in the ways others talk to them and from the appreciative comments of others on their leadership styles. Example 7.7 is an excerpt from an interview with Gretel, a Pākehā section manager. She provides a much more detailed description of Quentin's role in the events that Yvonne and Quentin refer to more indirectly and generally in the previous extracts.

EXAMPLE 7.7

Context: Kiwi Productions: Interview with Gretel, a Pākehā Section Manager

1	Gretel:	one example is one of our staff last year
2		in fact almost yeah in April last year lost a child
3		um and + the arrangements around you know all the stuff
4		that happened after Deb died
5		Quentin played a huge role in that
6		you know he was at the house every day um +
7		you know he went out and bought food
8		he and various other people went up there and cleaned...
9		it's an example of the way his role
10		transcends the day to day work stuff
11		but you know when at Deb's *tangi* ["funeral"]
12		he was there he was there
13		well we we were all most of us were there all day
14		but you know he actually I watched him
15		in terms of the role he played you know
16		when we had a cup of tea after the service
17		when when Ben and Madeline had taken
18		Deb to the crematorium
19		and you know he got round everybody
20		in Ben and Madeline's extended family and spoke to them
21		he was looking after people from our work
22		who were clearly well we were all very upset
23		but there were some people who were having
24		a really hard time with the whole thing you know
25		and after afterwards he would basically go up
26		and see Ben and Madeline you know
27		he blessed the house he did all that
28		well he organised the blessing of the house
29		so he kind of plays a role like this yeah
30		if there's something that happens
31		within the kind of the extended *whānau* if you like
32		Quentin plays a big part in actually helping everybody
33		through that and actually um making sure
34		that Kiwi Productions is contributing
35		to to to helping in that situation
36		in the right kind of way

Gretel here describes the far-reaching support that Quentin provides to staff members under stress, support that goes well beyond what might be expected of a company manager, extending to talking to all the family members of the bereaved couple, organising the blessing of the house (as required by Māori protocol after a death), and supporting other staff who were also upset by the death of their colleague's child. As noted previously, this is appropriate behaviour from a leader in a Māori organisation, in which traditional Māori values are paramount. It is interesting that it was a Pākehā staff member who provided this detailed example of Quentin's approach to leadership. It is possible that she made these observations because she considered his behaviour noteworthy, whereas for Māori staff members, such behaviour would be much less marked and simply taken-for-granted as the appropriate way for a good Māori leader to behave.

The recorded data also provided abundant evidence of the caring and supportive leadership identities enacted by both Yvonne and Quentin in their interactions within the organisation. Chapter 6 provided examples of both these leaders explicitly expressing appreciation of the work of their staff. Example 7.8 demonstrates how Quentin protects and defends members of his team from criticism in a one-to-one meeting with Yvonne.

EXAMPLE 7.8

Context: Kiwi Productions: Meeting between Yvonne, managing director, and Quentin, senior manager. They are discussing a problem raised by a client

1	Yvonne:	during the spot checks she finds a
2		[laughs]: problem every time: and so
3		that makes her nervous
4		and then she starts going back through all of them
5		um like that item without a credit
6		I mean that's just a simple little thing
7		but something like that just automatically
8		seems to cause worry //cos\
9	Quentin:	/yeah\\ and I mean it doesn't have a credit
10		in the guidelines and that's what we go by
11		//+ you see\ so I mean
12	Yvonne:	/[laughs] mm\\
13	Yvonne:	well well in that case //you see\
14	Quentin:	/yes I realise that\\
15	Yvonne:	it's just a matter of just saying that to Laura
16		um cos Laura's the one who's doing that sort of checking
17	Quentin:	when I saw it this morning and I I thought
18		oh you know we should have ( ) checked it through
19		but I went back to our guidelines
20		it doesn't have a credit in the guidelines

21		and I mean we're trying to be consistent + and (that's what)
		our guidelines say +
22		so and that's just it

Yvonne and Quentin are discussing the quality of the work of one of Quentin's team members. Yvonne describes a problem that suggests that the work is not meeting professional standards: the client has been spot-checking the quality of the company's work and she has identified errors (lines 1–2). She gives a specific example of a missing credit as one instance of concern (line 5). Quentin responds, defending his staff member by pointing out that she has precisely followed the guidelines they have established, and this is, therefore, not her error: *it doesn't have a credit in the guidelines and that's what we go by* (lines 9–10). Yvonne takes the point and notes that they should give this information to the client's checker, Laura (lines 15–16). Quentin then expands on his defense, making it clear that he had himself mistakenly thought this was an error, but, on checking, had identified it as an instance in which the staff member had exactly followed the guidelines (lines 17–22). He repeats *it doesn't have a credit in the guidelines* (line 20), and emphasises the fact that the staff member behaved correctly by adding *and I mean we're trying to be consistent* (line 21).

This is just one example of a pattern that is evident in a number of meetings: Quentin takes his responsibilities as a senior manager very seriously and looks after the interests of his staff, defending them from criticism (e.g., for apparently being slow or not keeping to deadlines). There are also many examples in our recorded data of Quentin providing extremely patient mentoring to staff involved in learning aspects of their job (Holmes, 2009), as well as detailed guidance to his team in their regular meetings. Yvonne, too, acts as a mentor and provides helpful direction to members of her staff in one-to-one sessions (Holmes and Marra, forthcoming), as well as steady support and consistently positive feedback to members of her senior management team (Holmes, 2005b). There is extensive evidence, then, that Kiwi Productions can be described as subscribing to a culture of care that is fostered by Yvonne, and which is particularly evident in the way Quentin enacts leadership.

At Kiwi Consultations, Daniel is the most obvious contrast to Yvonne and Quentin. Daniel is also very aware of his leadership role and responsibilities, but he constructs a rather different identity; he projects a somewhat brash and deliberately informal and unconventional image, adopting a relatively contestive style in his dealings with his senior management team. Daniel is quite aware of the fact that his approach is different from that of traditional Māori leaders, as indicated by his comments in interview.

EXAMPLE 7.9

Context: Kiwi Consultations: Interview with Daniel, CEO

| 1 | Daniel: | the other week we got (   ) the former guy |
| 2 | | he came in he he spoke to the board |

3	so he spent twenty minutes saying very little
4	and I was like oh jeez
5	imagine what it was like in the olden days
6	and er whereas I try and say as little possible...
7	I'm after results
8	I've seen some of the people here flourish
9	because of um my approach to things and and and
10	I think it's because not so much
11	that they're copying me or anything
12	but because I can see that there's potential there
13	I've been able to create an environment
14	where that has been able to flourish

It is clear, even from this brief excerpt, that Daniel portrays a contemporary new style of Māori leadership. He dispassionately notes what he assesses as the (lack of) content of the contribution to a board meeting of the former CEO (described rather dismissively as *the former guy* (line 1), and comments critically and informally: *oh jeez imagine what it was like in the olden days* (lines 4–5). In these frank comments, there is no sentimentality, nor evidence of the traditional respect for elders generally expressed by Māori people.

On the other hand, in describing his own style, Daniel does not explicitly talk himself up. Rather, using an approach consistent with Māori ways of assessing performance, he points to the benefits for others of his low-key approach, and emphasises his focus on developing potential by *creating an environment where that has been able to flourish* (lines 13–14). This comment in interview is supported by his interactions with his managers. Like Yvonne, he provides frequent positive feedback, and in the role of mentor to one of his Māori managers, he explicitly comments that it is important to do so: *you've got to um make sure that they understand that you value them...don't try fooling them I I don't think that's good eh.*

In enacting his role as CEO within the organisation, Daniel provides further evidence that he is aware of the tension between providing good leadership and maintaining appropriate mana as a leader, while also respecting the cultural value represented by whakaiti. Orienting to the need to provide new direction and authoritative leadership, he reports that he began, like Seamus in NZ Productions, by restructuring the senior management in Kiwi Consultations. His analysis of the changes needed is incisive. Example 7.10 is a short excerpt from a much longer detailed account of the steps he took.

EXAMPLE 7.10

Context: Kiwi Consultations: Interview with Daniel, CEO

1	Daniel:	I reshaped the the er the um
2		the reporting lines you know

3	the previous CEO had eight people
4	reporting to him directly
5	and that just comes about from when you start an outfit
6	I just expands and expands and it m-
7	they may as well report to you
8	um and you don't you don't notice
9	with an incremental increase like that
10	just how how much more work you've got
11	and when people come you know titles
12	and reporting lines are a big deal to them you know
13	[voc] I wouldn't want to be reporting to anyone else
14	except the CEO
15	so when I did that we had a few casualties
16	er in terms of you know people who felt that
17	they'd been + um treated less respectfully
18	than they'd thought and they don't work here anymore

It is clear that Daniel's leadership philosophy is rather different from Quentin and Yvonne's. Indeed, in some respects Daniel's account of his strategy echoes Seamus's hero story (see Example 3.2). As expressed in this interview, Daniel's attitudes contrast markedly with those of the leaders at Kiwi Productions. Although, inevitably, people also have to be asked to leave from time to time at Kiwi Productions, the leaders' attitude to their situations is overtly very much more person oriented and sympathetic than the decisive, hard-nosed approach that Daniel depicts here. He goes on to describe how he reshaped the senior management, creating *an elite group*, and then proceeded to dramatically change the ways of interacting that existed between the board and the management team. In all this, Daniel constructs himself as a modern leader, familiar with current western conceptions of management theory. A number of features of his discourse contribute to this construction, such as his choice of lexical items (e.g., *reshaped the reporting lines, incremental increase*), and his preference for simple syntactic constructions (e.g., *they don't work here anymore*), expressed fluently in a steady rhythmic delivery. These all encode a decisive and unsentimental stance, indexing an authoritative leadership identity. There is no hint of traditional Māori cultural values in Daniel's rather abstract description of how he approached the restructuring process.

However, as we indicated earlier, in his day-to-day interactions with the staff in his organisation, Daniel behaves in ways that are quite consistent with Māori values and beliefs. One way in which this is evident is his way of taking account of the Māori cultural value of whakaiti (which was introduced in chapter 3). His main interactional strategy for managing the tension between the need to appear authoritative and leader-like on the one hand, and the Māori cultural requirement to behave in an unpretentious way on the other, is to adopt a distinctly informal leadership style. Daniel manages even the most formal meetings with a light hand, and he uses many different linguistic devices to emphasise the lack of formality. In particular, as illustrated in Example 7.11, he makes extensive use of the New Zealand pragmatic tag, *eh,* a feature associated with both informality and Māori ethnicity, as mentioned in chapter 5.

EXAMPLE 7.11

Context: Kiwi Consultations: Management meeting

1	Daniel:	okay just have it for Wednesday //um\ eh
2	Frank:	/yeah\\
3	Frank:	…knowing how I feel about them
4		making time to go and have the games and various
5		other things but not doing the stuff that we'd
6		promised to do by Thursday
7	Daniel:	oh well shout at them a bit eh +
8		cos it's all fun it's great to have fun
9		and get dressed up
10		but it's gotta fit in with everything else eh

Daniel's frequent use of *eh* (lines 1, 7, 10) clearly contributes to the informal, egalitarian style that he cultivates, even in formal meetings of senior staff. This informality is also evident in his joking advice, *oh well shout at them a bit eh* (line 7), in response to Frank's complaint that his staff are spending time on frivolous pursuits rather than attending to their core work responsibilities. Daniel's reply further exemplifies his preference for a very casual style of spoken interaction. The use of the pragmatic particle *eh,* then, with its associations of informality and Māori ethnicity, is an effective strategy that Daniel uses, not only to index his ethnic identity, but also to construct solidarity, a strongly articulated feature of his leadership philosophy.

Another feature that contributes to Daniel's informal style is his extensive use of swear words. We did not record Quentin or Yvonne using a single swear word—even in informal one-to-one interactions, and although swear words occur in meetings in the relatively masculinist context of interactions in the Pākehā, NZ Productions, they do not occur in our recordings from NZ Consultations, and they are generally rare in our recordings from the wider corpus of professional, white-collar workplaces. Daniel's usage is thus relatively marked in our data, suggesting this may be a conscious strategy for indexing an unconventional, contemporary leadership style that contrasts with that of former leaders in his Māori organisation. Daniel's utterances are peppered with strong swear words, as illustrated in Example 7.12 from a one-to-one meeting with his finance manager, and Example 7.13 from a large formal meeting of the senior management team.

EXAMPLE 7.12

Context: Kiwi Consultations: Daniel, CEO, is meeting Frank, finance manager

1	Daniel:	he was + making Mary shit herself eh
2		and I just went down there and said
3		well what is it and then nothing to say eh
4		you know [politician's name] just a-
5		he pissed me off when we were at that conference eh

EXAMPLE 7.13

Context: Kiwi Consultations: Management meeting

1	Frank:	Company V got a new chairman they just got sick of him
2	Daniel:	oh yeah + fuck that's the sort of article
3		we got to send out to keep on [company name] eh
4		so that they don't think that fiddling
5		around with the board
6		won't do that you know

These examples illustrate some of the ways in which Daniel projects an aggressively informal style even in formal contexts, a style consistent with the contestive, teasing approach to humour associated with this CofP, described in chapter 5. He provides an alternative model of Māori leadership in a rapidly changing commercial context.

This section has illustrated a range of ways in which the leadership styles adopted in our two focus Māori workplaces contrast, identifying aspects of leadership construction that differentiate the Māori leaders in our data. Although these Māori leaders share a fundamental commitment to working for the benefit of Māori, the way they approach the accomplishment of their objectives differs, at least as they portray their perspectives on this challenge. In their day-to-day interactions, the evidence of an orientation to Māori cultural values takes different forms in the different organisations. Through their discourse in a range of contexts, Yvonne and especially Quentin construct themselves as dignified, gentle, supportive, and caring leaders, using more traditional ways of indexing these stances, including consciously, culturally appropriate ways. Daniel, by contrast, adopts a much more relaxed and informal leadership style, which is frequently permeated with humour and profanities. Like Yvonne and Quentin, his thoughtful reflections in interview indicate that he takes his leadership role very seriously, including his role as mentor to younger Māori in particular, but the analysis of his workplace discourse indicates a very different style of enacting this identity.

Although he opens and closes formal meetings using Māori protocol, there is little further evidence of respect for ceremony or formal procedures. Humour, a relaxed attitude, and derision of what he regards as old-fashioned rituals characterise his style; even his mentoring is suffused with teasing, banter, and challenging witty repartee. In sum, although Daniel's style includes a number of familar indices of leadership identity, it also indexes a much more contemporary Māori identity than that of Quentin, in particular.

CONCLUSION

Using the concept of the ethnicised CofP, this chapter has illustrated some of the ways in which Māori values pervade all aspects of interaction in the Māori organisations with whom we worked. In this concluding section, we briefly discuss our contention that no New Zealand workplace can be impervious to those values, and that, at some level, as our theoretical model suggests, all New Zealanders are conscious of Māori discourse norms and values. Even in the most distinctively Pākehā organisations, there is evidence of awareness that Māori ways of doing things are often different from Pākehā, that Māori place greater emphasis on consideration and obligations to the extended family, for instance, than Pākehā generally do, and that kinship links, and thus genealogy, are typically more important to Māori than to Pākehā New Zealanders.

Although this implicit awareness often takes the form of unquestioned, taken-for-granted background assumptions about appropriate ways of doing things in New Zealand, on occasion it may be made quite explicit. At Kiwi Consultations, for example, on one occasion, Frank, the Pākehā finance manager, had been delegated to represent the company in some important negotiations with external Māori groups. Discussing how he will handle the negotiation, Daniel teases him: *cos you have to check your whakapapa* ["Māori ancestry"] ... *if you wanna go*. Frank ruefully admits that, unlike many Pākehā, he has no trace of Māori ancestry in his family tree. The exchange clearly indicates that Frank is very aware of how even a small trace of Māori lineage would smooth the path of the negotiations.

Similarly, the Pākehā managers in NZ Productions convey their awareness of the importance of Māori kinship links and genealogy in New Zealand society in an extended humourous exchange while waiting for everyone to arrive at the beginning of a meeting. Seamus claims Māori ancestry traced back to tribal links in a particular area of New Zealand, and the others challenge him and ask for details, which he supplies, along with a great deal of banter, including the statement *I got a land claim going*, a patently joking statement that generates a lot of laughter. Example 7.14 is a brief excerpt from the subsequent talk, which conveys the joking tone of the exchange.

EXAMPLE 7.14

Context: NZ Productions: Management meeting

1	Evan:	I want to be Māori too
2	Veronica:	[laughs]
3	Evan:	better go and do some genealogy pretty quickly
4		see if I can turn up something
5	Seamus:	no you won't //+ can tell by\ your legs…
6		/[laughter]\\
7	Evan:	that's right the skinniest whitest Māori legs
8		you've ever seen
9		actually mum's done all our genealogy
10		and sadly they're Scots and English ( )
11		long skinny Scots people

Though this exchange is full of sarcasm, laughter, and contestive humour, it nevertheless testifies that Pākehā New Zealanders are very conscious of the importance of Māori kinship ties and descent lines in New Zealand society.

It is interesting to reflect, then, on the extent to which Māori norms may influence Pākehā interactional norms in New Zealand workplaces. Overt self-promotion is expected and normal in business settings in many cultures, and there are some contexts in New Zealand, such as in job or career interviews, in which this is evident. Our interviews with the Pākehā leaders on their leadership styles confirmed this, for example. However, in more public contexts, at least, leaders are expected to present their accomplishments in more self-deprecating ways. The "tall poppy" syndrome has its roots in envy and intolerance of others putting their heads up above the parapet. This is very different from the superficially similar concept of whakaiti, which has its roots in the Māori expectation that the individual should subjugate their needs to those of the group, and which values modesty as a positive virtue. Nevertheless, both concepts require individuals to behave in similar ways. And it seems likely that awareness of the positive value of the Māori concept reinforces the broader New Zealand respect for those who lead without self-aggrandisement. Sir Edmund Hillary is perhaps the most obvious exemplar here.

To take another example, there are many different ways of handling criticism and conflict in interaction. Concern for the face needs of others results in less direct strategies for handling these discourse moves in many organisations, but there are some where confrontation and challenge are considered desirable ways of dealing with differences of opinion, disagreements, and underperformance (Holmes and Marra, 2004a). Chapter 3 provided some evidence that cultural values are relevant here, too, indicating that strategies for expressing criticism and complaint, in the Māori organisations with whom we worked, tended to be more often indirect, implicit, and group oriented. By contrast, in NZ Productions, although indirect censure did occur, criticisms were often on record, explicit, and focused on an individual.

Māori values that respect the individual's dignity mean that Māori leaders tend to avoid direct confrontation that could shame the individual; rather they seek alternative ways of dealing with problems, which are respectful and safer, and typically less direct. Frequently they focus on weaknesses in processes rather than targeting an individual's limitations. Many Pākehā are aware that Māori ways of managing conflict and complaint favour indirect strategies that avoid causing embarrassment and shame to the individual. Our analysis suggests that Māori norms are steadily influencing Pākehā norms in this area and that patterns seem to be changing. Our model emphasises that norms are not set in concrete; constraints change as people contest them and adopt new ways of enacting their identities and indexing different social roles.

This chapter has also considered the variation evident in current styles of Māori leadership in ethnicised CofPs. Different Māori leaders construct their leadership identity along different dimensions, indexing different stances. Whereas Quentin tends to draw on discourse features associated with more traditional, Māori cultural values, Daniel provides an alternative approach, contesting some of the traditional discourse norms (e.g., appropriate ways of contributing to meetings and providing feedback). These differences were also reflected in the different interactional norms of their respective CofPs, as described in chapter 4. Whereas Quentin's team make extensive use of the Māori language for discussion of everyday work issues, the discourse of Daniel's senior management team is characterised by the use of informal discourse features, such as the pragmatic particle *eh,* and the relaxed use of swear words. Daniel's more casual ways of interacting may herald the development of a new style of Māori leadership, a style that values informality and downplays hierarchy built along traditional cultural dimensions.

There is, then, some evidence of change within the range of what is considered an acceptable way of enacting Māori leadership in contemporary New Zealand society. Daniel's leadership style provides interesting evidence of convergence between Māori and Pākehā ways of doing things, a pattern that is also apparent in other contexts. After centuries of interaction when Pākehā norms have tended to dominate in the wider society, it seems that gradually Māori values and Māori behaviours may be beginning to influence the ways that Pākehā New Zealanders behave and interact with each other, a point also noted in the next chapter.

Nevertheless, it is equally clear that there are many ways in which working in a Māori organisation is a very different experience from working in one dominated by Pākehā majority group norms. Through their talk and their behaviour toward their colleagues both within and outside the workplace, members of Kiwi Productions and Kiwi Consultations construct the workplace as Māori space (cf. Valentine, 2002; Bell et al., 1994). This point is also explored further in the next and final chapter, which focuses on areas of potential intercultural miscommunication, examining some of the interactional and sociopragmatic challenges that face minority group leaders operating in a society dominated by majority group norms and values, as well as the challenges facing Pākehā working with Māori in Māori organisations in New Zealand.

CHAPTER 8
Learning from Intercultural Research

"I have a sense of enrichment from this layered, many-faceted identity that is still in the process of evolution". (Michael King)[1]

Michael King was a friend and historian who died in 2004. He was one of a small number of Pākehā academics who are deeply respected by Māori elders and scholars for their efforts to understand Māori culture, Māori values, and the Māori language. As a result of many years of commitment, interaction with Māori elders, and a great deal of attentive listening in Māori contexts, Michael was unusually skilled in intercultural communication. This final chapter explores some of the implications of our analysis of leadership, ethnicity, and discourse in workplace interaction for the areas of intercultural and cross-cultural pragmatics.[2]

Our research has illustrated that effective leadership is a discursively complex achievement, jointly accomplished by a range of different people in different contexts, and sometimes co-constructed by several individuals working together to achieve specific goals. We have emphasised, in particular, that appropriate ways of enacting leadership are very context-dependent, and demonstrated that relevant contextual factors include, not only the kind of setting, participant-relationships, and goals of the interaction, but also the characteristics and norms of the particular community of practice (CofP), including culturally distinctive norms of interaction.

1. Michael King (1991: 79).
2. As noted in chapter 1, *intercultural interaction* refers to interactions involving participants from more than one culture, whereas research on *cross-cultural interaction* compares the interactional norms of different cultural groups. In researching these areas, we have drawn on insights from a range of earlier international research, including Roberts, Davies, and Jupp (1992), Clyne (1994), Ting-Toomey (1999), Ting-Toomey and Oetzel (2001), Bargiela-Chiappini (2004), Geluykens and Kraft (2008), Kotthoff and Spencer-Oatey (2007), Spencer-Oatey (2008).

At the macro-level, as indicated in chapter 3, our research raises questions concerning cultural bias in the results of the large-scale surveys used in many previous leadership studies. Our analyses of meetings in Māori workplaces in chapter 4 indicate the complexity of the interaction of leadership and ethnicity; they suggest that generalisations about individualistic versus collective orientations, for instance, as discussed in the survey-based leadership literature, do not always play out as predicted at the level of face-to-face interaction in specific workplaces. Specific contextual constraints, including degrees of formality and indispensable cultural protocols, proved much more relevant, especially in indicating areas of potential misunderstanding. At the micro-level, as illustrated in every chapter, our analyses suggest a number of areas of potential miscommunication and unintentional offense in intercultural interaction. However sensitive a researcher may be to potential misunderstandings due to cultural differences, there is always more to learn. Deeply rooted differences in the way behaviours are perceived and discourses interpreted can only be appreciated through extensive experience of and interaction with people who live and negotiate the "other" culture in their daily lives. The best we can do in many cases is to raise our awareness so that we are constantly open to learning more. In this chapter, we examine some of the sociopragmatic implications of these insights for those working in intercultural contexts, whether as researchers, as employers and employees, as colleagues, or in more informal relationships.

An example from our own workplace provides a useful illustration of the complexity of what must be learned. When new staff members arrive at Victoria University of Wellington, they are given the opportunity to join a group to be welcomed to the university marae, Te Herenga Waka, and thus become part of the Māori university community (Holmes, 2007c). The marae "provides a *tūrangawaewae* (a standing place where Māori custom prevails) for the students and staff of Victoria University to promote, disseminate, and maintain the use of the language and tikanga Māori".[3] The welcome follows a well-established ritual of encounter (see Salmond, 1975) with (typically) two or three formal speeches by the hosts and by the visitors in a preset order, and then a formal *hongi* ("pressing noses") between the host group and the visiting group, followed by a meal. Once staff members have been welcomed on to the University marae in this way, they are considered *tangata whenua*, or people who belong to the university marae community. Or are they?

One of our colleagues expressed bewilderment and annoyance because some months after his formal welcome, he volunteered to attend the marae when a new vice chancellor was being welcomed. To his surprise, he was told that his appropriate place was not in the welcoming party, as he had expected, but rather with the "visitors", the new vice chancellor's group. Since, in previous months, he had taken his place as tangata whenua to welcome visitors from another tribal area and another

3. Victoria University of Wellington university web site (www.victoria.ac.nz)

university, he could not understand why he had been suddenly relegated to the status of visitor. The issue of one's standing on any marae is always complex; the simplest explanation is that it is always context dependent—"it all depends"! On this occasion, the hosts judged that the visiting party needed some experienced people on their side to assist them with following Māori protocol. My colleague knew some Māori and could sing a Māori *waiata* ("song") and was, therefore, able to provide appropriate support for the vice chancellor's party. So, in fact, he was being honored with the responsibility for shepherding the visitors onto the marae, and, far from being offended at what he perceived as his "demotion", he should have recognised that he was being given a responsible role in the ritual of encounter. However, no one explicitly explained all this to him; he was expected to learn as Māori people typically learn about Māori protocol—by observation and experience, indirectly. One is expected to infer implicit social meaning rather than needing it spelled out.

Such lessons about culturally different behaviours often take Pākehā a long time to learn, because we do not thoroughly understand the dimensions of analysis. Even after many years, it is not always possible to predict what one's specific status will be on a particular occasion. It may be that the relevant dimensions involve seniority, or tribal area, or degree or kind of relationship to the visitors, or expertise in the area of the topic of the hui, or some subtle combination of different criteria. They will always be negotiated and negotiable in the specific context. There are many Māori stories of admired individuals who challenged the "rules" or flouted expectations, and who increased their mana as a result. However, these were people with a profound knowledge of the norms. As Pita Sharples comments, "I've broken kawa on the marae when I felt my kaupapa was strong enough to do so, and I could handle the hammering" (Diamond, 2003: 210). Learning how to analyse the relevant contextual dimensions involves learning about subtle aspects of Māori culture that are often not easily made explicit. It all depends, and what it depends on takes deep immersion in Māori culture to comprehend.

As this book has illustrated, the same fundamental principles apply in workplace interaction. People become familiar with the communicative norms of their workplace on the basis of experience. Many aspects of workplace interaction build on general sociopragmatic principles that apply across a wide area. It is only when things do not fit our expectations that we begin to wonder if we have understood the specific principles that apply in a particular workplace or CofP. Because Pākehā are the majority group in New Zealand, it is Pākehā communicative norms that predominate in most New Zealand workplaces (Metge, 1995). The way Pākehā do things is considered "normal" from the point of view of the majority of New Zealanders (Holmes et al., 2008). This hegemony sometimes results in misunderstandings between Pākehā and members of other ethnic groups. However, as the earlier quotation from Michael King suggests, by turning the tables and attempting to see things from a different cultural perspective, we also have the opportunity for enrichment. In the sections that follow, we explore some aspects of what we, as Pākehā researchers, learned about intercultural and cross-cultural communication from three different perspectives: first, a brief comment on what we learned about developing flexible methodologies; second, some examples of what we learned from our analyses of leadership construction in Māori and Pākehā New Zealand organisations; and, third, a discussion of what we learned from Pākehā employees working in Māori CofPs.

LEARNING TO DO RESEARCH WITH MĀORI PARTNERS

As chapter 2 demonstrated, we learned a great deal as researchers about the potential for misinterpretation and for causing offense by assuming "our" ways of behaving in the research context were normal. We learned to listen and observe for a much longer period in Māori workplaces than was appropriate in Pākehā workplaces. We learned to be present and available throughout the research process, rather than keeping out of sight, that is, to conduct our research with our Māori partners *kanohi ki te kanohi* ("face-to-face") (Wong, 2006: 54). At every stage, we talked through issues very thoroughly, rather than assuming people were not interested in the detail of data collection processes, and the range of possible interpretations of the recorded material. Overall, then, we adopted a more participatory, involved, and collaborative approach with our co-researchers and data collectors in the Māori workplaces than was appropriate in most Pākehā workplaces, where we were expected to be as unintrusive as possible.

Moreover, with one of these ethnicised workplaces, after providing extensive feedback in the form of workshops and reports, the research partnership has continued in a range of different ways that have proved of mutual benefit. The leaders who worked most closely with us have continued to willingly read and comment on drafts of our material before we present or publish it. And we have been called upon to support them in complementary areas of our expertise, such as advice on funding applications, acting as referees, providing methodology training workshops and technical advice for their apprentice researchers, and providing advice on effective data-collection strategies in a range of social contexts in which Pākehā norms predominate. In sum, we continue to maintain a warm and mutually beneficial social and scholarly relationship with our research partners in this workplace.

The most obvious lessons to be learned, then, involve respect for and sensitivity to the cultural and communicative norms of the groups with whom one is conducting research. Assumptions about "normal" research processes and practices deriving from methodologies developed in majority-group research contexts are likely to be at least misleading, and potentially counterproductive when working with people who bring a different set of expectations to the research collaboration.

LEADERSHIP IN CROSS-CULTURAL AND INTERCULTURAL PERSPECTIVE

We have examined a range of aspects of leadership construction in this book, drawing out similarities and differences in the ways that Māori and Pākehā leaders discursively index their leadership identities. In this section, we use the different levels of our theoretical model to discuss some of the cultural insights that emerged from the analysis, and we discuss their consequences for intercultural communication, focusing for illustration purposes first on a more transactional aspect, namely meeting protocols, and second on relational practice.

INTERCULTURAL COMMUNICATION AND WORKPLACE MEETINGS

Hegemony means that societal and institutional constraints are experienced differently by those for whom they are "normal" and unnoticed, and by those from minority cultures. Thus, leaders in organisations with an explicit commitment to furthering the objectives of their ethnic group, working in ways compatible with their ethnic values, often experience pressure from (their perceptions of) majority-group expectations. Comments offered in interview as well as in their workplace discourse indicated that the Māori leaders we worked with were very aware of being under scrutiny as leaders of Māori organisations operating in a Pākehā business world. In Kiwi Productions, for instance, the managing director, Yvonne, states quite unequivocally her awareness that their activities are constantly subject to an ethical microscope reserved for Māori organisations who are expected to be "whiter than white" (Marra, 2005). She noted that Māori companies have to deliver on time, meet deadlines, keep to budget, and be exemplary in all respects. They need to be vigilant about expenditure on accommodation and travel, she said, especially when they had accepted a government contract. In discussion with her managers, she regularly made this quite explicit, emphasising that it was crucial to avoid providing any basis for public criticism or complaint. Example 8.1 is an excerpt from a discussion that indicates that her managers have clearly taken this point.

EXAMPLE 8.1

Context: Kiwi Productions: Gretel, a senior manager, is discussing strategic and financial issues with Yvonne, the managing director

1	Gretel:	this is government it's the Ministry's money
2		and if people could actually view that rather dimly
3		because these two women who were doing (website) stuff
4		they were going to take them out for a meal
5		and Raewyn said oh we could take them

6		I've got a half price thing we could take them
7		to the seafood buffet at the Sheraton
8		and I said look I know it's probably cheaper
9		but I don't want you to take them there
10		you know imagine what it would look like
11		if someone from the Ministry saw you
12		wining and dining with some clients
13		on the Ministry's dollar at the Sheraton

Providing effective leadership in an ethnicised CofP clearly involves sensitivity to the way one's business activities may be perceived and interpreted in the wider community and society.

The converse of this issue is the failure by many Pākehā to recognise the worth or value of the knowledge and experience that leaders from different ethnic backgrounds bring to the core business that they are involved in. Daniel, the Chief Executive Officer (CEO) of Kiwi Consultations, makes this important complementary point, noting that Pākehā often do not appreciate what Māori accomplish, do not recognise, for instance, that negotiations with tribal groups on a marae visit constitute important "work". Pākehā, he claims, do not recognise the costs in terms of time and effort that are incurred by the negotiations required to accomplish Kiwi Consultations' business or transactional objectives. Discussions on different marae, for example, are immensely time consuming and frequently involve weekends and evenings, time that is discounted or overlooked ("disappeared" in Fletcher's (1999) terms) by many Pākehā. As Daniel comments to one of his senior managers, Hinerau, *they think that's not really business.*

EXAMPLE 8.2

Context: Kiwi Consultations: Daniel, CEO, and Hinerau, senior manager, are discussing the fact that he and Māori members of their board are working for the organisation without adequate financial recompense

1	Daniel:	well that list that he did [inhales]
2		there's a lot of stuff in that
3	Hinerau:	(mm) and it's not just arriving at five and go
4		yeah arriving at nine //and going back five\
5	Daniel:	/we had to come the night\\ before eh travel
6	Hinerau:	yeah yeah...
7	Daniel:	no they think someone's walking
8		across the road to do it eh
9		and they don't they would say
10		[with broad Pākehā accent]: well that's not

11	really business you know going to a *marae*: +
12	well hang on a minute what do you know
13	can you do oh you can't do it
14	you'd have to pay someone to do it wouldn't you yeah
15	so (that) means it's commercial [inhales]

Daniel here articulates Māori perceptions that what is required of Māori working for a Māori organisation is rendered invisible and not counted as valuable by Pākehā. Its commercial value is not recognised because Māori rather than Pākehā expertise is involved. It is seen as just part of being Māori and the specialised knowledge and skills required are not valued.

We noted in chapter 7 that Daniel's discourse provides some evidence of a potentially new style of Māori leadership, one that is less formal and traditional and that involves a more challenging attitude to the expectations of Pākehā. His wickedly satirical picture of hypocritical Pākehā attempting to be polite to new Māori neighbors (Example 5.14) suggests a growing confidence among young Māori leaders who are increasingly resistant to the expectation that Māori should conform to Pākehā discourse norms in commercial and business contexts. Nevertheless, even such contestive, challenging, and subversive comments indicate that participants in ethnicised CofPs are constantly orienting to Pākehā perceptions of their behaviour, whereas comments on ethnic difference and ethnic group boundaries are rare in Pākehā workplaces.

These brief examples illustrate some of the societal and institutional pressures that Māori leaders experience on a daily basis as they engage with Pākehā. When they venture into the wider New Zealand business environment, they must constantly monitor their discourse in response to their awareness of widespread stereotypes and prejudices about Māori behaviour or risk being misunderstood, misjudged, and criticised. Unlike Pākehā leaders, Māori leaders are effectively bicultural, drawing on a range of skills to construct their complex leadership identities. In public contexts, they draw on their knowledge of the discourse norms of the wider society, whereas, within their own Māori organisations, they make use of appropriate Māori ways of managing workplace interaction.

Moving to the level of interaction in particular workplaces, meeting management is one specific area in which differences in Māori and Pākehā leadership practices become apparent, as discussed in chapter 4. The opening sections of meetings in Māori workplaces, for example, often include features that are quite distinctive from a Pākehā perspective. Ignorance or lack of understanding of the underlying values reflected in the structure and form of such openings can lead to potential friction. New members of workplace teams and visitors invited to attend meetings of teams who follow Māori protocol can offend by behaving disrespectfully during these formal openings. They sometimes betray impatience at what appear to them to be empty rituals, as mentioned in chapter 4. Even those who are sympathetic to other cultures may fail to grasp the deep-seated significance for minority-group employees of the inclusion of such rituals in their workplace interactions.

One much publicised example of an incident that highlighted how cultural norms and values involving meeting procedures may clash concerned a Pākehā female probation officer, Josie Bullock. Ms. Bullock complained publicly about the use of Māori kawa or formal discourse rules at a *poroporoaki* ("farewell") for male offenders who had completed a violence-prevention program. In most tribal areas, formal speaking rights are assigned only to senior men during the formal ritual components of such a speech event. Consequently, it is the male speakers who are entitled to occupy the front bench (the *paepae*), while others, including all women, however senior, are expected to take a position behind the men. Ms. Bullock challenged this procedure and particularly her exclusion from the front bench. More generally, she contested the appropriateness of a government department adopting what she regarded as sexist Māori protocol for such occasions. In her view, the adoption of Māori protocol represented unacceptable and inappropriate overconvergence to another group's cultural norms.[4] This brief summary does not do justice to the complexities of the behaviours involved. Nonetheless, it indicates the potential for offense that may arise from different perceptions of what constitutes (culturally) appropriate meeting protocol on a particular occasion in a specific sociocultural context.

Conversely, employees from ethnic minorities may feel offended when some features of a welcome or greeting are ignored as a result of the emphasis on informality that pertains in Pākehā organisations. More than 30 years ago Metge and Kinloch (1978) commented on the fact that, for Polynesian people, the Pākehā tendency to omit a formal welcome with explicit greetings to those attending could be offensive. For many ethnic groups, omitting a formal greeting at the meeting opening is not an option, even for a relatively informal meeting between people who work together regularly and who know each other well. In Polynesian contexts, as well as in many Asian cultures, visitors are always formally welcomed, even if their role and expected contribution to the meeting is known to all. Our analyses confirm this as a relevant norm for all the Māori organisations that have participated in our research. This is, then, one obvious source of discomfort for people from ethnic minorities working in predominantly Pākehā workplaces. From their perspective, Pākehā openings are inappropriately abrupt and leave people feeling inadequately welcomed. They expect greater explicit attention to the relational aspects of interaction so that participants are formally welcomed and introduced and their concerns identified. Instead, Pākehā leaders typically cut greetings to a minimum, and "dispense with formalities" in order not to "waste time". The culturally specific assumptions apparent in the metaphors are revealing.

4. Josie Bullock was later dismissed for repeatedly breaching the Department of Corrections' code of conduct by speaking to the media without authorisation. Interestingly, however, the Department subsequently adopted a less formal ritual for such occasions, which included the same roles and seating arrangements for men and women. Available at: http://www.nzherald.co.nz/nz/news/article.cfm?c_id=1&objectid=10364273.

It is interesting to reflect on these different orientations to the dimensions for analysing cross-cultural interaction provided by the theoretical model outlined in chapter 1. Although Pākehā workplace meetings generally open and close in a low key and understated way, Māori meetings often open with a formal ritual that is explicit and structured and makes specific reference to the interests and concerns of those present. Using the dimensions of cross-cultural contrast identified in the model (modified from House, 2005), the Māori speech event involves more direct, explicit, other-oriented discourse, and ad hoc, creative formulations, whereas Pākehā meeting openings tend to be less direct, more implicit, content-oriented and formulaic. Moreover, during meetings, as discussed in chapter 4, Māori partici-pants tend to provide more explicit feedback to speakers, compared to the silence that is the norm during contributions to Pākehā formal meetings. Respect for others and for their discursive contributions is, thus, often explicitly expressed in Māori contexts, whereas it tends to be implicit and taken-for-granted in Pākehā contexts.

These features are worth attention, because they contrast with findings in other areas, such as social talk and humour in which, as discussed in the next section and illustrated in chapter 5, Māori discourse is often characterised by indirectness and implicitness, based on shared assumptions and understandings.

INTERCULTURAL COMMUNICATION AND RELATIONAL PRACTICE

Paying attention to workplace relationships makes good sense in all organisations. Using our model to frame consideration of these contrasts, we observed that, at the institutional level, English is undoubtedly the unmarked language of most New Zealand workplaces. In Māori organisations, however, although English is also the dominant language, a good deal more Māori is heard, ranging from informal greet-ings to the discussion of core business in some CofPs. As chapter 4 indicated, the use of Māori, even in routines, is a very appropriate and strongly encouraged means of constructing rapport and strengthening workplace relationships. The language also implicitly but powerfully references Māori values and attitudes, and thus serves as a resource for Pākehā who want to express empathy with Māori objectives.

More generally, as illustrated in chapter 5, social talk and humour are important ways in which people construct sound collegial links, establishing and maintaining rapport. However, the precise ways in which these strategies are instantiated varies in different contexts within different CofPs, and the analyses in this book have indi-cated some of the contrasting emphases which may characterise workplace interac-tions in Māori and Pākehā organisations.

Although participants in all the workplaces in our database engage in social talk at work, we identified some interesting and quite subtle differences in some Māori CofPs. In particular, the topics of pre- and post meeting talk were much more likely to refer to family and personal issues in the Māori organisations, reflecting the greater orientation of Māori to family as a priority in general. Perhaps most interesting in this area is that what is considered peripheral social talk, as opposed to material relevant to workplace discussion, often differs quite markedly between different workplaces, reflecting different priorities and cultural values. For Pākehā working in Māori workplaces, this raises interesting issues of perception. It would be easy to dismiss as inappropriate gossip a discussion that included, from a Māori perspective, very useful information about, for example, how to approach an upcoming meeting, or how best to make contact with an important client. Information about kinship connections and links is just the most obvious example of such potentially valuable information.

Humour is another relational resource that can be used to construct and maintain positive workplace relationships and, especially in Māori workplaces, to reinforce important cultural values. Self-deprecating humour is one very useful indirect strategy for Māori leaders to indicate humility and modesty, alongside the enactment of more decisive leadership behaviours. Although different Māori CofPs tended to be characterised by different preferred overall styles of humour (collaborative and supportive versus contestive and challenging), the commitment to Māori ethnic values was consistently evident. From a sociopragmatic perspective, humour is a complex and multifunctional interactional strategy, and sensitivity to appropriate ways of using it in different CofPs is crucial, especially in intercultural interactions. Many Māori in majority-group workplaces find the boasting and contestive skiting that characterise some, especially masculinist, workplaces (Collinson, 1988; Plester, 2003; Plester and Sayers, 2007) objectionable, or at least uncomfortable. On the other hand, Pākehā in Māori workplaces find that they must develop sensitivity to Māori values and ways of doing things, so that they do not unwittingly offend (see further discussion below). Example 4.11 provided a classic instance of this, in which a Pākehā staff member, Steve, betrayed ignorance of a Māori interactional norm and publicly criticised his CEO and the senior finance manager for talking during his presentation. Daniel, the Māori CEO, and Frank, a Pākehā manager with greater experience of Māori norms, used humour very effectively to handle this intercultural misunderstanding, thus maintaining a positive atmosphere in a situation that could have generated embarrassment and offense.

In this section, we have used two areas that emerged from our focus on leadership discourse in Māori and Pākehā workplaces, namely, meeting protocols and relational practice, to illustrate potential areas of intercultural miscommunication. We turn finally to a brief consideration of some insights about intercultural communication afforded by Pākehā members of a Māori CofP.

BEING PĀKEHĀ IN A MĀORI WORKPLACE

Sadly, many Pākehā never have the opportunity to engage with Māori culture in any but the most superficial manner, and their understanding of Māori concepts and values is consequently only partial. We were reminded of this when a Pākehā colleague recently opened a meeting by saying, "I suppose I should begin with a mihi". As chapter 4 demonstrated, a mihi or formal greeting is an appropriate way to open any Māori meeting, and its length and complexity typically reflects the context in which it occurs. When the speaker and audience do not know each other, it is appropriate for the mihi to include some background information about the speaker. This usually includes information about region of origin (e.g., one's local mountain and river), and kinship links, so listeners can identify how the speaker fits into their networks. Experienced Pākehā speakers generally find some appropriate alternative or additional dimensions to link themselves to their audience, for example, where they were educated and who their Māori teachers were. Omitting this information on potential links to his audience, my colleague proceeded to list all the reasons why he was the best person to be talking about the topic, explicitly making claims concerning his unique expertise in the area. From a Māori perspective, this came over as a prolonged boasting session (whakahīhī), though the Pākehā students in the audience were clearly impressed and reassured by this assertion of his qualifications as an expert on the topic he was to address. A Pākehā participant from one of our ethnicised CofPs was an audience member, and she later commented that this session helped her recognise how different her workplace was from mine, and how much she had absorbed Māori ways of doing things.

Learning how to work effectively and appropriately alongside leaders of different ethnicities in workplaces where minority ethnic norms of interaction are dominant is undoubtedly a challenge. In this final section, in order to throw additional light on the complexities of intercultural interaction, we draw on the reflections of Pākehā participants with whom we worked to focus more explicitly on the implications of our research for Pākehā working in Māori workplaces. These people have direct experience of what it feels like to be an outsider, or "other", and how it feels to be made constantly aware of areas of naïvety and ignorance (cf. Campbell and Roberts, 2007). They experience the unfamiliar discomfort of having one's taken-for-granted assumptions about normal ways of interacting challenged on a regular basis.

In Pākehā workplaces, ethnicity is simply not an issue for Pākehā participants; it is taken for granted and goes unnoticed. By contrast, as we have demonstrated throughout this book, ethnicity is always a significant dimension in Māori workplaces, and the boundary between Māori and Pākehā is a constant area of sensitivity. The behaviour of both Pākehā and Māori in Kiwi Consultations and Kiwi Productions indicates their awareness of the salience of this boundary, though the extent to which it is made explicit is situationally relative and varies from one team and from one individual to another.

Gretel, a Pākehā manager working at Kiwi Productions, indicates through her discourse both in interview and in interaction with other members of the CofP that she is very aware of the omni-relevance of ethnicity in the company's business, and the implications of this for what constitutes appropriate and effective behaviour on her part in a range of situations. In interview, for example, she articulated her perceptions of her role as follows.

EXAMPLE 8.3

Context: Kiwi Productions: Interview with Gretel, a Pākehā manager

1	Gretel:	I think the two biggest things are er
2		knowing what you don't know
3		or at least having an inkling of what you don't know
4		I mean you never know everything you don't know
5		and knowing knowing when to sit down and shut up
6		actually knowing when your input
7		when your direct input is not appropriate is very helpful

This reflection is illuminating and unusual. The predominantly monolingual make-up of New Zealand society (Starks, 1998) alongside widespread myopic ethno-centrism, means that it is generally those who come from cultural backgrounds other than the majority Pākehā group who are expected to make the adjustments and learn to interact appropriately according to Pākehā norms. Employers simply expect those from other countries and cultures to adapt to New Zealand norms, as if this "goes without saying". The concept of "tolerability" (Grin, 1995; May, 2000; de Bres, 2008) of the language and cultural norms of those from another culture is never considered. And the even more revolutionary notion that Pākehā might adapt to different sociocultural norms, as well as vice-versa, is rarely contemplated. Example 8.3 indicates, however, that being a Pākehā employee in a Māori work-place, and thus a minority-group member, can promote useful insights on intercul-tural communication.

Gretel also notes that, as a Pākehā, it is often appropriate for her to take a back-stage role when the company is negotiating outside contracts, even in areas of her expertise.

EXAMPLE 8.4

Context: Kiwi Productions: Interview with Gretel, a Pākehā manager

1	Gretel:	some people prefer to work with
2		a Māori consultant
3		they're happy for me to be in the background
4		but they really don't want me
5		having too much hands on stuff
6		so in in those cases the work I do
7		is more behind the scenes
8		working with the senior who's actually
9		dealing with the client…

10	I never really had a problem with that
11	because sometimes that Māori perspective
12	is pretty essential to the work
13	and that's something I I don't have
14	so it's about having a bit of an instinct
15	for when people are not comfortable necessarily
16	and backing off

Gretel is not at all inhibited in interaction within the CofP itself, and especially within her own team. She describes her management style as typically Pākehā and "very direct", and she constantly jokes and exchanges jocular insults with her own team members. However, in the wider context of the company as a whole, she is aware of the necessity of adopting a much more backstage role along with a much lower key approach.

Paula, another Pākehā member of Kiwi Productions, comments that she, too, has learned how to behave in ways that will not attract negative reactions. She does not, for instance, parade her knowledge in meetings, even when the discussion is in an area in which she was hired for her expertise (Holmes et al., 2009). She behaves in accordance with the respected Māori proverb, *Kaua e māhaki* "don't flaunt your knowledge".

This is very different behaviour from that we have observed in meetings in Pākehā organisations where it is usual for people to offer, and, indeed, to be expected to offer, explicit comments based on their knowledge and expertise. Paula described her role as a "very tricky" one.

EXAMPLE 8.5

Context: Kiwi Productions: Interview with Paula, a Pākehā member of the organisation

1	Paula:	I have to be very careful to be *whakaiti*
2		and I'm not coming across like that to my team
3		which is interesting you know
4		and it's because I know the stuff
5		and they don't know the stuff…
6		although I'm trying to provide them
7		with strong roles in it
8		but I'm in control of the information you know
9		in some way…
10		because you know they've got this idea
11		that I'm you know that I'm calling the shots
12		I mean I'm a manager I should be calling the shots

13	it shouldn't be a problem
14	that I'm calling the shots [laughs]
15	I know the stuff and they don't know the stuff
16	I know what has to happen
17	and they're working out what has to happen um
18	and I could make their life a lot easier
19	by just saying do it like this just do it like this
20	and it'll be fine and I can't be like that you know

Paula expresses very clearly here what she has learned, namely, that in a Māori context it is not appropriate for Pākehā co-leaders to take over and dictate how things should be done, even if they feel they have greater knowledge and expertise than their colleagues, and even if they have the appropriate formal status with its attendant responsibilities. Such behaviour is likely to attract censure and to be perceived as whakahīhī or bossy. Working out how to act in a professional way in such culturally sensitive contexts is not at all straightforward.

In another Māori organisation, a Pākehā employee, Joy, who had worked there for a considerable time and who, in other contexts, was rather voluble, commented that she had learned to keep quiet in meetings: *I felt it might be quite easy to dominate ... so I I shut up most of the time you know.* Some of the Pākehā we interviewed expressed a certain element of puzzlement over this issue, indicating that it was difficult for them to comprehend why someone would be discouraged from displaying the expertise for which they had been employed. The answer to this riddle is undoubtedly multifaceted; determining how to make effective use of one's expertise as a Pākehā in a Māori CofPs requires careful attention to the sociopragmatic complexities of the specific context in which one is operating. As Joy commented, it was often inappropriate to state what you knew directly and explicitly, *there was a process,* she said, which often led people indirectly to a solution, and in the end, she considered, it was better for others to arrive at the solution in their own way.

Clearly, being a member of a minority group in the workplace can be a challenging experience. However, there was also evidence that working in a Māori organisation could lead to greater intercultural understanding and contribute to the development of stronger workplace relationships. Our final example illustrates how Pākehā members of Kiwi Productions aligned themselves with their Māori colleagues over the issue of mispronunciation of a Māori phrase. The excerpt comes from a monthly staff meeting at Kiwi Productions where staff members are discussing the pronunciation of Māori by participants in an award ceremony. This particular excerpt focuses on a specific Māori phrase.[5]

---

5. The specific Māori lexical item used has been changed to protect confidentiality.

EXAMPLE 8.6[6]

Context: Kiwi Productions: Meeting of all staff. There is constant positive feedback and supportive laughter throughout

1	Gretel:	Quentin deserves an award too
2		for teaching [her] how to say *kia kaha*
3		["have courage, be strong"]
4		[laughter]
5	Gretel:	as opposed to key a car ha
6		[laughter]
7	April:	//key a car ha\
8	Gretel:	/which is\\ what she was saying
9		up to the nth hour before the presentation
10	Lillian:	get it right she could say Versace
11		but she can't say *kia kaha*
12		[laughter]

Gretel and Lillian are Pākehā staff members in this Māori workplace. By drawing attention to the fact that many Pākehā mispronounce Māori words, Gretel inevitably emphasises the ethnic boundary between the two groups. However, as stated in chapter 1, ethnicity is always salient in this workplace, and Māori issues are constantly on the radar. Moreover, Gretel's point is precisely to criticise those Pākehā who are not prepared to make the effort involved in correctly pronouncing Māori. Lillian's supportive comment is even more critical—*she could say Versace but she can't say kia kaha* (lines 9–10)—making the point that some Pākehā are willing to make a special effort to pronounce words in other languages, such as Italian, but will not make the effort with the Māori language.

Gretel and Lillian clearly differentiate themselves from the Pākehā pronouncers who are the butt of their joke, and align themselves with their Māori colleagues, a successful example of "crossing" ethnic boundaries (Rampton, 1995; de Bres et al., 2010). April's laughing imitation of Gretel's parodic *key a car ha* (line 6) indicates approval of their critical stance, implying shared attitudes and values, as does the supportive minimal feedback and appreciative laughter from others. The humourous exchange, thus, does valuable work in strengthening collegiality within this Māori workplace and assists these Pākehā employees to define themselves as "in-group" members.

It is also worth noting Gretel's explicit expression of approval for Quentin's patient and effective teaching: *Quentin deserves an award too for teaching [her] how to*

---

6. This example appeared in de Bres, Holmes, Marra, and Vine et al. (2010) where it is discussed in much greater detail.

say kia kaha (lines 1–2). Other staff members would regard Gretel's appreciative comment about Quentin's contribution very positively, because she is a senior manager, thereby effectively furthering work in building in-group solidarity.

There are many such constructive interactional possibilities in multicultural workplaces, providing Pākehā with opportunities to learn more about the norms of other cultures, and some are very open to these, regarding them as a source of cultural enrichment. Being sensitively responsive to the specific sociopragmatic meanings relevant in particular contexts is a challenging task, but the results can be rewarding.

CONCLUSION

Effective professionals in many areas, and especially those in leadership positions, are now expected to excel across a wide range of professional competencies. They must provide vision and inspiration, they need to be knowledge experts in their area, and they are also required to exercise well-honed relational skills, enabling them to interact effectively with a range of colleagues and clients. In addition, they are expected to be skilled in sharing different facets of leadership, as chapter 6 demonstrated, complementing each other's strengths to guarantee success. Leaders with non-mainstream ethnicities also face additional challenges; they must conform to the cultural norms of their groups and stay true to their ethnic beliefs and values.[7] These are hefty requirements. The analyses in this book have illustrated some of the ways in which different leaders respond constructively and creatively to such demands.

Our research has also made clear the importance of as thorough an understanding as possible of the culture of groups with whom one is undertaking research, as indicated in chapter 2. As Pākehā in Māori workplaces, we were aware of treading on eggshells and of the danger of causing offense. We found repeated evidence, both in workplace interactions and the comments that participants made about their leaders, of the Māori value of *manaaki tangata*, "respect and care for others" (Metge, 1995: 79), one component of spirituality that imbues all aspects of traditional Māori life and activity (Metge, 1995: 82–8; Henare, 2003). Our analyses of meetings provided further support for our observations regarding the omni-relevance of Māori values, such as respect for the dead, concern for whānau and family responsibilities, and so on. These important cultural issues were directly and explicitly brought to workplace meetings.

It is important to emphasise that even the extended discussion provided in this book can give only a tiny snapshot of what goes on in any workplace. We have

7. Note that Baxter (2010) suggests that women leaders face similar challenges in professional organisations. She argues that they need to pay more attention to their talk at work than men do because they are constantly contending with negative stereotypes and expectations. They need to undertake additional conversational work, she suggests, "to sustain a credible identity as a leader" (Baxter, 2010: 113).

Leadership, Discourse, and Ethnicity

focused on ethnicity, but as the discussion has often indicated, many other dimensions of identity are also relevant in workplace interactions. People index their identities, not only as Pākehā or Māori, but also as leaders or supporters, or as feminine and masculine, at different points, even in the same interaction. Moreover, the analysis has emphasised ways in which Pākehā and Māori communicative norms contrast, but it has been apparent throughout that the Māori workplaces in which we have recorded are by no means interchangeable; they also contrast in interesting ways. Within each workplace, different teams constitute distinct CofPs with their own norms and boundaries for acceptable behaviour and ways of interacting.

Almost every interaction provides evidence of the small and subtle ways in which people adapt their talk to the precise situation, including the specific discourse context, in which they are operating. Even in the same meeting with the same person, participants alter and adapt their ways of interacting in response to their perceptions of the effect their arguments are (or are not) having. There has not been space to illustrate this process in detail, but it is important to avoid overgeneralising. Inevitably, we have aimed to draw out patterns and themes in order to reflect on what can be learned from our research, but we are very aware of the danger of oversimplifying the rich complexity of workplace talk. Interactional behaviour varies in many ways from context to context, and variation is always a matter of degree rather than of absolutes. Recognising this, we suggest that our model provides a way forward in terms of assisting in the development of awareness of potential areas of intercultural miscommunication, discomfort, and potential offense. As we have demonstrated, the model provides a valuable means of discussing and analysing features of workplace interactions that may instantiate contrasting cultural values.

Finally, as suggested in chapter 7, it is also important to recognise that, in contemporary New Zealand society, there are many contexts in which there is a good deal of convergence between Māori and Pākehā ways of doing things. In addition to those formal occasions and contexts in which a conscious effort has been made to incorporate a Māori perspective or a Māori component into an event or a process (such as university graduation ceremonies and some formal government events), there are many more, less obvious areas where it could be argued that Māori values and Māori behaviours have influenced, often unconsciously, the way New Zealanders behave and interact with each other. It is totally unacceptable in Māori culture for instance to sit on a table: food surfaces are not available as seating. Many New Zealand Pākehā have adopted this norm and feel uncomfortable when a visitor from overseas or someone ignorant of this *tapu* ("restriction") sits on a table. Similarly, using the same basin for washing the body or clothes and for washing food is unacceptable in Māori culture, and some Pākehā are sensitive to this cultural tapu and respect it. Another, perhaps less obvious, example that involves discourse norms is the tendency to begin a conversation with a stranger by ascertaining their place of origin. This is standard among Māori people because it is an important way of establishing tribal affiliations and kinship links, with all their implications of relative rights, responsibilities, and mutual respect (Metge, 1995). Many Pākehā begin conversations with a stranger in a similar way. It could be argued that this is not surprising in a small country characterised by many close-knit and multiplex networks, but it is at least plausible that this is an area in which Māori norms have influenced even informal Pākehā "rituals of encounter". In our workplace data, we found references among Pākehā to the need for knowledge of one's kinship links and genealogy, which indicated the widespread awareness among non-Māori New Zealanders of the importance of such relationships for Māori. As a result of such intercultural convergences, it is often difficult to clearly identify distinctive areas of cultural contrast within mainstream contexts, such as the workplace. This book has taken a preliminary step in this direction.

The research outlined in this book has addressed issues that are of direct interest, not only to academics, but also to workplace practitioners. There is very little previous research that focuses on the discourse of leaders in white-collar organisations, and even less that examines the influence of ethnicity on discourse patterns in workplace interaction. Our analyses begin to fill these gaps. We have also addressed issues that, on the basis of our collaborative approach, we are confident are of interest to our co-researchers in the workplaces described in this study. Reviewing current trends in applied linguistics, Bygate (2004: 18) points out that many studies of real-world problems are "not explicitly located in problems perceived by the lay communities", and for those few that are "it is even rarer for them to discuss submitting their responses back to those communities". Our research meets both these criteria. We have collaborated with workplaces in identifying and addressing issues of mutual interest and concern, and we have provided feedback to those workplaces. We hope that the results will also be of interest to others interested in issues of intercultural communication at work. Finally, we hope that this book contributes to the development of a deeper understanding of the challenges and rewards of undertaking discourse analysis in diverse sociocultural contexts.

TRANSCRIPTION CONVENTIONS

Examples have been edited to protect the anonymity of the contributing organisations and all names used in extracts are pseudonyms. Minimal feedback and overlaps are sometimes edited out for ease of reading when the edited features are irrelevant to the point being made. Line divisions are intended to support understanding and typically represent sense unit boundaries. The main conventions used are outlined below:

iwi	Māori words are written in italics
["tribe"]	Translations are provided in square brackets
[laughs] : :	Paralinguistic features and editorial information in square brackets, colons indicate start/finish
+	Pause of up to one second
...//......\...	Simultaneous speech
.../........\\...	
( )	Unclear utterance
(hello)	Transcriber's best guess at an unclear utterance
#	Signals end of "sentence" where it is ambiguous on paper
-	Utterance cut off
...	Section of transcript omitted
=	Turn continuation

GLOSSARY

Standard spellings are taken from:
Te Taura Whiri i te Reo Māori Orthographic conventions http://www.tetaurawhiri
.govt.nz/,
He Pātaka Kupu http://www.koreromaori.co.nz/
Williams Dictionary http://www.nzetc.org/tm/scholarly/tei-WillDict.html and
http://www.maoridictionary.co.nz/

aroha – love
aroha ki te tangata – respect for people/love for people
haka – war dance
he kanohi kitea – seen faces
hongi – greeting involving pressing noses
hui – meeting/to meet/to gather
iwi – a tribe or a people
kai – food
kanohi – face
kanohi kitea – seen face
kanohi ki te kanohi – face to face
karakia – prayer, recitation, a formal greeting in the form of a prayer used to open
Maori events
kaumātua – respected Māori elder
kaua e takahia te mana o te tangata – do not trample over the mana of people
kaua e māhaki – don't flaunt your knowledge/be humble
kaupapa – objectives, priorities, core business
kawa – formal discourse rules, protocol
kei te pai – all right, that's good
kia ora – literally "your health", i.e., hello, thank you
kia tūpato – be cautious
kōhanga reo – language nests, i.e., a total immersion Māori language program for
young children

kōrero – discuss, talk, speak, communication
māhaki – humility, humbleness, modesty
mana – power, prestige or authority that is earned (not assigned)
manaaki – generosity
manaaki ki te tangata – share and host people, be generous
manaaki tangata – respect and care for others
manaakitanga – hospitality
Māori – language, people
Māoritanga – Maori culture
marae – Maori meeting complex; traditional meeting ground
mihi – greeting
mōrena – good morning
Ngāi Tahu – name of tribe
Ngāti Kahungunu – name of tribe
Ngāti Porou – name of tribe
Ngāti Whātua – name of tribe
paepae – front bench of a marae where elders speak
Pākehā – New Zealander of European descent, English language
poroporoaki – farewell
pōwhiri – formal welcome
rangatira – chief
reo – language
taha wairua – the spiritual dimension
te tangata – person
ngā tangata – people
tangata whenua – people of the land, indigenous people
tangi(hanga) – funeral
tapu – sacred, restriction
te reo – Maori language, voice
te reo Māori – the Maori language
tikanga – custom, protocol
tikanga Māori – Māori ways of doing things, Māori protocol
titiro – look
tūrangawaewae – a standing place where Māori customs prevail
whakaaro nui ki te hunga mate – respect for the dead
whakahīhī – boasting, being arrogant, conceited
whakaiti – being humble, modest, belittle, discriminate
whakamā – embarrassment, shame
whakapapa – heritage, genealogy
whakarongo – listen
whakatau – welcome
whānau – family, extended family
whanaungatanga – relationships, kinship

REFERENCES

Alvarez, José Luis, and Silviya Svejenova. 2005. *Sharing executive power: Roles and relationships at the top.* Cambridge, UK: Cambridge University Press.

Alvesson, Mats, and Yvonne Due Billing. 1997. *Understanding gender and organizations.* London: Sage.

Angouri, Jo, and Meredith Marra. 2009. Don't you know who I am? Corporate meetings and professional identity. Paper presented at 11th International Pragmatics Conference, Melbourne, 12–17 July 2009.

Angouri, Jo, and Meredith Marra. 2010. Corporate meetings as genre: A study of the role of the chair in corporate meeting talk. *Text & Talk* 30(6), 615–636.

Antonakis, John, Bruce J. Avolio, and Nagaraj Sivasubramaniam. 2003. Context and leadership: An examination of the nine-factor full-range leadership theory using the multifactor leadership questionnaire. *Leadership Quarterly* 14(3): 261–295.

Asmuss, Birte, and Jan Svennevig. 2009. Meeting talk: An introduction. *Journal of Business Communication* 46(1): 3–22.

Atkinson, J. Maxwell, and Paul Drew. 1979. *Order in court.* Cambridge, UK: Cambridge University Press.

Avolio, Bruce J., Nagaraj Sivasubramaniam, William D. Murry, Don Jung, and John W. Garger. 2003. Assessing shared leadership: Development and preliminary validation of a team multifactor leadership questionnaire. In *Shared leadership: Reframing the hows and whys of leadership*, ed. Craig L. Pearce and Jay A. Conger, 143–172. Thousand Oaks, CA: Sage.

Avolio, Bruce J., and Francis J. Yammarino, eds. 2002. *Transformational and charismatic leadership: The road ahead.* Oxford, UK: JAI.

Baragwanath, Willliam David, Margaret Lee, D. F. Dugdale, Timothy Brewer, and Paul Heath. 2001. *Māori custom and values in New Zealand law.* Wellington, NZ: The Law Commission.

Bargiela-Chiappini, Francesca. 2004. Intercultural business discourse. In *Linguistic Insights*, ed. Maurizio Gotti, 29–52. Bern, CH: Peter Lang.

Bargiela-Chiappini, Francesca, and Sandra J. Harris, eds. 1997a. *The languages of business: An international perspective.* Edinburgh: Edinburgh University Press.

Bargiela-Chiappini, Francesca, and Sandra J. Harris. 1997b. *Managing language: The discourse of corporate meetings.* Amsterdam: John Benjamins.

Bargiela-Chiappini, Francesca, Catherine Nickerson, and Brigitte Planken. 2007. *Business discourse.* New York: Palgrave Macmillan.

Barnes, Rebecca. 2007. Formulations and the facilitation of common agreement in meetings talk. *Text & Talk* 27(3): 273–296.

Bass, Bernard M. 1990. *Bass and Stogdill's handbook of leadership: Theory, research and managerial applications*. 3rd ed. New York: Free Press.

Baxter, Judith. 2003. *Positioning gender in discourse: A feminist methodology*. Basingstoke, UK: Palgrave.

Baxter, Judith. 2010. *The language of female leadership*. London: Palgrave Macmillan.

Bell, Allan. 2000. Maori and Pakeha English: A case study. In *New Zealand English*, ed. Allan Bell and Koenraad Kuiper, 221–248. Wellington, NZ: Victoria University Press.

Bell, Allan, and George Major. 2004. "Yeah right": Voicing Kiwi masculinity. Paper presented at New Zealand Language and Society Conference. Massey University, Palmerston North, 2–3 September 2004.

Bell, David, John Binnie, Julia Cream, and Gill Valentine. 1994. All hyped up and no place to go. *Gender Place and Culture* 1(1): 31–47.

Benton, Richard. 1991. "Maori English": A New Zealand myth? In *English around the world*, ed. Jenny Cheshire, 187–189. Cambridge, UK: Cambridge University Press.

Benton, Richard. 1996. Tokens and tokenism, models and metaphors: Facilitating the reacquisition of Te Reo Maori in the 1990s. Presentation to Applied Linguistics Association of New Zealand Research Seminar, August 2, 1996.

Berson, Yair, and Bruce J. Avolio. 2004. Transformational leadership and the dissemination of organizational goals: A case study of a telecommunication firm. *Leadership Quarterly* 15(5): 625–646.

Bilbow, Grahame T. 1998. Look who's talking: An analysis of "chair-talk" in business meetings. *Journal of Business and Technical Communication* 12: 157–197.

Bishop, Russell. 2005. Freeing ourselves from neocolonial domination in research: A Kaupapa Māori approach. In 3rd edition of *The SAGE handbook of qualitative research*, ed. Norman K. Denzin and Yvonna S. Lincoln, 109–138. Thousand Oaks, CA: Sage.

Blake, Robert R., and Jane S. Mouton. 1978. *The new managerial grid*. Houston, TX: Gulf.

Blommaert, Jan. 2005. *Discourse: A critical introduction*. Cambridge, UK: Cambridge University Press.

Blommaert, Jan. 2007. Sociolinguistics and discourse analysis: Orders of indexicality and polycentricity. *Journal of Multicultural Discourses* 2: 115–130.

Boden, Deidre. 1994. *The business of talk: Organizations in action*. Cambridge, UK: Polity Press.

Boje, David M. 1991. Consulting and change in the storytelling organization. *Journal of Organizational Change Management* 4: 7–17.

Brown, Penelope, and Stephen C. Levinson. 1987. *Politeness: Some universals in language usage*. Cambridge, UK: Cambridge University Press. (Orig. pub. 1978.)

Bryson, Jane, and Paul O'Neil. 2008. Developing human capability: Employment institutions, organisations and individuals. Victoria University of Wellington Developing Human Capability Project [Online]. Available at: http://www.victoria.ac.nz/vms/researchprojects/developg_human_cap_project-publicatns.aspx#Presentations [Accessed 18 August 2008].

Bucholtz, Mary, and Kira Hall. 2005. Identity and interaction: A sociocultural linguistics approach. *Discourse Studies* 7(4–5): 585–614.

Butler, Judith. 1990. Gender trouble: Feminism and the subversion of identity. New York: Routledge.

Button, Graham. 1987. Moving out of closings. In *Talk and social organization*, ed. Graham Button and John R. E. Lee, 101–151. Clevedon, Avon, UK: Multilingual Matters.

Bygate, Martin. 2004. Some current trends in applied linguistics: Towards a generic view. *AILA Review* 17(1): 6–22.

Cameron, Deborah. 1985. "Respect, please!" Subjects and objects in sociolinguistics. Unpublished manuscript.

Cameron, Deborah. 2009. Theoretical issues for the study of gender and spoken interaction. In *Gender and spoken interaction*, ed. Pia Pichler and Eva M. Eppler, 1–17. London: Palgrave Macmillan.

Cameron, Deborah, Elizabeth Frazer, Penelope Harvey, M. B. H. Rampton, and Kay Richardson. 1992. *Researching language: Issues of power and method*. London: Routledge.

Campbell, Sarah, and Celia Roberts. 2007. Migration, ethnicity and competing discourses in the job interview: Synthesizing the institutional and personal. *Discourse and Society* 18(3): 243–271.

Caudron, Shari. 1992. Humor is healthy in the workplace. *Personnel Journal* 71(6): 63–68.

Chan, Angela Chi Kuen. 2005. *Openings and closings in business meetings in different cultures*. Unpublished PhD thesis, Wellington, NZ: Victoria University of Wellington.

Chhokar, Jagdeep S., Felix C. Brodbek, and Robert J. House, eds. 2007. *Culture and leadership across the world: The GLOBE book of in-depth studies of 25 societies*. Mahwah, NJ: Lawrence Erlbaum.

Clouse, R. Wilburn, and Karen L. Spurgeon. 1995. Corporate analysis of humor. *Psychology: A Journal of Human Behaviour* 32(3–4): 1–24.

Clyne, Michael. 1994. *Inter-cultural communication at work*. Cambridge, UK: Cambridge University Press.

Coates, Jennifer. 1989. Gossip revisited: Language in all-female groups. In *Women in their speech communities: New perspectives on language and sex*, ed. Jennifer Coates and Deborah Cameron, 94–122. London: Longman.

Coates, Jennifer. 2003. *Men talk: Stories in the making of masculinities*. Oxford, UK: Blackwell.

Coates, Jennifer. Forthcoming. Gender and humour in everyday conversation. To appear in *Gender and humor*, ed. Delia Chiaro and Raffaella Baccolini. Bologna: University of Bologna Press.

Collinson, David L. 1988. "Engineering humour": Masculinity, joking and conflict in shop-floor relations. *Organizational Studies* 2: 181–200.

Cook-Gumperz, Jenny. 2001. Cooperation, collaboration and pleasure in work. In *Culture in communication: Analyses of intercultural situations*, ed. Aldo Di Luzio, Susanne Günthner, and Franca Orletti, 117–139. Amsterdam: John Benjamins.

Corder, Saskia, and Miriam Meyerhoff. 2007. Communities of practice in the analysis of inter-cultural communication. In *Handbook of applied linguistics*, vol. 7, *Intercultural communication*, ed. Helga Kotthoff and Helen Spencer-Oatey, 441–461. Berlin: Mouton de Gruyter.

Coupland, Justine, ed. 2000. *Small talk*. Harlow, UK: Longman.

Coupland, Nikolas. 2001. Introduction: Sociolinguistic theory and social theory. In *Sociolinguistics and social theory*, ed. Nikolas Coupland, Srikant Sarangi, and Christopher N. Candlin, 1–26. London: Longman.

Cuff, E. C., and W. W. Sharrock. 1985. Meetings. In *Handbook of discourse analysis*, vol. 3, *Discourse and dialogue*, ed. Teun A. Van Dijk, 149–159. London: Academic Press.

Day, David V., Peter Gronn, and Eduardo Salas. 2004. Leadership capacity in teams. *Leadership Quarterly* 15(6): 857–880.

de Bres, Julia. 2008. Planning for tolerability: Promoting positive attitudes and behaviours towards the Māori language among non-Māori New Zealanders. Unpublished PhD thesis, Wellington, NZ: Victoria University of Wellington.

de Bres, Julia, Janet Holmes, Meredith Marra, and Bernadette Vine. 2010. Kia ora matua: Humour and the Māori language in the workplace. *Journal of Asian Pacific Communication* 20(1): 46–68.

De Fina, Anna. 2007. Code-switching and the construction of ethnic identity in a community of practice. *Language in Society* 36(3): 371–392.

Dennehy, Robert F. 1999. The executive as storyteller. *Management Review* 88(3): 40–43.

Diamond, Paul. 2003. *A fire in your belly: Maori leaders speak.* Wellington, NZ: Huia Publishers.

Dorfman, Peter W. 2003. International and cross-cultural leadership research. In *Handbook for international management research,* ed. Betty Jane Punnett and Oded Shenkar, 265–355. Ann Arbor, MI: University of Michigan Press.

Drew, Paul, and John Heritage. 1992. *Talk at work: Interaction in institutional settings.* Cambridge, UK: Cambridge University Press.

Drucker, Peter. 1955. *The practice of management.* New York: Harper & Row.

Dwyer, Judith. 1993. *The business communication handbook.* New York: Prentice Hall.

Eckert, Penelope. 2008. Variation and the indexical field. *Journal of Sociolinguistics* 12(4): 453–476.

Eckert, Penelope, and Sally McConnell-Ginet. 1992. Think practically and look locally: Language and gender as community-based practice. *Annual Review of Anthropology* 21: 461–490. (Reprinted in *The Women and Language Debate,* ed. Camille Roman, Suzanne Juhasz, and Christanne Miller, 432–460. 1994. New Brunswick, NJ: Rutgers University Press).

Ehrlich, Susan. 2008. Sexual assault trials, discursive identities and institutional change. In *Analysing identities in discourse,* ed. Rosana Dolón and Júlia Todolí, 159–177. Amsterdam: John Benjamins.

Eisenberg, Eric, and H. L. Goodall Jr. 2004. *Organizational communication: Balancing creativity and constraint.* New York: St. Martin's Press.

Elkin, Graham, Brad Jackson, and Kerr Inkson. 2008. *Organisational behaviour in New Zealand.* 3rd ed. Auckland, NZ: Prentice Hall.

Erez, Miriam, and Efrat Gati. 2004. A dynamic, multi-level model of culture: From the micro level of the individual to the macro level of a global culture. *Applied Psychology: An International Review* 53(4): 583–598.

Fairclough, Norman. 1989. *Language and power.* London: Longman.

Fairclough, Norman. 1992. *Discourse and social change.* Cambridge, UK: Polity Press.

Fairclough, Norman. 2003. *Analysing discourse: Textual analysis for social research.* London: Routledge.

Fairclough, Norman, and Anna Mauranen. 1998. The conversationalisation of political discourse: A comparative view. In *Political linguistics,* ed. Jan Blommaert and Chris Bulcaen, 89–121. Amsterdam: John Benjamins.

Fairhurst. Gail T. 2007. *Discursive leadership.* London: Sage.

Fairhurst, Gail T., and Robert A. Sarr. 1996. *The art of framing: Managing the language of leadership.* San Francisco, CA: Jossey-Bass.

Firth, Alan. 1995. *The discourse of negotiation: Studies of language in the workplace.* Oxford, UK: Pergamon Press.

Fisher, Sue. 1982. The decision-making context: How doctors and patients communicate. In *Linguistics and professions,* ed. Robert J. Di Pietro, 51–81. Norwood, NJ: Ablex.

Fleming, David. 2001. Narrative leadership: Using the power of stories. *Strategy & Leadership* 29(4): 34–36.

Fletcher, Joyce K. 1999. *Disappearing acts: Gender, power, and relational practice at work.* Cambridge, MA: MIT Press.

Ford, Celia. 2010. Questioning in meetings: Participation and positioning. In *"Why do you ask?": The function of questions in institutional discourse,* ed. Susan Erlich and Alice Freed, 211–234. Oxford, UK: Oxford University Press.

Ford, Jackie. 2006. Discourses of leadership: Gender, identity and contradiction in a UK public sector organization. *Leadership* 2(1): 77–99.

Foucault, Michel. 1982. The subject and power. In *Michel Foucault: Beyond structuralism and hermeneutics*, ed. Hubert L. Dreyfus and Paul Rabinow, 208–222. Chicago, IL: University of Chicago Press.

Foucault, Michel. 1988. Technologies of the self. In *Technologies of the self: A seminar with Michel Foucault*, ed. Luther H. Martin, Huck Gutman, and Patrick H. Hutton, 16–49. Amherst, MA: University of Massachusetts Press.

Fought, Carmen. 2006. *Language and ethnicity*. Cambridge, UK: Cambridge University Press.

French, John R. P., and Bertram Raven. 1959. The bases of social power. In *Group dynamics*, ed. Dorwin Cartwright and Alvin Zander, 150–167. New York: Harper and Row.

Gardner, John, and Deborah Terry. 1996. Communication, leadership and organisational change. In *Leadership research and practice: Emerging themes and new challenges*, ed. Ken W. Parry, 153–161. Melbourne: Pitman.

Garner, Mark, Christine Raschka, and Peter Sercombe. 2006. Sociolinguistic minorities, research and social relationships. *Journal of Multilingual and Multicultural Development* 27(1): 61–78.

Gee, James Paul. 1999. *An introduction to discourse analysis: Theory and method*. London and New York: Routledge.

Geertz, Clifford. 1973. Thick description: Towards an interpretive theory of culture. In *The interpretation of cultures*, ed. Clifford Geertz, 3–30. New York: Basic Books.

Geluykens, Ronald, and Bettina Kraft, eds. 2008. *Institutional discourse in cross-cultural contexts*. Munich: Lincom Europa.

Geyer, Naomi. 2008. *Discourse and politeness: Ambivalent face in Japanese*. London: Continuum.

Goffman, Erving. 1963. *Behavior in public places: Notes on the social organization of gatherings*. New York: Free Press of Glencoe.

Goffman, Erving. 1974. *Frame analysis: An essay on the organization of experience*. Cambridge, MA: Harvard University Press.

Grin, François. 1995. Combining immigrant and autochthonous language rights. In *Linguistic human rights: Overcoming linguistic discrimination*, ed. Tove Skutnabb-Kangas and Robert Phillipson, 31–48. Berlin: Mouton de Gruyter.

Gumperz, John. 1982a. *Discourse strategies*. Cambridge, UK: Cambridge University Press.

Gumperz, John. 1982b. *Language and social identity*. Cambridge, UK: Cambridge University Press.

Gumperz, John. 1996. The linguistic and cultural relativity of inference. In *Rethinking linguistic relativity*, ed. John J. Gumperz and Stephen C. Levinson, 374–406. Cambridge, UK: Cambridge University Press.

Hackman, Michael Z., and Craig E. Johnson. 2004. *Leadership: A communication perspective*, 4th ed. Long Grove, IL: Waveland Press.

Harris, Sandra J., and Francesca Bargiela-Chiappini. 1997. The languages of business: Introduction and overview. In *The languages of business: An international perspective*, ed. Fransesca Bargiela-Chiappini and Sandra J. Harris, 1–18. Edinburgh: Edinburgh University Press.

Hecht, Michael L., Jennifer R. Warren, Eura Jung, and Janice L. Krieger. 2005. A communication theory of identity: Development, theoretical perspective, and future directions. In *Theorizing about intercultural communication*, ed. William B. Gudykunst, 257–278. Thousand Oaks, CA: Sage.

Hede, Andrew. 2001. Integrated leadership: Multiple styles for maximal effectiveness. In *Leadership in the Antipodes: Findings, implications and a leader profile*, ed. Ken W. Parry, 6–21. Wellington, NZ: Institute of Policy Studies Centre for the Study of Leadership.

Heenan, David A., and Warren Bennis. 1999. *Co-leaders: The power of great partnerships*. New York: John Wiley and Sons.

Henare, Manuka. 2003. The changing images of the nineteenth century Maori society: From tribes to nation. Unpublished PhD thesis, Wellington, NZ: Victoria University.

Henry, Ella Y. 1994. *Rangatira wahine: Maori women managers and leadership*. Unpublished MPhil thesis, Auckland, NZ: University of Auckland.

Hofstede, Geert. 1997. *Cultures and organizations: Software of the mind*. Rev. ed. New York: McGraw-Hill.

Hofstede, Geert, and Gert Jan Hofstede. 2005. *Cultures and organizations: Software of the mind*. 2nd ed. New York: McGraw-Hill.

Holmes, Janet. 1997. Women, language and identity. *Journal of Sociolinguistics* 2(1): 195–223.

Holmes, Janet. 1998a. No joking matter! The functions of humour in the workplace. Proceedings of the Australian Linguistics Society Conference. Brisbane: University of Queensland, July 1998. Available at: http://emsah.uq.edu.au/linguistics/als/als98/.

Holmes, Janet. 1998b. Why tell stories? Contrasting themes and identities in the narratives of Maori and Pakeha women and men. *Journal of Asian Pacific Communication* 8(1): 1–29.

Holmes, Janet. 2000. Doing collegiality and keeping control at work: Small talk in government departments. In *Small talk*, ed. Justine Coupland, 32–61. London: Longman,

Holmes, Janet. 2004. Monitoring, mentoring and managing: The complexities of workplace discourse. *Wellington Working Papers in Linguistics* 16: 44–67.

Holmes, Janet. 2005a. Power and discourse at work: Is gender relevant? In *Feminist critical discourse analsysis*, ed. Michelle Lazar, 31–60. London: Palgrave

Holmes, Janet. 2005b. Leadership talk: How do leaders "do mentoring", and is gender relevant? *Journal of Pragmatics* 37: 1779–1880.

Holmes, Janet. 2006. *Gendered talk at work: Constructing social identity through workplace inter-action*. Malden, MA: Blackwell.

Holmes, Janet. 2007a. Politeness, power and provocation: How humour functions in the work-place. In *Discourse studies*, vol. 3, ed. Teun van Dijk, 76–101. London: Sage.

Holmes, Janet. 2007b. Humour and the construction of Maori leadership at work. *Leadership* 3(1): 5–27.

Holmes, Janet. 2007c. Relativity rules: Politic talk in ethnicised workplaces. Closing Plenary at the Third International Symposium on Politeness, University of Leeds, 2–4 July 2007.

Holmes, Janet. 2008. *An introduction to sociolinguistics*. 3rd ed. London: Longman.

Holmes, Janet. 2009. Men, masculinities and leadership: Different discourse styles at work. In *Gender and spoken interaction*, ed. Pia Pichler and Eva M. Eppler, 186–210. London: Palgrave Macmillan.

Holmes, Janet. 2011. Discourse in the workplace. In *Continuum companion to discourse analysis*, ed. Ken Hyland and Brian Paltridge, 185–198. London: Continuum.

Holmes, Janet, and Tina Chiles. 2010. "Is that right?" Questions as control devices in workplace meetings. In *"Why do you ask?": The function of questions in institutional discourse*, ed. Alice Freed and Susan Ehrlich, 187–210. Oxford, UK: Oxford University Press.

Holmes, Janet, and Jennifer Hay. 1997. Humour as an ethnic boundary marker in New Zealand interaction. *Journal of Intercultural Studies* 18(2): 127–151.

Holmes, Janet, and Meredith Marra. 2002a. Having a laugh at work: How humour contributes to workplace culture. *Journal of Pragmatics* 34: 1683–1710.

Holmes, Janet, and Meredith Marra. 2002b. Humour as a discursive boundary marker in social interaction. In *Us and others: Social identities across languages, discourses and cultures*, ed. Anna Duszak, 377–400. Amsterdam: John Benjamins.

Holmes, Janet, and Meredith Marra. 2004a. Leadership and managing conflict in meetings. *Pragmatics* 14(4): 439–462.

Holmes, Janet, and Meredith Marra. 2004b. Relational practice in the workplace: Women's talk or gendered discourse? *Language in Society* 33(3): 377–398.

Holmes, Janet, and Meredith Marra. 2005. Narrative and the construction of professional identity in the workplace. In *The sociolinguistics of narrative*, ed. Joanna Thornborrow and Jennifer Coates, 193–213. Amsterdam: John Benjamins.

Holmes, Janet, and Meredith Marra. 2006. Humor and leadership style. *Humor* 19(2): 119–138.

Holmes, Janet, and Meredith Marra. Forthcoming. Leadership discourse in a Māori workplace: Negotiating gender, ethnicity and leadership at work. *Gender and Language*.

Holmes, Janet, Meredith Marra, and Stephanie Schnurr. 2008. Impoliteness and ethnicity: Māori and Pākehā discourse in New Zealand workplaces. *Journal of Politeness Research* 4(2): 193–219.

Holmes, Janet, Meredith Marra, and Bernadette Vine. 2009. Preparing Pakeha for working with people from other cultures. In *Proceedings of the Language Education and Diversity Conference*, ed. Stephen May, 21–23 November 2007. Hamilton, NZ: Waikato University.

Holmes, Janet, and Stephanie Schnurr. 2005. Politeness, humor and gender in the workplace: Negotiating norms and identifying contestation. *Journal of Politeness Research* 1(1): 121–149.

Holmes, Janet, Stephanie Schnurr, Angela Chan, and Tina Chiles. 2003. The discourse of leadership. *Te Reo* 46: 31–46.

Holmes, Janet, and Maria Stubbe. 2003a. *Power and politeness in the workplace*. London: Pearson.

Holmes, Janet, and Maria Stubbe. 2003b. "Feminine" workplaces: Stereotype and reality. In *Handbook of language and gender*, ed. Janet Holmes and Miriam Meyerhoff, 573–599. Oxford, UK: Blackwell.

Holmes, Janet, and Maria Stubbe. 2003c. Doing disagreement at work: A sociolinguistic approach. *Australian Journal of Communication* 30(1): 53–78.

Holmes, Janet, Maria Stubbe, and Bernadette Vine. 1999. Constructing professional identity: "Doing power" in policy units. In *Talk, work and institutional order: Discourse in medical, mediation and management settings*, ed. Srikant Sarangi and Celia Roberts, 351–385. Berlin: Mouton de Gruyter.

Holmes, Janet, Bernadette Vine, and Meredith Marra. 2009. Māori men at work: Leadership, discourse and ethnic identity. *Intercultural pragmatics* 6(3): 345–366.

House, Juliane. 2005. Politeness in Germany: Politeness in Germany? In *Politeness in Europe*, ed. Leo Hickey and Miranda Stewart, 13–28. Clevedon, UK: Multilingual Matters.

House, Robert J., Paul J. Hanges, Mansour Javidan, Peter Dorfman, and Vipin Gupta, eds. 2004. *Culture, leadership and organisations: The GLOBE study of 62 societies*. Thousand Oaks, CA: Sage.

Huisman, Marjan. 2001. Decision-making in meetings as talk-in-interaction. *International Studies of Management and Organization* 31(3): 69–90.

Huxham, Chris, and Siv Vangen. 2000. Leadership in the shaping and implementation of collaboration agendas: How things happen in a (not quite) joined up world. *Academy of Management Journal* 43(6): 1159–1175.

Jackson, Brad, and Ken Parry. 2001. *The hero manager: Learning from New Zealand's top chief executives*. Auckland, NZ: Penguin.

Jackson, Brad, and Ken Parry. 2008. *A very short, fairly interesting and reasonably cheap book about studying leadership*. London: Sage.

Jackson, Brad, Dale Pfeifer, and Bernadette Vine. 2006. The co-leadership of transformational leadership. In *Proceedings of the 20th Australia and New Zealand Academy of Management Conference*. Rockhampton, Queensland, Australia. 6–10 December 2006.

Jaworski, Adam. 1993. *The power of silence: Social and pragmatic perspective*. Newbury Park, CA: Sage.

Jenkins, Richard. 1996. *Social identity*. London: Routledge.

Johnson, Sally. 1997. Theorising language and masculinity: A feminist perspective. In *Language and masculinity*, ed. Sally Johnson and Ulrike Hanna Meinhof, 8–26. Malden, MA: Blackwell.

Jones, Deborah, Judith Pringle, and Deborah Shepherd. 2000. Managing diversity meets Aotearoa/New Zealand. *Personnel Review* 29(3): 364–380.

Jones, Rod, and Joanna Thornborrow. 2004. Floors, talk and the organisation of classroom activities. *Language in Society* 33(3): 233–423.

Ka'ai, Tānia M., and Michael P. J. Reilly. 2004. Rangatiratanga: Traditional and contemporary leadership. In *Ki te whaiao: An introduction to Māori culture and society*, ed. Tānia M. Ka'ai, John C. Moorfield, Michael P. J. Reilly and Sharon Mosely, 91–102. Auckland, NZ: Pearson Longman.

Kaye, Michael. 1996. *Myth makers and story-tellers*. Chatswood, N.S.W., Australia: Business and professional publishing.

Kell, Susan, Meredith Marra, Janet Holmes, and Bernadette Vine. 2007. Ethnic differences in the dynamics of women's work meetings. *Multilingua* 26(4): 309–331.

Kennedy, Graeme, and Shunji Yamazaki. 1999. The influence of Māori on the New Zealand English lexicon. In *Corpora galore: Analyses and techniques in describing English*, ed. John M. Kirk, 33–44. Amsterdam: Rodopi.

Kerfoot, Karlene. 2003. Organizational intelligence/organizational stupidity: The leader's challenge. *Nursing Economics* 21(2): 91–93.

Kiesling, Scott Fabius. 2001. "Now I gotta watch what I say": Shifting constructions of masculinity in discourse. *Journal of Linguistic Anthropology* 11(2): 250–273.

King, Michael. 1991. *Pakeha: The quest for identity in New Zealand*. Auckland, NZ: Penguin.

Koller, Veronika. 2004. Businesswomen and war metaphors: Possessive, jealous and pugnacious? *Journal of Sociolinguistics* 8(1): 3–22.

Kotthoff, Helga. 2007. Ritual and style across cultures. In *Handbook of Intercultural Communication*, ed. Helga Kotthoff and Helen Spencer-Oatey, 173–198. Berlin: Mouton.

Kotthoff, Helga, and Helen Spencer-Oatey, eds. 2007. *Handbook of intercultural communication*. Berlin: Mouton.

Kramsch, Claire. 1998. *Language and culture*. Oxford, UK: Oxford University Press.

Kuiper, Koenraad. 1991. Sporting formulae in New Zealand English: Two models of male solidarity. In *English around the world: Sociolinguistic perspectives*, ed. Jenny Cheshire, 200–209. Cambridge, UK: Cambridge University Press.

Labov, William. 1972. *Sociolinguistic patterns*. Philadelphia: University of Pennsylvania Press.

Lave, Jean, and Etienne Wenger. 1991. *Situated learning: Legitimate peripheral participation*. Cambridge, UK: Cambridge University Press.

Laver, John. 1975. Communicative functions of phatic communion. In *The organization of behavior in face-to-face interaction*, ed. Adam Kendon, Richard Harris, and Mary Ritchie Key, 215–238. The Hague: Mouton.

Lemke, Jay L. 2008. Identity, development and desire: Critical questions. In *Identity trouble: Critical discourse and contested identities*, ed. Carmen Rosa Caldas-Coulthard and Rick Iedema, 17–42. London: Palgrave McMillan.

Linell, Per. 2001. *Approaching dialogue: Talk, interaction and contexts in dialogical perspectives*. Amsterdam: John Benjamins.

Locher, Miriam. 2004. *Power and politeness in action: Disagreements in oral communication.* Berlin: Mouton De Gruyter.

Locher, Miriam. 2006. Polite behavior within relational work: The discursive approach to politeness. *Multilingua* 25(3): 249–267.

Locher, Miriam. 2008. Relational work, politeness, and identity construction. In *Handbook of interpersonal communication,* ed. Gerd Antos and Eija Ventola (in cooperation with Tilo Weber), 509–540. Berlin and New York: Mouton de Gruyter.

Locher, Miriam, and Richard J. Watts. 2005. Politeness theory and relational work. *Journal of Politeness Research* 1(1): 9–34.

Macalister, John. 2003. The presence of Māori words in New Zealand English, Unpublished PhD thesis, Wellington, NZ: Victoria University of Wellington.

Magee, Ann. 2001. Women. *Asia Pacific Viewpoint* 42(1): 35–45.

Mahuika, Api. 1992. Leadership: Inherited and achieved. In *Te ao hurihuri: Aspects of Māoritanga,* ed. Michael King, 86–113. Auckland, NZ: Reed Books.

Marra, Meredith. 2003. Decisions in New Zealand business meetings: A sociolinguistic analysis of power at work. PhD thesis, Victoria University of Wellington.

Marra, Meredith. 2005. "Whiter than white": Constructing ethnic and professional identity in a Maori workplace. Paper presented at the language in the media conference, Leeds University, 12–14 September 2005.

Marra, Meredith. 2006. Talking up, talking down: Ethnicised communities of practice at work. Paper presented at the New Zealand language and society conference, Christchurch Arts Centre, 19–20 August 2006.

Marra, Meredith. 2008a. Meeting talk: Aligning the classroom with the workplace. *Communication Journal of New Zealand* 9(1): 63–82.

Marra, Meredith. 2008b. Recording and analyzing talk across cultures. In 2nd ed. of *Culturally speaking: Managing rapport through talk across cultures,* ed. Helen Spencer-Oatey, 304–321. London: Continuum.

Marra, Meredith, and Janet Holmes. 2005. Constructing ethnicity and leadership through storytelling at work. In *Communication at work: Showcasing communication scholarship,* ed. Colleen Mills and Donald Matheson. Publication of the Annual Meeting of the Australia New Zealand Communication Association 2005. Available at: http://www.mang.canterbury.ac.nz/ANZCA/CommAtWork.shtml.

Marra, Meredith, and Janet Holmes. 2008. Constructing ethnicity in New Zealand workplace stories. *Text & Talk* 28(3): 397–420.

Marra, Meredith, Stephanie Schnurr, and Janet Holmes. 2006. Effective leadership in New Zealand workplaces: Balancing gender and role. In *Speaking out: The female voice in public contexts,* ed. Judith Baxter and Allyson Jule, 240–260. Basingstoke, UK: Palgrave Macmillan.

Marra, Meredith, Bernadette Vine, and Janet Holmes. 2008. Heroes, fathers and good mates: Leadership styles of men at work. In *Proceedings of the Australia and New Zealand Communication Association Conference,* ed. Elspeth Tilley. 1–15. Wellington, NZ, 9–11 July 2008. Available at: http://anzca08.massey.ac.nz/.

May, Stephen. 2000. Uncommon languages: The challenges and possibilities of minority language rights. *Journal of Multilingual and Multicultural Development* 21(5): 366–385.

McRae, Susan. 2009. It's a blokes thing: Gender, occupational roles and talk in the workplace. In *Gender and spoken interaction,* ed. Pia Pichler and Eva M. Eppler, 163–185. London: Palgrave Macmillan.

Mead, Hirini Moko. 2003. *Tikanga Māori. Living by Māori values.* Wellington, NZ: Huia.

Mead, Hirini Moko, and Neil Grove. 2003. *Ngā Pāpeha a ngā Tāpuna.* Wellington, NZ: Victoria University Press.

Metge, Joan. 1976. *The Maoris of New Zealand: Rautahi*. London: Routledge.

Metge, Joan. 1995. *New growth from old: The whanau in the modern world*. Wellington, NZ: Victoria University Press.

Metge, Joan. 2001. *Kōrero tahi: Talking together*. Auckland, NZ: Auckland University Press.

Metge, Joan. 2005. Working in/playing with three languages: English te reo Maori and Maori body language. *Sites New Series* 2(2): 83–90.

Metge, Joan, and Patricia Kinloch. 1978. *Talking past each other: Problems of cross-cultural communication*. Wellington, NZ: Victoria University Press.

Meyerhoff, Miriam. 1994. Sounds pretty ethnic eh? A pragmatic particle in New Zealand English. *Language in society* 23(3): 367–388.

Morreall, John. 1991. Humor and work. *Humor* 4(4): 359–373.

Mullany, Louise. 2004. Gender, politeness and institutional power roles: Humour as a tactic to gain compliance in workplace business meetings. *Multilingua* 23(1–2): 13–37.

Mullany, Louise. 2007. *Gendered discourse in the professional workplace*. London: Palgrave Macmillan.

Murata, Kazuyo. Forthcoming. A contrastive study of the discourse of business meetings in New Zealand and in Japan. PhD thesis, Wellington, NZ: Victoria University of Wellington

Nathan, Siaan Barbara. 1999. Tikanga Maori in Aotearoa/New Zealand clinical psychology training programmes: A follow up of Abbott and Durie's (1987) study. Unpublished MA thesis, Wellington, NZ: Victoria University of Wellington.

Nga Tuara. 1992. *Nga toka tu Moana: Māori leadership and decision making*. Wellington, NZ: Te Puni Kokiri.

Nielsen, Jeffrey S. 2004. *The myth of leadership: Creating leaderless organizations*. Palo Alto, CA: Davies-Black.

Northouse, Peter. 1997. *Leadership: Theory and practice*. London: Sage.

Ochs, Elinor. 1992. Indexing gender. In *Rethinking context: Language as an interactive phenomenon*, ed. Alessandro Duranti and Charles Goodwin, 335–358. Cambridge, UK: Cambridge University Press.

Omi, Michael, and Howard Winant. 1994. *Racial formation in the United States: From the 1960s to the 1990s*. New York: Routledge.

Onyx, Jenny. 1999. Power between women in organizations. *Feminism and Psychology* 9(4): 417–421.

O'Toole, James, Jay Galbraith, and Edward Emmet Lawler. 2002. When two (or more) heads are better than one: The promises and the pitfalls of shared leadership. *California Management Review* 44: 65–83.

Parry, Ken, ed. 2001. *Leadership in the Antipodes: Findings, implications and a leader profile*. Wellington, NZ: Institute of Policy Studies Centre for the Study of Leadership.

Pennycook, Alastair. 2001. *Critical applied linguistics: A critical introduction*. Mahwah, NJ: Lawrence Erlbaum.

Phillips, Jock. 1996. *A man's country? The image of the Pakeha male, a history*. Rev. ed. Auckland, NZ: Penguin.

Plester, Barbara. 2003. "Work hard: play hard": Using humour at work. Unpublished Masters thesis, Massey University, Albany, New Zealand.

Plester, Barbara, and Janet Sayers. 2007. "Taking the piss": Functions of banter in the IT industry. *Humor* 20: 157–187.

Potter, Jonathan, and Margaret Wetherell. 1987. *Discourse and social psychology*. London: Sage.

Pringle, Judith K. 2005. Reflections on amplifying "others" voices: Dilemmas that face "white" researchers who aim to make research and scholarship more inclusive by "writing in" the experiences of the "others"—those that are members of historically disadvantaged groups. Paper presented in the Advanced Research Methodologies Seminar Series

2005, Faculty of Commerce and Administration, Victoria University of Wellington, 11 November 2005.

Raelin, Joseph A. 2003. *Creating leaderful organizations: How to bring out leadership in everyone.* San Francisco, CA: Berrett-Koehler.

Rampton, Ben. 1995. *Crossing: Language and ethnicity among adolescents.* London: Longman.

Ready, Douglas A. 2002. How storytelling builds next-generation leaders. *MIT Sloan Management Review* 43(4), 63–69.

Reed, Michael. 2005. Reflections on the "realist turn" in organisation and management studies. *Journal of Management Studies* 42(8): 1621–1644.

Richards, Keith. 2006. *Language and professional identity.* Houndmills, UK: Palgrave Macmillan.

Ritchie, James. 1992. *Becoming bicultural.* Wellington, NZ: Huia Publishers.

Robbins, Stephen P., Bruce Millett, Ron Cacioppe, and Terry Waters-Marsh. 1998. *Organisational behaviour: Leading and managing in Australia and New Zealand.* 2nd ed. Sydney: Prentice Hall.

Roberts, Celia, Evelyn Davies, and Tom Jupp. 1992. *Language and discrimination: A study of communication in multi-ethnic workplaces.* London: Longman.

Rodrigues, Suzana B., and David L. Collinson. 1995. "Having fun?" Humour as resistance in Brazil. *Organization Studies* 16(5): 739–768.

Ruwhiu, Diane, and Rachel Wolfgramm. 2006. Kaupapa Māori research: A contribution to critical management studies in New Zealand. In *Organisation, identity and locality (OIL) II conference proceedings,* ed. Craig Pritchard, Deborah Jones, and Roy Jacques, 51–58. Palmerston North, NZ: Department of Management, Massey University. Available at: http://www.massey.ac.nz/~cprichar/Oil%20Conference%20Proceedings_revised.pdf [Accessed 21 June 2007].

Sacks, Harvey, Emanuel Schegloff, and Gail Jefferson. 1974. A simplest systematics for the organization of turn-taking for conversation. *Language* 50: 696–735.

Sally, David. 2002. Co-leadership: Lessons from the republican Rome. *California Management Review* 44: 65–83.

Salmond, Anne. 1974. Rituals of encounter among the Maori: Sociolinguistic study of a scene. In *Explorations in the ethnography of speaking,* ed. Richard Bauman and Joel Sherzer, 192–212. Cambridge, UK: Cambridge University Press.

Salmond, Anne. 1975. *Hui: A study of Māori ceremonial gatherings.* Wellington, NZ: Reed.

Sarangi, Srikant. 2006. The conditions and consequences of professional discourse studies. In *Language, culture and identity in applied linguistics (British studies in applied linguistics 21),* ed. Richard Kiely, Pauline Rea-Dickens, Helen Woodfield, and Gerald Clibbon, 199–220. London: Equinox.

Sarangi, Srikant. 2009. Culture. In *Culture and language use,* ed. Gunter Senft, Jan-Ola Ostman, and Jeff Verschueren, 81–104. Amsterdam: John Benjamins.

Sarangi, Srikant, and Celia Roberts, eds. 1999. *Talk, work and institutional order: Discourse in medical, mediation and management settings.* Berlin: Mouton de Gruyter.

Sayers, Janet. 1997. Managing conflict at work. In *Perspectives in business communication: Theory and practice,* ed. Frank Sligo, Su Olsson, and Catherine Wallace, 241–253. Palmerston North, NZ: Software Technology New Zealand.

Schegloff, Emauel A. 1979. Identification and recognition in telephone conversation openings. In *Everyday language: Studies in ethnomethodology,* ed. George Psathas, 23–78. New York: Irvington.

Schiffrin, Deborah. 1994. *Approaches to discourse.* Oxford, UK: Blackwell.

Schnurr, Stephanie. 2005. Humour and leadership discourse in different workplace cultures. Unpublished PhD thesis, Wellington, NZ: Victoria University of Wellington.

Schnurr, Stephanie. 2008. Surviving in a man's world with a sense of humour: An analysis of women leaders' use of humour at work. *Leadership* 4(3): 299–319.

Schnurr, Stephanie, Meredith Marra, and Janet Holmes. 2007. Being (im)polite in New Zealand workplaces: Māori and Pākehā leaders. *Journal of Pragmatics* 39(4): 712–729.

Schnurr, Stephanie, Meredith Marra, and Janet Holmes. 2008. Impoliteness as a means of contesting power relations in the workplace. In *Impoliteness in language: Studies on its interplay with power in theory and practice*, ed. Derek Bousfield and Miriam Locher, 211–230. Berlin: Walter de Guyter.

Schwartzman, Helen. 1989. *The meeting*. New York: Plenum Press.

Silverstein, Michael. 2003. Indexical order and the dialectics of sociolinguistic life. *Language and Communication* 23: 193–229.

Sinclair, Amanda. 1998. *Doing leadership differently: Gender, power and sexuality in a changing business culture*. Melbourne: Melbourne University Press.

Sinclair, Amanda. 2005. Body possibilities in leadership. *Leadership* 1(4): 387–406.

Smith, Graham Hingangaroa. 1990. The politics of reforming Maori education. In *Towards successful schooling*, ed. Hugh Lauder and Cathy Wylie, 73–88. London: Falmer Press.

Smith, Linda Tuhiwai. 1999. *Decolonizing methodologies: Research and indigenous peoples*. Dunedin, NZ: University of Otago Press.

Sollitt-Morris, Lynnette. 1996. Language, gender and power relationships: The enactment of repressive discourse in staff meetings of two subject departments in a New Zealand secondary school. Unpublished PhD thesis, Victoria University of Wellington.

Spencer-Oatey, Helen. 2000. Rapport management: A framework for analysis. In *Culturally speaking: Managing rapport through talk across cultures*, ed. Helen Spencer-Oatey, 11–46. London: Continuum.

Spencer-Oatey, Helen, ed. 2008. *Culturally speaking: Managing rapport through talk across cultures*. 2nd ed. London: Continuum.

Spreckels, Janet, and Helga Kotthoff. 2007. Communicating identity in intercultural communication. In *Handbook of applied linguistics*, vol. 7, *Intercultural communication*, ed. Helga Kotthoff and Helen Spencer-Oatey, 415–440. Berlin: Mouton.

Starks, Donna. 1998. Monolingual speakers of New Zealand's languages. *NZSAL* 4: 71–76.

Stubbe, Maria. 1998a. Researching language in the workplace: A participatory model. Proceedings of the Australian Linguistics Society Conference, Brisbane University of Queensland July 1998, Available at: http://www.cltr.uq.edu.au/als98/.

Stubbe, Maria. 1998b. Are you listening? Cultural influences on the use of supportive verbal feedback in conversation. *Journal of Pragmatics* 29(3): 257–289.

Stubbe, Maria. 2001. From office to production line: Collecting data for the Wellington Language in the Workplace Project. *Language in the Workplace Occasional Papers* 2. Available at: http://www.vuw.ac.nz/lals.

Stubbe, Maria, and Janet Holmes. 2000. Talking Māori or Pākehā in English: Signalling identity in discourse. In *New Zealand English*, ed. Allan Bell and Koenraad Kuiper, 249–278. Wellington, NZ: Victoria University Press.

Swann, Joan. 2009. Doing gender against the odds: A sociolinguistic analysis of educational discourse. In *Gender and spoken interaction*, ed. Pia Pichler and Eva M. Eppler, 18–41. London: Palgrave Macmillan.

Swann, Joan, and William L. Leap. 2000. Language in interaction. In *Introducing sociolinguistics*, ed. Rajend Mesthrie, Joan Swann, Andrea Deumert, and William L. Leap, 184–215. Edinburgh: Edinburgh University Press.

Te Awekotuku, Ngahuia. 1991. Mana wahine Maori. *New Zealand Sociology* 6(2): 204–205.

Thomas, David C. 2001. Leadership across cultures: A New Zealand perspective. In *Leadership in the Antipodes: Findings, implications and a leader profile*, ed. Ken Parry, 22–45. Wellington, NZ: Institute of Policy Studies.

Thornborrow, Joanna. 2002. *Power talk. Language and interaction in institutional discourse*. London: Longman.

Thornton, Agatha. 1985. Two features of oral style in Maori narrative. *Journal of the Polynesian Society* 94: 149–177.

Ting-Toomey, Stella. 1999. *Communicating across cultures*. New York: Guilford.

Ting-Toomey, Stella, and John G. Oetzel. 2001. *Managing intercultural conflict effectively*. London: Sage.

Toulmin, Stephen E. 2003, updated ed. *The uses of argument*. Cambridge, UK: Cambridge University Press.

Trevor-Roberts, Edwin, Neal M. Ashkanasy, and Jeffrey C. Kennedy. 2003. The egalitarian leader: A comparison of leadership in Australia and New Zealand. *Asia Pacific Journal of management* 20(4): 517–540.

Turner, Roy. 1972. Some formal properties of therapy talk. In *Studies in social interaction*, ed. David Sudnow, 367–396. New York: The Free Press.

Vaara, Eero. 2003. Post-acquisition integration as sensemaking: Glimpses of ambiguity, confusion, hypocrisy, and politicization. *Journal of Management Studies* 40(4): 859–894.

Valentine, Gill. 2002. Queer bodies and the production of space. In *Handbook of lesbian and gay studies*, ed. Diane Richardson and Steven Seidman, 145–160. London: Sage.

van Dijk, Teun A. 1993. Principles of critical discourse analysis. *Discourse and Society* 4: 249–283.

Vine, Bernadette. 2004. *Getting things done at work: The discourse of power in workplace interaction*. Philadelphia, PA: John Benjamins.

Vine, Bernadette. 2009. Directives at work: Exploring the contextual complexity of workplace directives. *Journal of Pragmatics* 41(7): 1395–1405.

Vine, Bernadette, Janet Holmes, Meredith Marra, Dale Pfeifer, and Brad Jackson. 2008. Exploring co-leadership talk through interactional sociolinguistics. *Leadership* 4(3): 339–360.

Vine, Bernadette, Gary Johnson, Jennifer O'Brien, and Shelley Robertson. 2002. Wellington archive of New Zealand English transcriber's manual. *Language in the Workplace Occasional Papers* 5. Available at: http://www.victoria.ac.nz/lals/lwp/docs/ops/op5.htm.

Vine, Bernadette, Susan Kell, Meredith Marra, and Janet Holmes. 2009. Boundary-marking humor: Institutional, gender and ethnic demarcation in the workplace. In *Humor in interaction*, ed. Neal R. Norrick and Delia Chiaro, 125–139. Amsterdam: John Benjamins.

Vine, Bernadette, and Meredith Marra. 2008. EH and Māori men: A vernacular feature at work. Paper presented at 5th Biennial International Gender and Language Association Conference (IGALA5), Victoria University of Wellington, 3–5 July 2008.

Vine, Bernadette, and Sharon Marsden. Forthcoming. Eh at work in New Zealand English. Submitted to *English Worldwide*.

Walker, Ranginui. 1993. *Tradition and change in Māori leadership*. Auckland, NZ: University of Auckland.

Warner, Linda Sue, and Keith Grint. 2006. American ways of leading and knowing. *Leadership* 2(2): 225–244.

Watts, Richard J. 2003. *Politeness*. Cambridge, UK: Cambridge University Press.

Watts, Richard J. 2005. Linguistic politeness research: Quo vadis? In *Politeness in language: Studies in its history, theory, and practice*, ed. Richard J. Watts, Sachiko Ide, and Konrad Ehlich, 2nd ed, xi–xlvii. New York: Mouton.

Wenger, Etienne. 1998. *Communities of practice: Learning, meaning and identity*. Cambridge, UK: Cambridge University Press.

Wodak, Ruth. 1995. Critical linguistics and the study of institutional communication. In *The German language and the real world: Sociolinguistic, cultural and pragmatic perspectives on contemporary German*, ed. Patrick Stevenson, 205–223. Oxford, UK: Clarendon.

Wodak, Ruth. 2008. Controversial issues in feminist critical discourse analysis. In *Gender and language research methodologies*, ed. Kate Harrington, Lia Litosseliti, Helen Sauntson, and Jane Sunderland, 193–210. London: Palgrave.

Wong, Marge. 2006. Researching in a Maori cultural context: The moral, ethical and cultural obligations. In *Challenging the notion of "other": Reframing research in the Aotearoa New Zealand context*, ed. Carol Mutch, 45–61. Wellington, NZ: NZCER Press.

Yukl, Gary A. 2002. *Leadership in organizations*. 5th ed. Englewood Cliffs, NJ: Prentice-Hall.

Zaleznik, Abraham. 1977. Managers and leaders: Are they different? *Harvard Business Review* 55: 67–78.

INDEX